W9-CAN-676

WHAT MAN HAS MADE OF MAN

WHAT MAN HAS MADE OF MAN

A Study of the Consequences of Platonism and Positivism in Psychology

By

MORTIMER J. ADLER

Director, Institute for Philosophical Research, San Francisco

With an Introduction by

DR. FRANZ ALEXANDER

Director, Institute for Psychoanalysis, Chicago

FREDERICK UNGAR PUBLISHING CO.

NEW YORK

Republished 1957

Second Printing

Printed in the United States of America

Library of Congress Catalog Card Number 57-9409

TO

MY PARENTS

CONTENTS

NOTE

At the time of first publication of this volume, Dr. Adler was Associate Professor of the Philosophy of Law, University of Chicago.

INTRODUCTION

BY DR. FRANZ ALEXANDER

It is unusual to write an introduction to a book of an author whose conclusions, approach to his problems and whole outlook are diametrically opposite to those of the author of the introduction. Why did I then accept Mr. Adler's suggestion to write an introduction to his book and why did Mr. Adler ask me to do so, are both questions which require an explanation. The circumstances under which these four lectures originated will elucidate this paradox.

Engaged in psychoanalytic teaching and clinical studies for a long period of time, I gradually came to the conviction that in this field as in others where students are using a highly standardized technical procedure and are mainly absorbed in minute observation of facts,—briefly in all preeminently empirical fields,—the students are apt to lose perspective towards their own work. This conviction goes back to those early days that I spent as a research worker in physiology in an experimental laboratory. There, I became first acquainted with the characteristic mentality of modern scientific research. There I learned the *mores* and virtues of modern research and first recognized the danger which confronts the scientific worker of the present day. This danger is not restricted to scientific laboratories, it is a general problem of the present age. Man, the inventor of the machine, has become the slave of the machine, and the scientist, in developing highly refined methods of investigation, has become not the master but the slave of his laboratory equipment. An extreme amount of specialization of interest and mechanization of activity has taken place and a scotoma for essentials has developed; a naive belief in the magic omnipotence of specific technical procedures leads to a routine, often sterile submersion in details without interest in or understanding of larger connections.

It is no exaggeration to say that in many scientific centers not the interest in certain fundamental problems but the fortuitous possession of some new apparatus directs the research work: a new laboratory technique is introduced which spreads like a fad to all laboratories; then everywhere problems are selected which can be approached by this new technique or apparatus. Scientific interest in the fundamentals is lost, research is dictated more or less at random by the technical facilities at the worker's disposal.

This attitude necessarily must lead to that caricature of scientific ethics which regards suspiciously everything that entails reasoning and not merely observation and is contemptuous about theories, not to say hypotheses that are not as yet proven. There is a naive adoration of "pure facts" which are collected without any leading ideas.

Psychoanalysis is a highly empirical field in which the student is exposed to an extreme variety of observations and—in a certain sense—unique facts, as every patient presents a unique combination of common elements. Today the psychoanalytic clinician is undergoing a healthy reaction against the present abundance of theory and generalizations. He is in the process of accepting the mentality of the natural scientist and is assuming all the virtues and weaknesses of our era of laboratory research. Like his other clinical colleagues also he uses a highly standardized and refined technique but pays a high price for his technical skill: he is gradually losing perspective and correct judgment regarding the validity and limitations of his technique and of his scientific work in general.

To expose the students and the members of the staff of the Psychoanalytic Institute of Chicago to a lecture course dealing with epistemology and methodology seemed to me therefore highly indicated. I hoped that such a course would make them more conscious of and critical toward the methods, achievements and significance of their own field. Although one could not anticipate full agreement with all of Mr. Adler's conclusions, it was to be expected that the discussion of problems of psychological methodology by an expert such as Mr. Adler would be a real challenge and a healthy stimulus for all of us, which would stop us for a moment in our daily work and induce us to give ourselves an account of what we are really doing.

This experiment was successful in one respect. Although Mr. Adler was not able to convince his audience of the validity of any of his major statements, he aroused interest in this type of reflection, so direly needed in any group of specialists.

During the discussions that followed each of his lectures Mr. Adler has realized the basic disagreement of his audience with his theses and was therefore hesitant to publish his lectures without giving me an opportunity to state these fundamental controversies in the form of an introduction to his book.

During these discussions it became evident that our disagreement represents two diametrically opposite points of view, and illustrates the unsurmountable gap between what could be called a scientific *Weltanschauung* and the dogmatic attitude of a Thirteenth Century scholastic. As Mr. Adler himself very correctly put it, his lectures represent something which might have been the attitude of a contemporary pupil of Thomas Aquinas, or perhaps of Thomas himself if he could come to life again and be confronted with the new discoveries of Sigmund Freud. If for nothing else, then as such an anachronism, Mr. Adler's lectures may have the interest and value of a curiosity. It became obvious that according to Mr. Adler since the times of Aristotle and his belated scholastic pupil, Thomas Aquinas, man really did not contribute anything much of value to the inventory of his knowledge about the surrounding world and himself. Such radical new accomplishments as the recognition of the fact of biological evolution, the technical achievements of physics, chemistry and medicine, the better understanding of mental diseases, which have resulted in an ever-growing capacity of modern psychiatry to cure psychopathological processes, are of no great importance for him. This contempt for "practical" accomplishments explains why he considers the futile speculations and meditations about human nature of ancient and medieval philosophers like Aristotle and Thomas Aquinas to be superior to our detailed and precise knowledge of normal and pathological mental processes which enable us to influence these processes in a desired direction and thus cure mental ailments. Mr. Adler does not evaluate scientific concepts according to the degree to which they increase our ability to control and influence natural phenomena but according to their ability to be fitted into some preconceived rigid and abstract logical construction. The gap between these two attitudes cannot be bridged. In the following I shall state the main points of our controversy.

1. Mr. Adler defines philosophy as a body of logical conclusions drawn from common sense observations, and science as a body of conclusions drawn from specific observations obtained by specific investigative methods. I agree with Mr. Adler's definition of science but not with his definition of philosophy. Mr. Adler

reduces philosophy to reasoning about inadequate (common sense) observations, science representing at the same time reasoning about more adequate observations obtained by refined and improved methods of investigation. And yet, in order to save the medieval hegemony of philosophy, with a peculiar twist of reasoning Mr. Adler tries *to subordinate science*—that is to say conclusions drawn from improved observations—to philosophy, which according to his own definition consists of conclusions from inadequate observations. If Adler's definition of philosophy is correct, philosophy should be discarded in the proportion to which scientific knowledge progresses by the use of steadily improving special techniques of investigation. With this definition, Adler himself speaks the death sentence of philosophy. However I am much more inclined to accept the view of those philosophers (a view which was most convincingly expressed by Bernard Alexander) who consider philosophic reflection as the manifestation of a deep and universal need in human beings to orient themselves towards the universe with which they are confronted. Science must necessarily leave this deep need for orientation to a high degree unfulfilled because due to its nature its answers are disconnected and restricted to isolated portions of reality, namely to those fields that have already been scientifically explored, and also because scientific answers are necessarily incomplete due to the high claims regarding validity which science sets to itself. In view of this incomplete nature of science, only two attitudes remain for a human being in handling his desire to orient himself in the world in which he lives:

a. A kind of agnosticism, contenting himself with the answers which science can offer at any given time, abandoning the wish for an integrated concept of the universe.

b. An attempt to integrate the isolated and disconnected answers of science into a *Weltbild*. This is philosophy. Such a philosophical picture of the world however must be consistent with what is known by science. It tries to integrate the results of scientific investigations into the best possible synthesis of current knowledge. Therefore philosophy never can disprove science, on the contrary it must always be ready to be corrected by new scientific discoveries. In this sense philosophy never can become superfluous as long as human beings continue to ponder over the world in which they live.

2. One of Mr. Adler's fundamental convictions is that the act of reasoning itself cannot be studied scientifically: that in this regard it has an exceptional position among all psychological

processes. Since the reasoning faculties have been subjected successfully both to psychological and physiological investigation, this statement does not need further discussion. Freud's studies of rational thinking, his understanding of it as motor innervations with small quantities of energy on a trial and error basis, his comparative studies of rational thinking in contrast to thinking in dreams, his classical study of denial, and finally his demonstration of the influence of emotional factors upon rational thought have shown that the reasoning process can be psychologically analysed and genetically understood as the result of a process of adjustment of the biological individual to its environment. Furthermore the first promising steps have been made by the method of brain operation to establish the relation of rational processes such as the faculty for abstraction, to brain functions.

3. Perhaps the greatest gap between Adler's concepts and the viewpoint assumed by psychoanalysts consists in his insistence upon the non-animal nature of human beings, in his contention that there is no evolutionary continuity between men and brutes. Adler belongs to that rapidly diminishing, in fact today almost extinct species of thinkers who still try desperately to disregard the solid facts of evolution. The type of argument which is used can be best characterised by quoting the distinguished American thinker, James Harvey Robinson.[1]

"Having myself given much time to the comings and goings of beliefs in the past, I see how great a part mere ignorance and confusion always play in blocking the ready acceptance of new knowledge. . . . It is true the biologists have, many of them, given up what *they* call 'Darwinism'; they have surrendered Spencer's notion of the hereditary transmission of acquired characters, and they even use the word 'evolution' timidly and with many reservations. *But this does not mean that they have any doubts that mankind is a species of animal, sprung in some mysterious and as yet unexplained manner from extinct wild creatures of the forests and plains.* This they simply take for granted; for, unlike the public at large, they distinguish carefully between the varied and impressive evidence which appears to confirm man's animalhood and the several theories which have been advanced from time to time by Lamarck, Darwin, Spencer, Haeckel, and others, to account for the process by which organic life, including man, has developed. The first confusion of which we must relieve ourselves is that between the *facts*, on the one hand, revealed by geology, biology and comparative anatomy, and, on the other hand, the *conjectures* suggested to

1 Robinson, James Harvey: The Human Comedy, New York, Harper & Bros., 1937, pp. 23–4.

explain the history of life. As time has gone on the facts which compel anyone acquainted with them to accept man's essentially animal nature have become more abundant and unmistakable, while many of the older theories of evolution have, as a result of further study and increasing knowledge, shown themselves to a great extent untenable. Much light has been cast of late on the history of life, but in some respects it seems more mysterious than ever before."

Adler, like some theologists, in order to refute the unassailable fact of evolution, takes advantage of recent controversies regarding those detailed mechanisms by which man has developed into his present form from more primitive beings.

His methodological discussion about the discontinuity of the different realms of knowledge, his insistence upon unsurmountable gaps between the inanimate world, animals and man, are based on a refusal to draw the correct conclusion from the factual evidence which we possess regarding the relationships between these different sections of the universe. Even though scientists are not able to reduce the processes of life to physics and chemistry there is no doubt that the process of life consists in a specific combination of exactly the same processes as are known in the physics and chemistry of nonliving substances. The specificity of life consists *in the specificity of the combination* of those partial processes which constitute life and which are identical with the chemical processes of nonliving substances. It is true that the specific principles of this coördination are not known as yet. Nevertheless it is quite possible that some time in the future when we shall possess the knowledge of the characteristic combination of physico-chemical processes in the living cell we shall be able to create living substance from nonliving substance. It is needless to say that the difference between the higher animals and man is far less incisive than that between animals and inanimate nature. The psychoanalyst considers the difference between man and animals as definitely of quantitative nature because he can observe that the new-born infant shows no human but merely animal characteristics. The difference between men and animals, which is one of Adler's fundamental theses, comes gradually about during the individual's development from an ovum to an adult.

4. Adler's efforts to demonstrate that the Freudian concepts of personality have been anticipated if not more completely elaborated by Aristotle are based upon entirely formalistic and verbal comparisons. Aristotle's theory of personality has the same relation to the Freudian as Democritus' concept of the atom bears

to the scientific concepts of Dalton or as Edward von Hartmann's "unconscious" has to the Freudian concept of the unconscious. The similarity is based mainly on the use of the same word. Democritus' "atom" was the result of deductive speculation and did not contribute to a better knowledge of matter, whereas Dalton's atomic concept was concluded from specific observations regarding certain permanent quantitative relationships in chemical compounds and has led to the body of knowledge represented by modern chemistry. Similarly Aristotle's speculations about human nature did not enable any contemporary physician to understand better the nature of paranoia or hysterical blindness, whereas Freud's concepts were derived from painstaking minute observations made by the help of a refined technique of psychological inquiry and have made possible a better understanding and methodical influencing of psychological processes.

5. Mr. Adler's statement that the Aristotelian concepts about personality in a certain respect were more complete than Freud's is obviously true. But this completeness is anything but an asset as compared with the incompleteness of the Freudian concepts. The Freudian concepts are necessarily incomplete; they are, like every scientific concept, in a continuous process of change and improvement because, being of a scientific nature, they must remain in accordance with new observational material whereas the systematic philosophic concepts of Aristotle are "eternal," since they had to be only consistent in themselves, had to fit not observations but vague generalizations and an abstract system of thought.

6. The gap between the scholastic attitude of Adler and the scientific views of Freud becomes widest when Adler takes a stand regarding the psychoanalytic concepts of moral phenomena. Adler evaluates the Aristotelian concepts of morals as superior because they are absolute whereas the Freudian concepts are relative. Freudians consider moral concepts to be the results of parental influences, the nature of which are determined by the structure of the civilization in which the parents live. Aristotle has an anthropomorphic concept and declares the moral ideas of the Greek Peninsula to be absolute values. Freud's concept of morality compares to the Aristotelian as the concept of present cosmology is related to the Aristotelian concept of the earth as the center of the universe. The facts of modern anthropology and ethnology fully corroborate the Freudian view and disprove the Aristotelian, showing that the concepts of good and bad radically differ in different cultural settings depending upon the political, economic and cultural history and situation of a group.

If there is such a thing as turning back the clock of history and science, here we see a classical example of it. Scholasticism, a sterile form of deductive thinking, developed as a harmless outlet for the reasoning powers of man in a period of intellectual servitude when man could not observe the world around himself lest any observation come in contradiction with prevailing dogmas. He had to content himself with flawless deductions from incorrect premises. Free observation of facts was forbidden; rigid acceptance of preconceived ideas was the highest requisite of these medieval centuries. What else remained for the human mind to do but indulge in playful deductive meditations starting from the accepted and prescribed dogmas as premises? Our present freedom of inquiry is nothing but the continuation of that great period of the liberaation of the mind which started in the Renaissance, with Galileo, Giordano Bruno, and Bacon. It took centuries before this freedom of investigation was fully achieved. At first the realm of the celestial bodies, the stars, then the human body, was claimed as a legitimate subject for scientific study. The last step in this process of emancipation of the human mind was the accomplishment of Sigmund Freud, the objective unbiased study of the human personality, including its reasoning and moral powers.

In spite of these fundamental disagreements, I am very much indebted to Mr. Adler for his courage in presenting his scholastic philosophy to a group which was so thoroughly biased by what is a scientific credo. The consistency of his presentation, the astuteness and skill of his logical deductions, aroused in us the same admiration as those of some medieval scholasticists. The internal consistency of his lectures representing literally a medieval viewpoint, through the effect of contrast, afforded unprecedented opportunity for his audience to understand better the nature of psychoanalytic methods and the position which this science takes in the present realm of knowledge.

Chicago, January 25, 1937

PREFACE

THESE lectures were delivered before the Institute of Psychoanalysis in Chicago in the Spring of 1936. I was asked to discuss methodological problems, especially in relation to the scientific procedures of psychoanalysis. But it seemed important, almost unavoidable, to shift the discussion to more fundamental considerations about the nature of any science of psychology, its limited subject-matter, the scope of its problems. Only in such light could questions about method be properly answered. This, furthermore, necessitated a distinction, in general, between the scope of philosophy and of science; and, in particular, a determination of the parts which philosophy and science contribute to the knowledge of man.

As Dr. Alexander says in his Introduction, it became evident during the course of these lectures that my analysis provoked sharp differences of opinion on the part of the audience. I must confess to having been naively unsuspecting. I was surprised to discover that psychoanalysts were just as ready to tell me what philosophy was about and how to solve its problems, as they were willing to instruct me concerning the scientific facts they had learned from clinical experience. Furthermore, what I had to say seemed to me high praise of the contribution of psychoanalysis as a body of scientific knowledge. I did not expect that the praise would seem so faint because it did not glorify psychoanalysis, or even the whole of natural science, by abolishing all other knowledge, by condemning philosophy as empty talk or futile speculation. But the chief issue of the contemporary world, whether science is enough, once agitated, obscures all other questions, or determines the acceptance or rejection of the answers which are proposed. That was the case in the forum of the Institute last Spring.

I, therefore, felt it would be desirable to have Dr. Alexander write the Introduction to this book, in order to bring the line of these disagreements more sharply into focus. The dialectic would benefit from the expression of opposite voices on the same points. Dr. Alexander could not, of course, do more than indicate his position briefly. In fairness to him, the reader must be referred to the works of Freud and to Dr. Alexander's own writings for a fuller exposition of the view which psychoanalysts take of these basic questions. Since Dr. Alexander covers in ten pages the same points that I discuss in two hundred, it would hardly be fair to his position for the reader to make a final judgment on the issues involved. At the same time, it would not be fair to me for the reader to make a judgment about my position by *merely* consulting what Dr. Alexander says I say.

The lectures are here printed in the form in which they were given. The structure of an outline has the virtue of making explicit the progress of an analysis. It gives the leading propositions due prominence, and exhibits the order and relation of the parts of a complicated argument. But an outline is, strictly, not an argument. It is much more like an analytical index to one. This is its chief disadvantage. For those who know the full substance of the arguments, an outline can serve excellently the purpose of summarizing; it may even have the additional merit of putting a multitude of relevant discussions into the perspective of a single frame. But for those who do not know intimately what these arguments are, an outline must necessarily seem dogmatic, almost simple-minded in its brevity. On the surface it is dogmatic because, as a teaching instrument, it proceeds by the sequence of assertions, few of which it can stop fully to support. Yet whatever is affirmed is either self-evident or demonstrable, and in philosophy demonstrations can be given. I have attempted to show this, and also to compensate for the brevity and condensation of the outline form, by adding to the lectures a series of notes, appended at the rear and referred to by the bracketed numbers in the text. These notes are not only expansions of points made in the lectures; they are argumentative discussions of what the lectures may appear to say dogmatically because too simply or too briefly. The reader is asked to regard the lectures and the notes as integral parts of a unity, just as he would be obligated to examine the evidence on which the premises of a demonstration rested before judging the truth of the conclusion.

The issue which is central to this book, the relation of science and philosophy, is the crucial stumbling block of modern times. As Dr. Alexander recognizes, the issue is not merely between psychoanalysis and other psychologies, or between Freud and Aristotle. It involves all members of the household of human knowledge in the modern triangle of science, philosophy and theology. This, unfortunately, is not material for a domestic comedy. The issue is not a remote, academic one. The practical consequences of one or another solution are momentous. Science seems to be the modern hero. The *hybris* of science, the pride in its ability to answer all questions or to dismiss those it cannot answer as unanswerable,—a pride which is comic only when scientists pretend to tell philosophers what philosophy is about,—may make science the pivot of a tragic turn in modern affairs.

I would like to say, finally, that although what follows is written for the most part in the language of the philosophy of Aristotle and St. Thomas Aquinas, it is not "scholasticism," as that word is currently used to suggest necromancy with buried syllogisms. Even when not used opprobriously, scholasticism is an unfortunate designation. It confuses the fact that medieval philosophers were Christians with the fact that in the middle ages thinkers worked in a continuous tradition of philosophical thought, and did not seek to invent "systems" which would bear their separate names to posterity. Lack of education, combined with the burning desire to be original, prevents most modern philosophers from being scholastic in this latter sense. But what is more important to say to a contemporary audience is that although the truths of traditional philosophy are compatible with the dogmas of a revealed religion,—and therefore a man can be a Christian without ceasing to be a philosopher,—nevertheless, philosophy is not religion. Nor is it sacred theology. St. Thomas is a philosopher in the same sense that Aristotle and Santayana are. The truths of reason are formally established by reason independently of faith, even when they are truths in which faith concurs.

The passages I quote from the *Summa Theologica*,—the mere name of which may be misleading to some,—are entirely philosophical, as, indeed, all the points which I have argued in this book are philosophical. They rest neither on theological dogma nor on scientific fact. The citation of Aristotle and St. Thomas in the notes and footnotes is not an appeal to authorities on my part. It does not justify the dismissal of what I have to say as Aristotelian or Thomistic in the utterly absurd sense of a nostalgic return to the dead past. One can be an Aristotelian or a Thomist only by being a philosopher facing contemporary issues in the light of reason and experience, as they did in their day; and, as they were, through being respectful of the tradition of human knowledge wherever it bears witness to the truth.

MORTIMER J. ADLER

Chicago, 1937

WHAT MAN
HAS MADE OF MAN

LECTURE ONE

THE CONCEPTION OF SCIENCE IN THE MODERN WORLD

I. Introduction

1. Why the modern world? Because it is only in the modern world that science is self-conscious, that it considers itself distinct from other disciplines, as having a method and a mission. Because it is only in the modern world that science and philosophy are sharply separated and that there are supposed to be conflicts between science and philosophy and between science and religion. Because it is only in the modern world that the scientist wonders about himself and his methods. Because it is only in the modern world that positivism has rightly conceived science as different from philosophy, adding thereto a denial that philosophy is knowledge, if it claims to be different from science.
2. This does not mean that science is entirely a modern invention. It occurs and appears in the ancient and medieval worlds, but differently. It is only in the modern world that science has revolted from religion, revolted from philosophy. Thus, in the 17th century, physics revolted and gained autonomy; in the 18th, biology; in the 19th, psychology and the so-called social sciences. As a result of these revolts, it is in the modern world, and particularly in the 19th and 20th centuries, that it is supposed that any question worth answering is capable of being answered only by the method of the scientist; or, on the other hand, that any question which is not capable of being thus answered is not a genuinely answerable question.
3. There are, therefore, in modern times a number of peculiar problems which confront and perplex the scientist. (By the sciences I shall henceforth mean the natural sciences, including psychology. I shall, for the most part, ignore the social sciences.)

a. The difference between science and philosophy, and the relation between science and philosophy.

b. In considering this first problem, the scientist usually differentiates himself by his method, only to be further perplexed by the plurality of methods (procedures, techniques) which claim to be scientific. He must, therefore, determine what is common to all these different procedures.

c. He is, furthermore, aware of the plurality of the sciences as they are distinguished according to subject-matter as well as by method, and he is often embarrassed by their several claims to priority or independence. He faces here two sorts of questions:

(1) Questions of order: priority and dependence.

(2) Questions of composition: cooperating disciplines, hybrid subject-matters.

4. All of these problems are more intensified and, in a sense, more embarrassing for the psychologist than for any other natural scientist.

a. Thus, for example, his relation to the philosopher, because of the recency of his revolt. Boring's insight: "Psychology has never succeeded in taking philosophy to itself or in leaving it alone."[1]

b. Similarly, his attempt to define his subject-matter and his methods. Consider here the existence of "schools" of psychology; the fact that there are rival pretenders to the title of "scientific psychology." Consider the controversial character of these plural psychologies in contrast to the situation in physics or chemistry, where there is neither this plurality nor such polemic [1].

c. Finally, his relation to other scientists: particularly the relation of the psychologist to the physiologist, on the one hand, and to the social scientist, on the other.

5. And even more so are these problems exasperating for the psychoanalyst; and here the following should be noted:

a. His relation,–in both subject-matter and method,–to the rest of the psychologists. Is psychoanalysis a *part* of or the *whole* of psychology? Is it just another sect or school?

[1] *A History of Experimental Psychology*, New York, 1929: p. 660. Professor Boring goes on to say: "Such a diagnosis is not founded upon the necessary relation of science to philosophy, for this conflict is not to be found in the natural sciences. In psychology it lies very near the surface."

b. The character of his methods and of his research in relation to the better recognized and more certainly accepted canons of scientific procedure.

c. His acceptance of a philosophy,—the "philosophy of evolution",—and, at the same time, his opposition to philosophy.[2]

6. I propose, therefore, in this opening lecture to approach the problems of the psychologist and the psychoanalyst by considering, first, the two most general problems concerning science in modern times:

(1) The distinction between philosophy and science, and their relation.

(2) What is common to the plurality of scientific methods, procedures, techniques.

Then, subsequently, I shall consider the position of psychology in the order and relation of the natural sciences and in relation to philosophy.

II. Two Further Introductory Observations

1. We must understand a distinction within the field of logic, made according to differences in the relation of logic, as an organon, to knowledge and the types of cognition. (This is the distinction between the prior and posterior analytics in Aristotle's *Organon,* and between *petite logique* and *grande logique,* or formal and material logic, in the modern tradition.)

a. Formal logic: the analysis of terms, propositions, syllogisms, but not induction.

b. Material logic (which necessarily presupposes formal logic): the analysis of bodies of knowledge according to principles of order and system; the distinction of the kinds of knowledge; the formulation of the methods of knowing (evidence, proof, probability, induction, measurement, etc.)

[2] Freud proclaims himself a positivist. He regards philosophy, along with religion, as outside the realm of established knowledge,—as superstition, speculation, or "mere poetry." He speaks of his own "philosophy of life" as the rigorous *weltanschauung* of science. Unfortunately, this is not true. It would be better if Freud contented himself with being a scientist; but, like so many scientists who are positivists, Freud denies philosophers the right to their "opinions," but does not restrict himself to the "facts" of science. Vd. *New Introductory Lectures on Psychoanalysis,* New York, 1933: Ch. 7; also *The Future of an Illusion,* New York, 1928. Cf. Fritz Wittels, *Freud and His Time,* New York, 1931: Ch. II, "Freud, the Anti-Philosopher."

(1) Material logic is, in part, a sort of "theoretical rhetoric": the methods and types of exposition appropriate to the communication of different kinds of knowledge.

(2) Material logic is necessarily related to psychology: the analysis of human powers and acts of cognition.

c. In these lectures, I shall presuppose formal logic in order to discuss the larger material problems [2].

2. But, as we have seen, material logic involves psychological analysis. We cannot distinguish the kinds of knowledge, we cannot formulate the methods of knowing, without an account of the objects of human knowledge and of the cognitive processes of man. This fact has critical consequences:

a. Any scientist who entertains certain convictions about scientific method, about abstraction and induction, about observation and conception, about proof and probability, is necessarily, implicitly or explicitly, asserting propositions in psychology about the cognitive operations of man. Thus, for example, consider the ancient paradox of the strict atomic materialist who tried to explain himself as a scientist in terms of his own theory while at the same time appealing for the truth of that theory in terms of the rational canons of scientific method [3].

b. This paradox is even more embarrassing for the psychologist:

(1) It has been exposed by Lovejoy in the case of the "thinking behaviorist," and by Bradley in the case of the British associationists [4].

(2) In short, the psychologist in his capacity as a scientist appealing for the truth of his conclusions and their status as scientific knowledge, must assert or admit

(a) That man is in some sense rational, that he is bound by evidence and proof, seeks truth and avoids error, knows the difference between the better and the worse reason, etc. (In short, the man who claims to be a scientist cannot as a psychologist so conceive man that there is no difference between a scientist and a sophist).

(b) That man is intellectual as well as sensitive, that he knows by operations other than sensing, that he has abstract concepts, which are not sensory images, that, in short, he can generalize and thus go beyond all sense-data.

c. This point is particularly important for the Freudian, and particularly important for me to make clear at the beginning of this course of lectures.

(1) If psychoanalysis is a body of scientific knowledge which employs abstract concepts,—and it most certainly does employ such abstract concepts as *complex*, *regression*, *sexuality*, *cathexis*, *abreaction*, etc., —then the Freudian cannot without contradiction at one time be proud of his scientific knowledge and at another deny the intellect.[3] His position as a scientist considering his own knowledge must agree with his position as a psychologist considering man's cognitive powers.

(2) Furthermore and similarly, if psychoanalysis is scientific in its methods and appeals to the binding canons of reason in evidence and proof, then the Freudian as a psychologist cannot deny the independence of human reason from passion and prejudice. He cannot assert that everything which appears to be *rational* is merely *rationalization* without making psychoanalysis itself a mere rationalization instead of a body of objectively true scientific knowledge.

3. Therefore, as I proceed I shall not hesitate to present a psychological analysis,—an account of man as a scientific knower,—which I shall expect the Freudian to accept, not only because he is a scientist, but in his capacity as a psychologist as well.

III. The Kinds of Knowledge [4]

1. There are two basic ways in which one body of knowledge can be distinguished from another:

[3] The intellect is denied whenever it is held to be indistinguishable in operation from sense and imagination, or is treated as completely reducible thereto. The modern attempt to identify idea, the product of intellectual abstraction, with image, the product of sensitive memory, always fails. The "abstract image" is as self-contradictory as the "round square." Vd. Locke, *An Essay Concerning Human Understanding*, Bk. II, Ch. 2, ¶ 9, 10; Bk. III, Ch. 3; Bk. IV, Ch. 6, 7, 17; Berkeley, *The Principles of Human Knowledge*, Introduction, ¶ 6–27; Hume, *An Enquiry Concerning Human Understanding*, Sections II, XII.

[4] For the fullest discussion of the distinctions indicated in this section of the lec-

a. By *subject-matter*, and here
   (1) Either in terms of *that which* is known: the knowable *thing* or material object of knowledge.
   (2) Or in terms of *what* is known of it: the thing *as known* or formal object of knowledge; the cognitive selection, the content of the knowledge.

b. By *method*.

c. All other distinctions,–such, for instance, as that made in terms of the modality of the knowledge (its certainty or probability),–can be ignored for the time being as subordinate.

2. But first we must consider what is common to *almost* all human knowledge.

a. Almost all human knowledge is a product of the cooperative activity of the senses and intellect, as these are involved in processes of observation and reflection.
   (1) By sense, or the powers of observation, I mean all those perceptual abilities which are exercised through the activity of bodily parts called sense-organs and brain.
   (2) By intellect, or the powers of reflection, I mean the following abilities: abstraction (the ability to conceive, define, distinguish, generalize, make inductions and analyses); judgment (the ability to formulate propositions and to assert them); reasoning (the ability to infer and demonstrate, to systematize knowledge deductively.)

b. The one exception is important: the kind of knowledge we call immediate experience,–and perhaps, also, the memory of such experiences,–*seems* to be purely sensitive.
   (1) No new reflective process is involved here in the act of knowing.
   (2) But even here there is an involvement of past reflections (the results of past intellectual activity) as evidenced by the fact that we cannot observe or remember without some interpretation. (This is

ture, see J. Maritain, *Les Degrés du Savoir*, Paris, 1932; vd. also my mimeographed *Analysis of the Kinds of Knowledge*, at the University Press Bookstore, Chicago, 1935; and *Art and Prudence*, New York, 1937: Ch. 9 on knowledge and opinion. This chapter is a refinement as well as a condensation of the earlier analysis.

what Kant meant by saying that percepts without concepts are blind.)

(3) This exception need not concern us now. We shall return to it in a later analysis of the observational process itself, in order to determine what are the "pure data" of scientific observation.

c. What is crucially important here is the basic proposition: *All human knowledge arises from the operation of the senses, and most human knowledge goes beyond sense, i.e., has a reflective development.*

(1) The first clause denies that ideas are primary objects of knowledge, capable of being directly or intuitively known by the intellect (supposedly the error of the Platonists); it must also be interpreted as denying innate ideas (the Platonic error made by Descartes and repeated in a somewhat disguised form by Kant), and the *a priori* in any of the absurd constructions which have been straw-men attacked by modern empiricism.

(2) The second clause asserts that although *all* human knowledge depends initially upon the activity of the senses, it does not depend exclusively thereon. It depends also upon intellectual activity, abstracting ideas from the presentations of sense. (Ideas are neither innate nor intuited, but the products of abstraction.)

d. The fact that most human knowledge goes beyond sense can be made clear simply by the limitations of the senses themselves.

(1) The senses apprehend only this particular thing or its qualities. This is true also of sensitive memory and imagination.

(2) But man is able to apprehend kinds of things, of which the particulars are recognizable instances; and man is able to conceive or to construct conceptually what is not observable at all by sense, even though the construction depends upon sense-data of some sort.

(3) Therefore we can say that understanding goes beyond sensation in grasping universals, knowing kinds, conceiving and constructing entities not observable. All of this depends upon the first intellectual act, the act of abstraction.

(4) If this were not the case, if man could not abstract as well as sense,—and the intellect is *primarily* the power of abstracting,—then induction and generalization would not be possible, and we could not distinguish between science and history, or even between history and aesthetic experience.

3. *The distinction between science and history.*
   a. By historical knowledge is here meant the conclusions of historical research, as by scientific knowledge we mean the conclusions of scientific research. It is necessary to say this in order to exclude the interpretation of historical fact which is made in the course of historical (i.e., narrative) writing.
   b. The historical proposition is singular: it is always about this particular thing, this change, this event, this agent, this action, etc.
      (1) This does not mean that historical knowledge is purely sensitive. Historical research involves inferences and hence general propositions. Moreover, the historical proposition usually reports knowledge of things not immediately experienced. Finally, the particulars we know historically are known as instances of kinds.
      (2) It means only that the historical proposition is like sensitive knowledge in that it refers to particular things.
   c. Scientific knowledge, considering now only the conclusions of scientific research, consists of general propositions: either propositions which are first generalizations, that is, inductions from the data of sense-experience, or derived generalizations, propositions which have been either inferred (i.e., deduced) from the primary inductions, or otherwise elaborated.
   d. In both history and science, observation is primary. In history, the basic evidences are discovered by observation, and from these the inferences to unobserved facts are made. In science, also, the basic evidences are matters of observation, and from these the primary inductions and further proofs are made.
   e. In both kinds of knowledge, *that which* is known are the things of the physical world: physical things in change. Both kinds of knowledge have the same material

object. The two kinds of knowledge can, however, be distinguished by reference to *what* is known of this common object:

(1) The formal object of historical knowledge is the thing in its particularity.

(2) The formal object of scientific knowledge is the thing in its universality.

There is a further distinction between history and science. The historian is primarily concerned with questions of existence,—whether or not his material object, a certain particular, exists, or existed. But the scientist is never concerned with the existence of his material object, physical things in general. He does not question the existence of the phenomenal order. (A full understanding of these distinctions depends not only upon a grasp of the distinction between sense and intellect, but also upon the comprehension of basic metaphysical distinctions between the form and matter, the essence and accidents, of *entia naturae*, as existing and as objects of knowledge.)

4. *The distinction between science and philosophy.*

a. They are alike in one essential respect as knowledge; and this differentiates them both from history. They are both knowledge of things in their universality.

(1) Their propositions, their conclusions, are general propositions.

(2) In both, the primary inductions,—on which everything else rests,—are inductions from sense-experience.

b. To the extent that they have the same material object, —the things of the physical world,—which is the proper or cognate object of all human knowledge, they cannot be distinguished in subject-matter. (Nor can we, at this point, completely distinguish them in terms of their formal objects. We shall return to this principle of distinction later, at 5. *infra.*)

c. They must be differentiated, then, by method. This differentiation can be made only with respect to the activity of the senses and not with respect to the activity of the intellect. In other words, philosophy and science do not differ methodologically in their reflective dimensions. In both induction is the same, judgment is the same, analysis is the same, proof is the same, etc. Hence, their difference in method must be in the observational dimension. This difference can be stated in terms of the difference between common and special experience [5].

(1) *Common experience:* perceptions not produced by, or in any way resulting from, processes of research or investigation, but rather arising from the normal operation of the sense-organs in the ordinary life of the animal. Common experience is the sense-experience of the ordinary man. It is constituted by undirected, unmethodic observations.

(2) *Special experience:* sense-data resulting from the special operations which we shall call "investigation," i.e., all the motions and manipulations, with or without apparatus and instruments, of men *seeking* and *doing something* for the sake of observing. The experience is special in the sense that the scientist differs from other men in what he does in order to observe, and therefore what he observes is different. Thus, we have the experience of the laboratory (usually with apparatus), of field research, of the clinic, etc.

(3) It is because investigation is a special kind of doing, a kind of physical activity or operation, that we speak of the *data* of science, the special observations resulting from such doing. We do not speak of the data of philosophy since the experience that philosophy reflects about is the common experience of all men. But the scientist reflects about his special data. This must not be interpreted to mean that he can ignore the common experience of all men; it means only that that is insufficient for him; and, therefore, he investigates.

(4) *Digression:* This difference is made clear by the analogous difference between investigative and non-investigative history. The knowledge which one has of one's own life as a matter of personal memory is non-investigative history; almost all other history is investigative.

(5) *Terminology:* We shall use the words "science" and "philosophy," without qualification, to name investigative and non-investigative knowledge, which

has generality. We can also speak of the investigative and the philosophical sciences.[5]

d. This distinction between philosophy and science explains a number of things that are generally recognized about their difference [6]:

(1) Their different relations to common sense.

(2) Their different degrees of change and progress, and the conditions of progress in the two fields.

(3) The difference between the locus of contingency and the possibility of error in the two fields.

(4) The utility of science and the inutility of philosophy, *in one meaning of utility*, namely, the use of knowledge to direct operations for the alteration or change of things, which is commonly called prediction and control. There is another meaning of utility: i.e., the use of knowledge to determine means and ends in human conduct, in which sense philosophy is practical, as in ethics and politics. But in the first sense philosophy is not useful. Metaphysics and mathematics, both of which are philosophical knowledge, illustrate this negative point. There is no metaphysical or mathematical engineering. Science, on the other hand, can become practical or applied in the technological sense because the knowledge it has achieved results from doing with respect to things and hence can again lead to doing with respect to things [6a].

e. Finally, we can understand why there *should* be no conflict between philosophy and science, no rivalry, but rather good order and cooperation.

(1) The reason is that special experience does not *alter* common experience; it merely *supplements* common experience with respect to details. But philosophical truths are the highest generalities of common experience. In respect to the sort of data phi-

[5] In the 17th century, the word "philosophy" was the commonly accepted name for knowledge which had generality, in contradistinction to history. Newton distinguished himself by taking the name of "experimental philosopher." The word "science" today, as it is commonly used, thus denotes what the phrase "experimental philosophy" did in the 17th century. The basic distinction between philosophy and science remains the same whether we name the kinds of knowledge distinguished as "abstract philosophy" and "experimental philosophy," or as "philosophical science" and "investigative science." The criterion of the distinction is method: the employment of investigative procedures.

losophy finds in common experience it is adequate. Hence, inductions properly made from common experience are not affected by the findings of investigation, as the latter, in turn, cannot be forecast by philosophy from its limited data. Nor can they be judged by philosophy so long as they are properly restricted. If the reflective processes are properly disciplined in both fields, scientific and philosophical knowledge must be compatible and complementary [6b].

(2) This does not mean that actually there have been or are no conflicts. There are always bad philosophers and bad scientists who go beyond their fields, who transgress upon domains not their own, and when this happens there is a bad order and antagonism instead of cooperation and harmony.

(3) The occurrence of such conflicts in modern times is a significant comment on the lack of intellectual discipline in this period. Whenever there is a conflict between science and philosophy, one or the other is out of order [7].

5. We can now differentiate the formal objects of philosophical and scientific knowledge, as before we distinguished the formal objects of historical and scientific knowledge.

a. The proper or cognate object of all human knowledge is the physical world: the order of physical things as sensible and intelligible. This is the case because only corporeal things are sensible, directly or indirectly, and all human knowledge involves the senses.

b. But, as we have seen, most human knowledge involves the intellect as well, and therefore we can distinguish, analytically, the proper objects of sense and intellect:

(1) The proper object of sense: the thing as particular; as *this*

(2) The proper object of intellect: the thing as universal; as *such and such*.

c. Within the sphere which is common to both science and philosophy, distinction can be made between two cognitive aims: the aim of science is to know what is universally observable about the nature of things; the aim of philosophy is to know what is universally intelligible about their nature, their substance and causes.

(1) The formal object of the natural sciences is the phenomenal order. Things are observable in their operations and changes. The phenomenal order is the changing surface of nature. Science studies this surface: it classifies, correlates, systematizes, measures the given phenomenal diversity.

(2) The formal object of philosophy is the noumenal order. Things are intelligible in the principles and causes of their being. The noumenal order is, in part, the substance of sensible nature. (We shall presently see that the noumenal includes objects which are purely intelligible.) Philosophy penetrates the phenomenal surface to the intelligible constitution of sensible things.

(3) This distinction in the formal objects of science and philosophy does not abrogate the point that both are intellectual knowledge, i.e., knowledge of things in their universality; nor does it violate the basic principle of human cognition, that intellectual knowledge is based upon the data of sense-experience. (The accidents which constitute the phenomenal order are both sensible and intelligible. Although the substance of things is, strictly, not sensible, the process of inference by which it is intellectually known originates from a knowledge of the accidents.)

d. Since what is characteristically human knowledge involves both sense and intellect, we must note

(1) The infra-intelligible object (below the intellect): the unique individual thing, known as *individual* and not as a particular instance of such and such a kind. (This object is always physical.)

(2) The supra-sensible object (above the senses): nonphysical things, such as souls separately existing, angels, God. (Such objects always transcend the physical order.)

(3) Since neither of these two objects are proper objects of human knowledge,—although both, let it be added, are intrinsically knowable, the latter more so than the former,—neither are known adequately. The infra-intelligible object is known

probably. The supra-sensible object is known *analogically*, by *a posteriori* modes of remotion from experience [8].

e. What further distinguishes science from philosophy is that it never seeks to know supra-sensible objects; in fact, it is prevented from doing so by its method, which requires that its objects be subject to human investigation. Philosophy, not bound by the limitations of the investigative method, can at least *seek* knowledge of transcendent objects, but in so doing it is, like science, bound by conditions common to all human knowledge: it must do so *a posteriori*, that is, it must learn about such objects from sense-experience, both with respect to their existence and their natures [8a].

f. Neither science nor philosophy, nor even history in the usual sense of that term, seeks to know the infra-intelligible object. That is the field of aesthetic or immediate experience.

6. In order to complete the distinction of philosophy and science, and to state their relation, we must indicate the formal divisions of philosophy.[5a] It should be noted that the fields of philosophy are distinguished formally in terms of grades of abstraction; whereas, we shall see, the different sciences, all of the same grade of abstraction, can be distinguished only materially. There are three grades of abstraction. Thus:

a. *Physics:* knowledge of physical things as such: i.e., with all their accidents and as changing. The range of physics includes everything from astronomy through chemistry and biology to human physiology and even psychology, in so far as man is a physical thing. It is this range of subject-matters which requires a careful formulation of the relation between philosophical physics and the special natural sciences.

Mathematics: knowledge of physical things not as such,

[5a] We are here concerned only with the divisions within speculative or theoretic philosophy. Theoretic philosophy as a whole must be divided against practical philosophy (ethics, politics, poetics), and these two together must be distinguished from the organon of knowledge (the liberal or speculative arts of grammar, logic and rhetoric) which it is the task of the philosopher to formulate. The Stoic tripartite classification of philosophical disciplines (logic, physics, ethics) is accurate if logic be taken as representing all the liberal arts, physics the whole of theoretic philosophy, and ethics all practical philosophy.

but as determined in quantity and quantitative order. In other words, mathematics is an abstraction from physics. It considers only one aspect of physical things, their quantity due to their matter, and apart from their changes, motions and other accidents.

Metaphysics: knowledge of physical things merely as being, abstracted from all special determinations due to matter and motion. In short, metaphysics is concerned with whatever is *as it is*, and thus extends from the knowledge of the being of physical things to the knowledge of the being of anything, both as possible and as actually existent. Metaphysics considers both physical and transcendent objects. The conditions of becoming presuppose the conditions of being, and the order of becoming presupposes an order of being both in and apart from the conditions of becoming.

b. Another way of saying this is: metaphysics is about being abstracted from any special determinations; mathematics is about being as determined by quantity and order but abstracted from the material conditions which determine change, and from change itself; and physics is about being as materially determined in the order of becoming [9].

c. Of these three philosophical subject-matters, distinguished not by that which is known but by what is known of that which is known, only one can be shared in common by philosophy and science, because only one is capable of supporting investigative procedures. That one obviously is physics.

(1) First, because only physical things *as such* are sensible and operable, and investigation can yield knowledge only of sensible, operable things.[6] Thus, the mathematical and metaphysical objects,—being abstractions from the physical thing *as such* and hence neither sensible nor operable,—are not capable of investigation in the sense defined. There is, in short, no empirical, experimental or investiga-

[6] A science can be experimental, in the strict sense of that term, only if its objects are both sensible and physically operable. If its objects are sensible but not physically operable, as in the case of astronomy, the science can be investigative or empirical, but not experimental.

tively observational mathematics or metaphysics [10].

(2) Second, because common experience is sufficient for both mathematics and metaphysics. Neither need to have more experience, as a source of reflective development, than that which the least inquiring ordinary man possesses as the result of his ordinary observations.

d. It must be added at once that although physics *can be investigative, it need not be*. Physics names a subject-matter that is common to both philosophical and scientific knowledge. Whereas physics may be either philosophical or investigative knowledge, all the sciences, all bodies of investigative knowledge, must be branches of physics.

(1) It is proper to identify science in its modern meaning with *natural* science, because science is investigative knowledge of natural, that is, changing things. Whether social phenomena are in a strict sense natural and can be proper objects of science need not be discussed here. If they are, then the social studies may some day become natural sciences. If they are not, then the social studies will never become scientific.[7]

(2) I shall refer to philosophical physics,—the philosophy of nature, the knowledge man has of the physical world by reflection about common experience,—as general physics (or as philosophy of nature); and to scientific physics, which includes the entire range of the particular sciences of nature resulting from the investigation of particular kinds of bodies, particular kinds of change, etc., as the particular physics. There is only one general phys-

[7] Societies are not natural substances, but as systems of phenomena they are not different from other phenomenal entities. If science were knowledge of the substantial order, social science would be impossible. But science is knowledge of the phenomenal order, and social science of either a non-mathematical or a mathematical sort can be constructed in the same way as any other natural science. The possibility of social science seems indisputable. Whether such science exists in any adequate development is another question. Vd. Notes 9 and 47 *infra*. The problems of social science must not be confused with those of social psychology; the latter tries to solve the philosophical problem of the causes of human behavior. Vd. my discussion of this point in *Art and Prudence*, New York, 1937: Ch. 9.

ics, or natural philosophy, and many particular physics, or natural sciences.

e. One further point is important. Since physics deals with changing things and with change itself, it treats of causes, the conditions of change; whereas mathematics, having abstract objects, i.e., quantities and orders apart from change, has nothing to do with causes.[8] It should be added here that the philosophy of nature treats of causes theoretically, while the natural sciences are concerned with causes only practically.[8a]

7. *Summary:* Physics, as the name for a domain of knowledge, a subject-matter determined by the lowest grade of abstraction, is both philosophical and scientific [10a].

a. *As philosophical*, it is what Aristotle developed in the eight books of the *Physics*, and in some part also the books of the *De Caelo* and the *De Generatione et Corruptione*. These books contain discussions of the causes, principles and elements of all change, the types of change, the nature of matter, space, time, infinity, and the types of physical existence. Such discourse is a philosophy of nature and constitutes an introduction to all of Aristotle's particular scientific works, his astronomy, his mechanics, his biology, etc.

b. *As scientific*, it consists of the whole range of investigative natural sciences, differentiated from each other materially by the kind of change or the kind of body (i.e., the selected phenomenal area) being investigated. (This differentiation is primarily in subject-matter; subordinate distinctions can be made in terms of method.)

(1) Thus, according to the kind of change: local mo-

[8] This is perfectly clear in Galileo's *Two New Sciences* (trans. by De Salvio and Favaro), New York, 1914. He conceives his study of acceleration as the kind of science "where mathematical demonstrations are applied to natural phenomena, as is seen in the case of perspective, astronomy, mechanics, music, and others, where the principles once established by well chosen experiments, become the foundation of the entire superstructure" (p. 178). Such a science, i.e. any mathematical physics or applied mathematics, is not concerned with causes, except in so far as causes are involved in the experimental operations. Galileo writes: "The present does not seem to be the proper time to investigate the cause of the acceleration of natural motion concerning which various *opinions* have been expressed by various *philosophers*. . . . Now, all these *fantasies*, and others too, ought to be examined; but it is not really worth while. At present it is the purpose of our Author merely to *investigate* and to *demonstrate* some of the properties of accelerated motion" (pp. 166–167). Italics mine.

[8a] Vd. Note 47 *infra*.

tion (mechanics); generation, growth, and decay (biology).

(2) Or, according to the kind of body: celestial or earthly, inanimate or animate (astronomy or geology, chemistry or botany).

c. The history of natural science is a history of increasing particularization of subject-matters and the separation of the particular physics. For our present purposes, we shall consider only the main grouping of these particular sciences into the physical (inanimate bodies) and the biological (animate bodies). We shall return to this point later.

d. It is clear from this analysis that general physics is illuminated by metaphysics because whatever holds for being in general must hold for beings which change. The particular natural sciences may, however, be informed by mathematical principles, thus giving rise to what the ancients treated as the mixed (or hybrid) science of mathematical physics, or mathematics applied to nature by measurement [11]. But, whether mathematical or not, these sciences presuppose the principles of philosophical physics, because whatever holds for any change and any body, must hold for particular types of change and particular kinds of bodies.[9]

e. In order to make this last point clear, in order to understand the relation of the natural sciences to philosophy (to general physics, to mathematics and to metaphysics) we must now consider the history of the natural sciences.

IV. The History of the Natural Sciences

1. In the ancient world there was no clear separation of science and philosophy according to method.

[9] Vd. J. Maritain, *La Philosophie De La Nature*, Paris, 1935. This dependence is clearly illustrated in the works of Newton and Galileo. Thus, in the opening discussion of the Third Day of the *Two New Sciences*, Galileo presupposes the distinction between local motion and other types of changes, and the distinction between natural and violent motion (*op. cit.*, pp. 153–54). These distinctions he learned and accepted from the traditional philosophy of nature, i.e., general physics. They are to be found, of course, in Aristotle's *Physics*, Bk. I, II, and *De Generatione et Corruptione*, Bk. I. The presupposition of an analysis of the principles, causes and elements of change, and of the distinction of the kinds of change, is even more obvious in works of empirical biology.

a. Aristotle's *Physics* is a work in general physics and is purely philosophical.

b. Aristotle's astronomical and biological works are works in particular physics. Being non-mathematical, they depend for their first principles upon general physics, and to this extent they are philosophical. But to apply the principles to particular types of physical phenomena, there is a large addition of investigative knowledge based upon special observations. To this extent they are scientific works. (*Note:* This composite character of ancient physical writings,–partly philosophical in method and partly scientific,–requires great care in the modern reader, who must distinguish philosophical principles from scientific knowledge of particular matters of fact. In the latter sphere it is to be expected that the ancients would make many errors; but these errors do not affect the validity of the principles.) Galen is another good example of such a composite work. In his treatise *Of Natural Faculties*, the principles of general physics are applied by investigation to human physiology.

c. Mixed or intermediate sciences: applied mathematics, such as astronomy of the Alexandrian sort, mechanics (Archimedes), harmonics (Aristoxenus), etc. These sciences are mixed in two senses:
   (1) In subject-matter: They are mathematics *formally* and physics *materially*.
   (2) In method: They are philosophical (in their mathematical dimension) and scientific or investigative (in their physical dimension).

d. The mixture to be found in mathematical physics is different from the mixture of philosophy and science to be found in Aristotle's non-mathematical physical works in particular fields. In the latter there is no mixture of subject-matter, but only a composition of two sorts of knowledge, of the same grade of abstraction, but obtained by different methods.[9a]

2. In the modern world there has been an ever sharper separa-

[9a] Aristotelian science was bad as science for a more fundamental reason than imperfect data or wrong conclusions. Innocent of the distinction between the formal objects of philosophical and scientific inquiry, Aristotle employed a substantive logic throughout and failed to see that data of investigation could yield purely relational generalizations. Vd. Notes 2 and 47 *infra*.

tion of the sciences from philosophy in terms of their investigative methods. (In fact, the great achievement of the modern world has been this separation of science from philosophy, and the understanding of its autonomy.)

a. Mixed science in the modern world.

(1) Galileo: *Two New Sciences*. (This work is of the same type as Newton's *Principia Mathematica*, the work of Clerk-Maxwell, Einstein, etc.) Analysis:

(a) Philosophical physics is presupposed.[10]

(b) The application of mathematics: the requirement of investigation in order to make metrical observations, and the need of measurement for the sake of applying mathematics.[11]

(c) By means of experiments: the construction of an approximation to the ideal to show that the mathematically possible is physically actual; also for the sake of precision in measurement. But there is a limited use of experiments. They are used to establish the definitions, from which all else follows deductively.[12]

[10] Vd. fn. 9 *supra*.

[11] "First of all it seems desirable to find and explain a definition best fitting natural phenomena. For anyone may invent an arbitrary type of motion and discuss its properties; thus, for instance, some have imagined helices and conchoids as described by certain motions which are not met with in nature, and have very commendably established the properties which these curves possess in virtue of their definitions; but we have decided to consider the phenomena of bodies falling with an acceleration such as actually occurs in nature and to make this definition of accelerated motion exhibit the essential features of observed accelerated motions. And this, at last, after repeated efforts we trust we have succeeded in doing. In this belief, we are confirmed mainly by the consideration that the experimental results are seen to agree with and exactly correspond with those properties which have been, one after another, demonstrated by us" (*op. cit.*, p. 160). It should be noted that the demonstration here referred to is not experimental but mathematical. Experiment is used not to demonstrate the truth of theorems but to test the agreement of a mathematically coherent analysis with observed nature.

[12] Vd. fn. 8 *supra*. This limited use of experiments,—to find observable exemplifications of an analysis,–is indicated by a number of passages. Thus, at one point Galileo says: "Without depending upon the above experiment, which is doubtless very conclusive, it seems to me that it ought not to be difficult to establish such a fact by reasoning alone" (*op. cit.*, p. 164). And at another: "Whether this acceleration is that which one meets in nature in the case of falling bodies, I am still doubtful; and it seems to me, not only for my own sake, but also for those who think as I do, that this would be the proper moment to introduce one of those experiments–and there are many of them, I understand–which *illustrate* in several ways the *conclusions reached*" (*op. cit.*, p. 178). Simplicio is the

(d) *Digression:* such mathematical physics is not inductive. But the relation between the conclusions and the data is nevertheless the same. This can be shown by supposing apparatus which Galileo did not have [12].

(2) The works of Kepler and Copernicus are examples of applied mathematics without experiments but with a tremendous amount of metrical data.

b. Inductive, non-statistical and non-mathematical physics. Newton's *Optics.* (The work is of the same type as that of Boyle, Rumford, Faraday, Kelvin, etc.) It is typical *experimental*, as opposed to *mathematical*, physics. Analysis:

(1) Difference in the use of definitions and in the meaning and use of axioms.[13]

(2) The experiment is used as the source of the induction, not as a means by which to apply mathematical formulae. It is a construction of the ideal case in order to be able to see the universal in the particular by abstraction of essence from accidents, i.e., the separation of relevant conditions from the irrelevant.

(3) There is both measurement and mathematics in the *Optics*, even though it is not applied mathematics, but pure physics. The mathematics is used for the sake of precision of formulation.

(4) There is "speculation" about causes,—the real na-

speaker at this point in the dialogue. The italics are mine to indicate that Simplicio has admitted the demonstration of the theorem, by mathematical reasoning, and asks to have its applicability to nature shown, by experiment. Cf. fn. 8 *supra.*

[13] Newton's *Principia Mathematica* is a work of the same sort as Galileo's *Two New Sciences.* It is applied mathematics. This can be seen in the way in which the mathematical demonstrations come first, and the tests of applicability to nature by reference to selected phenomena follow. In such works, the axioms and definitions are used probatively to demonstrate the theorems. But in the *Optics*, the definitions and axioms are not the premises whereby Newton demonstrates his theorems. Each of the theorems is an experimental induction. Of the axioms Newton says that they are "the sum of what hath hitherto been treated of in Opticks. For what hath been generally agreed on I content myself to assume under the notion of Principles, in order to what I have farther to write. And this may suffice for an Introduction to Readers of quick Wit and good Understanding not yet versed in Opticks: Although those who are already acquainted with this Science, and have handled Glasses, will more readily apprehend what followeth."

ture of light, the cause of its properties, etc.,—whereas Galileo, being a mathematical physicist, excluded causes.[14] (Here note the dependence of a particular physics on general physics. Newton unfortunately made the error of accepting Greek atomism as his "philosophy of nature.")

c. Mendel's work in genetics, and subsequent work by Morgan and Bateson. These works are examples of inductive science, which is non-mathematical, and yet may be either metrical or non-metrical, statistical or non-statistical. Even when statistical methods are employed, the conclusions are not statistical generalizations but genuine inductions. The experiments in this field are clearly different from the experiments in Newton's *Optics* and are, for the most part, merely devices for controlling the phenomena for the sake of special observation.

d. Lyell's *Principles of Geology* is non-experimental, and inductive without being statistical. The inductions state secular trends which are typical of all life-history patterns.

e. We can briefly summarize the foregoing by the following classification of all investigative natural sciences:

(1) Mixed sciences: applied mathematics. Either experimental or not. Thus, astronomy is not experimental; mechanics is.

[14] It should be noted, however, that the speculation about causes does not occur in the main body of the treatise, but rather at the end of the work in a series of queries, to stimulate, as Newton says, "a farther search to be made by others." See particularly, Book III, Part 1, Query 31, in which Newton propounds the atomic hypothesis for the causal explanation of natural phenomena. It is here also that Newton discusses scientific method: "As in Mathematics, so in Natural Philosophy, the Investigation of difficult Things by the Method of Analysis, ought ever to precede the Method of Composition. This Analysis consists in making Experiments and Observations, and in drawing general Conclusions from them by Induction, and admitting of no Objections against the Conclusions, but such as are taken from Experiments, or other certain Truths. For Hypotheses are not to be regarded in experimental Philosophy. And although the arguing from Experiments and Observations by Induction be no Demonstration of general Conclusions; yet it is the best way of arguing which the Nature of Things admits of, and may be looked upon as so much the stronger, by how much the induction is more general. . . . This is the Method of Analysis: And the Synthesis consists in assuming the Causes discovered, and established as Principles, and by explaining the Phaenomena proceeding from them, and proving the Explanations." Cf. Query 28.

(2) Purely physical sciences: essentially non-mathematical, although they may involve mathematics, measurements, and statistics in some subordinate use.

(a) They may be experimental or not. Thus, geology is not experimental; genetics is.

(b) They may be statistical or not. Either the generalizations are primary inductions or they are only statistical generalizations. The statistical sciences are quasi-mathematical.

(c) With respect to the way in which they describe the phenomena they study, they are:

(1) Taxonomic (merely classificatory)

(2) Physionomic (secular trends; life histories

(3) Analytic (quasi-aetiological).

Note: Mathematical physics is analytic, but not in the same way as the non-mathematical sciences. In either case, however, a practical knowledge of causes is involved [13].

f. In the light of this summary it can be seen that there is a rivalry between two philosophical fields for the control of the particular natural sciences: mathematics (which does not consider causes), on the one hand, and general physics (which is primarily aetiological), on the other. In fact, the story of modern science can be told in terms of this rivalry. The particular natural sciences must get their principles somewhere, since they have a limited scope of investigation. They borrow their principles either from mathematics or from the philosophy of nature. There are, as a result, two sorts of sciences and accordingly two different philosophies of science, i.e., two different conceptions of the nature, aims and scope of science. I shall now attempt briefly to summarize this.

V. The Relation of the Several Natural Sciences *Inter Se* and to Philosophy

1. The view one takes of the relation *inter se* of the particular natural sciences depends upon one's metaphysics and philosophy of nature (general physics).

a. Thus, in terms of an atomistic or Cartesian philosophy, all the physical sciences are reducible to a basic mathematical physics like mechanics, because the only properties of matter are quantitative and these are the properties to which mathematics is applicable. The mixed kind of physics (mathematical physics) looks forward to the day when all the other natural sciences will be reduced to it.

b. In terms of an Aristotelian philosophy,—and this is the only other alternative,[15]—there is an acknowledged and irreducible heterogeneity of the physical sciences, and the non-mathematical sciences are not regarded as inferior. In fact, they are more purely physical than the mixed sciences of applied mathematics. The systems of phenomena which constitute the subject-matters of the several sciences are based on deeper distinctions in the nature of physical things. The particular natural sciences can, therefore, be arranged according to the kinds of bodies studied.
   (1) The primary distinction would be between the animate and the inanimate.
   (2) Subordinate distinctions would be made within these two realms: thus, within the inanimate, mechanical and chemical systems; within the animate, biological, psychological and social systems. This denies continuity and reducibility in nature in one sense and affirms it in another, in so far as the philosophy of nature and metaphysics provide principles which are common to all the particular sciences of nature.

2. The view one takes of the relation between the sciences and philosophy depends, of course, upon one's conception of philosophy.
   a. In terms of many contemporary conceptions of philosophy,—the positivist's, the pragmatist's, the sociologist's,—philosophy is at best the handmaiden of the sciences.
      (1) It is not a body of knowledge having a content and validity independent of the results of scientific research.
      (2) It performs one or another literary or rhetorical function, which is ancillary to the acquisition of knowledge by the scientific method [14].
      (3) Like religion, it satisfies emotional needs, which a scientist is able to conquer or deprive. The pursuit

15 Vd. Lecture II *infra*.

of philosophy is the expression of a persistent human desire to know the world more fully and more profoundly than it can be known by science. But this desire must be fruitless if the only genuine knowledge is scientific. Dissatisfaction and impatience with the achievements of science is the regrettable emotional source from which philosophy,—the illusory quest for ultimates,—perpetually arises.[16]

b. In terms of a conception of philosophy which views it as the tradition of wisdom, prior logically, as well as historically, to the accomplishments of science, the sciences are at best the servants of philosophy.
   (1) Philosophy rules the sciences negatively.
      (a) It restricts them to their proper spheres, and governs them justly in that it recognizes their autonomy within their own domains.
      (b) In other words, it does not dictate the conclusions of scientific research, but it does require scientists to confine their "interpretations" to whatever can be concluded from their limited data. This negative rule is unfortunately often violated by modern scientists, particularly when they give Gifford lectures or win Nobel prizes [15]. It must be added that many modern philosophers have also exceeded their powers and have attempted to answer questions which should properly be reserved for scientific investigation. Such dogmatic and speculative excesses on the part of modern philosophers, both in the 17th and the 19th centuries, are in large part responsible for the bad reputation which philosophy has in the modern world [16].
      (c) That the sciences cannot rule themselves is simply indicated by the fact that any discussion of science, its methods, its scope, the nature

[16] This is the psychoanalyst's conception of philosophy. Vd. S. Freud, *op. cit.* in fn. 2 *supra.* It is shared, of course, by sociologists and anthropologists. Vd. K. Mannheim, *Ideology and Utopia,* New York, 1936; A. Herzberg, *The Psychology of Philosophers,* New York, 1929; P. Masson-Oursel, *Comparative Philosophy,* New York, 1926. That the pragmatist is a positivist in his denial of philosophy as knowledge of the noumenal, and that he is a sociologist in his conception of philosophy as nothing more than the highest rationalization of local cultural values is clearly seen in Dewey's *Reconstruction in Philosophy* (New York, 1920: pp. 22–27). Vd. also *Experience and Nature,* Chicago, 1929.

and validity of its knowledge, raises questions which are not answerable by scientific method, but belong to the province of the logician and the epistemologist, i.e., the philosopher. In short, the question, What is the relation of science to philosophy? is a philosophical and not a scientific question.

(2) The sciences serve philosophy positively by affording it additional materials with which to exemplify its principles.

VI. Conclusion

1. Summary of the basic distinctions:
   a. Science and philosophy, together, are distinguished from history in terms of generality and particularity: different formal objects.
   b. Science and philosophy are distinguished from each other *negatively* in terms of method.
      (1) Both are observational; both are reflective;
      (2) But philosophy is *not* investigatively observational, whereas science is impossible without investigation.
   c. Science and philosophy are distinguished from each other *positively* in terms of their different formal objects, i.e., their different cognitive aims. They are essentially different types of knowledge.
      (1) The positivist is right in his conception of science as concerned exclusively with the phenomenal order, as descriptive rather than explanatory, as systematizing and correlating phenomena rather than as seeking to know the substance and causes of things.
      (2) The positivist is wrong only in his denial of another type of knowledge, namely, philosophy which is concerned exclusively with the noumenal order, which explains rather than describes, and which succeeds in knowing the substance and causes of things. The goodness of positivism can be separated from its denials and exclusions, its *negativism* in short.
      (3) For a modern audience, philosophy can perhaps be most easily defined by saying that it is precisely the kind of knowledge which the positivist declares to be impossible. It is an unfortunate,

though an understandable, circumstance that the achievement of a sound conception of science, largely due to modern philosophers, should be accompanied by a misunderstanding and even a denial of philosophy [16a].

d. The fields of philosophy,—the philosophy of nature, mathematics, metaphysics,—are formally distinguished *inter se* by their different grades of abstraction.

e. The particular natural sciences are all determined by the same grade of abstraction which defines the province of the philosophy of nature, but they are materially distinguished *inter se* according to the phenomenal area they select for investigation. These material distinctions divide the sciences according to subject-matters. But there are also quasi-formal distinctions among the sciences according to their principles, their methods and their aims. Thus:

(1) They are mixed or pure: consisting of mathematical principles applied to natural things, or of physical principles applied to natural things.

(2) They are experimental or not; and if experimental, the experiments are either for the sake of applying mathematics by measurement or for the sake of induction.

(3) They are statistical or not; and if statistical, statistics is employed either for the sake of testing or qualifying generalizations made otherwise, or for the sake of making generalizations (statistical inductions).

(4) They are analytic, physionomic or taxonomic.

Note: These various traits combine in many different ways.

2. Summary of the basic propositions:

a. All human knowledge arises with sense-experience, but most human knowledge goes beyond sense by means of intellectual processes (abstraction, judgment, inference).

b. All scientific knowledge and all philosophical knowledge, consisting of generalities, must involve both sense and intellect as cognitive faculties.

c. Because they are different types of knowledge, employing different methods, there can be no conflict between the evidence and proper conclusions of scientific research and the principles and proper conclusions of philosophical analysis.

(1) "Proper" here does not mean "true in fact" but rather "achieved by the proper method and within the proper province." Thus, there are conflicts between trespassing scientists and dogmatic philosophers in the modern world.

(2) If a question cannot be answered by a given method, answers given to it cannot be refuted by knowledge achieved through the given method. Thus, mathematics and metaphysics are concerned with questions which cannot be answered by any process of investigation; hence no knowledge achieved by investigative procedures can be used to refute philosophical answers to such questions.

3. The problem which remains for us is formulated by the question: What is the position of psychology as a branch of philosophy, on the one hand, and as a particular natural science, on the other?

a. It is obviously a peculiar subject-matter. No other particular sphere of natural phenomena is the subject-matter of philosophical knowledge. In every other case, mechanics, chemistry, botany, etc., only investigative knowledge is possible.

b. Yet it can be shown that psychology is, in one sense, a particular branch of natural science, and, in another sense, a very special philosophical discipline. The positivistic denial of philosophy as knowledge of the real is, therefore, crucially important to psychology. If, as I shall try to show, the basic questions in psychology are entirely philosophical, then the attempt to construct a science of psychology on positivistic principles is doomed to failure and to perpetuate the misguided polemic of the "schools."

4. The themes of the lectures to follow are determined by the foregoing analysis, the insights it yields, the questions it raises. They are in order:

Lecture Two: THE POSITION OF PSYCHOLOGY AMONG THE SCIENCES AND IN PHILOSOPHY
Lecture Three: THE HISTORY OF PSYCHOLOGY
Lecture Four: THE POSITION OF PSYCHOANALYSIS

THE POSITION OF PSYCHOLOGY: IN PHILOSOPHY AND AMONG THE NATURAL SCIENCES

I. Introduction

1. However one conceives psychology, it is clear that the psychologist has a double status: on the one hand, he is a scientist or philosopher who is a special student of man (human nature); on the other hand, he is a psychologist who must give an account of man which accounts for himself as a man who is either a scientist or a philosopher. In short, the psychologist is himself the subject-matter of psychology as a field of knowledge.
   a. This double status of the psychologist as *knower* and as *object known* is related to the reflexivity of psychological knowledge. And this reflexivity imposes a peculiar burden on the psychologist. He cannot, as scientist or philosopher, claim to have knowledge of a certain sort, and then as a psychologist deny that men are capable of such knowledge.
   b. It is important to note here that the analysis of the kinds of knowledge, made in the first lecture, was philosophical, i.e., not the result of scientific research or investigation; that that philosophical analysis involved psychological considerations about man's cognitive powers and operations; and hence that there is psychological knowledge which is not scientific but philosophical. In other words, there is a philosophical psychology.
   c. The philosophical analysis of the kinds of knowledge and the nature of science included, at least, the two following propositions in psychology:

(1) There is a distinction between sense and understanding as powers of knowing, and between sensitive and intellectual knowledge as kinds of knowledge.

(2) Reason is autonomous. In both philosophy and science men assent to conclusions only because they are bound by evidence or premises to do so, and not as a result of their desires or passions. Men can reason as well as rationalize. Otherwise there is neither science nor philosophy. (Freud, in a recent lecture, recognized this point.)

(3) These two psychological points are crucial to the psychoanalyst in his double role as a scientist (or a philosopher sometimes) and as a psychologist.

2. At the conclusion of the first lecture, Dr. Alexander raised a number of questions which went immediately to the heart of the matter. His questions focus the chief issues for our present discussion. They follow:

a. Why all the reflective processes, attributed by me to a distinct and separate intellectual faculty, could not be reduced to, or treated as extensions of, man's sensitive powers and operations?

b. Whether such a reduction was not required by the physiology of cognition which showed that man's reflective processes were disturbed by brain pathology? (It was admitted, of course, that the brain is nothing but an elaborated sensorium plus complicated connections with a primary motorium. The essential structure of the brain is the same as that of the simplest spinal segment.)

c. Whether we must not consider reflective processes as serving biological functions, just as we consider the operations of sense in relation to the life of the animal?

d. Whether there is not perfect biological continuity, that is, whether man differs from brute animals essentially in *kind* or only accidentally in *degree?*

3. I must answer all of these questions in the course of this lecture because the answers are indispensable to a proper definition of the subject-matter of psychology and its place among the natural sciences.

a. But, first, I must make an inescapable phenomenological point. By phenomenology I mean a description of the facts, regardless of how they are explained. Thus, the answer to the first question phenomenologically must be made independently of the answer to the second question. In other words, physiology or neurology cannot determine the answer to the first question. The distinction between sense and intellect as an essential distinction, a distinction in kind, a distinction incapable of reduction, is made in terms of common experience.

(1) Sense and understanding are essentially different. The difference is that of the two intentions of the mind: the particular and the universal.

(2) This is best illustrated by mathematics, since mathematics is impossible if all knowledge is merely sensitive.

(a) First, geometry. There is a distinction between the defined object (a universal) and the drawn figure (a particular). No geometrical knowledge is about the drawn figure; nor can any sensitive knowledge of the drawn figure establish the simplest geometrical truth. For example, the truth that the number of diagonals in an n-sided figure is equal to $n(n-3)/2$, cannot be learned by counting the diagonals in any number of particular figures. It can be learned only by a process of demonstration employing universals. The examination of particular figures may, of course, be *suggestive* of this truth.

(b) Second, arithmetic. The obvious truth that any positive number over 100 multiplied by any positive number over 100 yields a product which is a positive number over 100, can be established only by intellectual processes. No sensitive evidence here is more than remotely relevant.

(3) The distinction is one which every one knows. It is the distinction between recognizing John Smith in a crowd (by sense) and understanding what a man is as distinct from a mouse (by intellect). We commonly distinguish the following items of knowledge: (1) that John Smith is; (2) what John Smith is, i.e., a man; (3) that men are in this room; (4) what men, in this room or elsewhere, are, i.e., rational animals [17].

b. I turn next to the physiology of cognition (because of Dr. Alexander's second question). This cannot possibly alter the foregoing distinction, although we shall have to understand the foregoing distinction in terms of our physiology.

(1) Physiology teaches us the distinction between the peripheral and central nervous system, between the organs of sense and movement and the organs of connection between senses, muscles and glands.

(2) The brain, in addition to being an elaborate system of connections, is the organ of imagination, because it contains the primary and secondary sensory projection areas. It is imagination which is an extension of sense, and it is imagination which is reducible to sense. Dr. Alexander's point applies properly to imagination but not to understanding.

(3) But the distinction between imagination and understanding is the same as the distinction between sensation and understanding. What is imagined is always a particular, even though what have been called "generic" or "abstract" images indicate the way in which the imagination contains the universal implicitly and potentially [18].

(4) I shall show, subsequently, that there is no bodily organ of understanding (no physiology of the intellect), but that, since intellect depends upon sensation and imagination (as providing the materials from which the intellect abstracts universal intentions), there is a physiological account that is relevant to the intellect. Thus, fatigue and brain lesions hinder understanding by hindering its indispensable condition, the activity of the imagination [19]. This does not reduce understanding to imagination any more than the fact that a fire needs oxygen reduces a fire to oxygen.

(5) The psychiatrist is right who refuses to surrender his subject-matter to the neurologist. The psychology of the organic psychoses shows the *essential*, not merely the *present*, inadequacy of brain physiology to account for psychological phenomena. (Neuropathology deals only with the material cause of insanity. It does not, and cannot, account for the individual content of the same psychosis in different individuals. This is a matter of psychogenesis.)

c. The remaining two of Dr. Alexander's questions I shall

answer later, since both depend upon the full demonstration of the answer I have given to the second, namely, that understanding is not directly physiological, but only indirectly in so far as understanding depends upon sense and imagination.

(1) I shall answer the third question by showing that the biological functions of sense and intellect are different; and

(2) I shall answer the fourth question by showing that there is a specific and essential difference between men and brute animals, animals lacking an intellect, though having intelligence of a sensitive and imaginative sort.

d. My answers to the first and second questions, with their consequent answers to the third and fourth, are fundamental propositions in philosophical, not scientific, psychology. I must, therefore, first consider the position of psychology in philosophy and among the natural sciences.

4. That I must do this at once is also indicated by the analysis made in the first lecture. That analysis showed a basic paradox about psychology as subject-matter, partly indicated by the reflexivity of psychological knowledge, and partly indicated by the following questions, which can be asked about psychology and only about psychology:

(1) Is it, as a body of knowledge, a branch of philosophy?

(2) Is it, as a body of knowledge, a particular natural science?

(3) Is there a unity of these two bodies of knowledge?

a. These three questions cannot be asked about metaphysics and mathematics, on the one hand, since they are entirely philosophical in method; nor, on the other hand, can they be asked about mechanics, geology, electricity, genetics, qualitative chemistry, etc., since they are entirely scientific in method.

b. If the affirmative answer is given to these three questions, this fact will then be true only of psychology, and this will indicate something unique about its subject-matter, a uniqueness already somewhat indicated by the fact of reflexivity.

c. The affirmative answer *must* be given to these questions. To show this,—and particularly to answer the second of these questions,—we must understand the relation *inter se* of the particular natural sciences. To do this, we must first analyze the prevailing issue in what is currently called the "philosophy of science." We turn to this at once.

II. The Philosophy of Science

1. The "philosophy of science," i.e., the sort of discussion to be found in the writings of Poincaré, Cassirer, Meyerson, Mach, Whitehead, Russell,[1] deals with four leading topics:
   a. The character of scientific knowledge. (This raises psychological questions.)
   b. The principles of scientific method. (This raises logical questions, viz., the issue about predicational vs. relational logic.[1a])
   c. The aims of science: description or explanation. (This is the issue raised by 19th century positivism.[1b])
   d. The order and relation of the particular sciences in terms of their subject-matters, their objects of knowledge. (This raises metaphysical questions about the different kinds of *knowable objects*.)
2. It is only the fourth question with which we are here concerned, and we must, therefore, enter the realm of metaphysics in order to answer it. (It is important to remember here that metaphysics is knowledge based upon observation, and developed by reflection from common experience. It is open to argument in the reflective dimension only.)
3. There are two "philosophies of science" in modern times:
   a. The first position is that all the natural sciences are homogeneous with respect to their object, hence continuous, and hence ultimately all reducible to the basic science of that one common object.
      (1) This is the position taken by some physicists with

[1] Vd. T. Merz, *History of European Thought in the 19th Century*, London, 1896; W. Whewell, *Philosophy of the Inductive Sciences*, London, 1840; J. B. Stallo, *Concepts and Theories of Modern Physics*, London, 1890; H. Poincaré, *Foundations of Science*, New York, 1921; E. Cassirer, *Substance and Function*, Chicago, 1923; E. W. Hobson, *Domain of Science*, Cambridge, 1926; J. S. Haldane, *The Sciences and Philosophy*, New York, 1929; A. S. Eddington, *Nature of the Physical World*, New York, 1928; E. Meyerson, *Identity and Reality*, New York, 1930; G. N. Lewis, *The Anatomy of Science*, New Haven, 1926; F. S. C. Northrop, *Science and First Principles*, New York, 1931; B. Russell, *The Scientific Outlook*, New York, 1931; F. R. Tennant, *Philosophy of the Sciences*, Cambridge, 1932.

[1a] Vd. Notes 2 and 47 *infra*.

[1b] Vd. Notes 16a and 47 *infra*.

regard to the biological sciences. Mechanics is the basic science of matter in motion, and all the other natural sciences are reducible thereto.

(2) This is the Cartesian philosophy of science, and it is based on the metaphysical point that matter exists as such, that its substantial nature is extension, and its essential operation is local motion. The Cartesian cosmology is a 17th century Christianized version of Plato's *Timaeus*. (The study of living matter must, therefore, be only a special case of the study of matter; the study of vital functions, of the kinds of change involved in digestion, sensation, reproduction, etc., must be reducible to the study of the proper change of matter in place, which is mechanics. It also involves the reduction of all causes to one type: the external, efficient cause, i.e., a local motion caused by a local motion).

(3) The Cartesian philosophy of science, furthermore, makes mathematical physics the supreme achievement of scientific endeavor, and presents it as the ideal toward which all scientific work must be directed. (The opposite position criticizes mathematical physics as a misleading ideal, a mixed science rather than real physics. But the Cartesian position idealizes it because if the essence of matter is quantity or extension or dimensionality, then all of the sciences of matter must be formally mathematical.)

(4) The Cartesian position with respect to the sciences is also taken by materialists, differing from Descartes in metaphysics in that they are monists whereas he is a dualist.[1c] In either case the properties

[1c] This sort of materialism is called by Marxists "natural-science materialism." Dialectical materialism goes beyond this by being "natural-science materialism" *plus* "historical materialism." Vd. A. Thalheimer, *An Introduction to Dialectical Materialism*, New York, 1936: Ch. VII, VIII; also Note 28a *infra*. It should be added here that the Cartesian position was taken by Kant; it was because of his Cartesian insistence upon dimensionality in science, that he despaired of "empirical psychology" as a science. The existence of psychometrics as an application of mathematics to psychical phenomena disposes of Kant as a prophet,—or, perhaps, Kant would have called this science "anthropometrics." Finally, it should be added here that the Cartesian position on the unity of science is taken by the logical positivists. Vd. R. Carnap, *The Unity of Science*, London, 1935. That they take this position is not due to their logic or, more properly, their grammar, but rather to their unacknowledged metaphysics which is simple-minded materialism.

of matter are the same, and hence the sciences of matter are homogeneous.

(5) The issue in the field of biology between mechanism and vitalism is to be understood in terms of the opposition between the first of these two philosophies of science and the second.

b. The second position is that the objects of natural science are heterogeneous, that there is only a partial continuity among the natural sciences, in which one may include the findings of another, but that the different sciences are ultimately irreducible to one another.

(1) This is the position taken by some biologists with respect to physics. The name "vitalist" is an ambiguous way in which to designate all those who resist the attempt to reduce all the natural sciences to mechanics and who insist that the heterogeneity of the animate and the inanimate is absolute and ultimate and, who, therefore, also insist that biology, though it may depend on knowledge gained by physicists and chemists, cannot be reduced thereto.[2]

(2) This is the Aristotelian philosophy of science, and it is based on the metaphysical point that matter does not exist as such, but only as formed; and that the forms under which units of matter can exist are never exclusively quantitative or dimensional, because quantity is at best an accidental and not a substantial determination of whatever exists materially. As a consequence of this basic point, it follows that matter existing under different substantial forms is radically different in nature. Hence the sciences of dead and of living matter belong to a different order because their objects belong to a different order of natural existence. (This philosophy of science insists not only upon different kinds of natural things, but upon different types of change, of which local

[2] Vd. J. S. Haldane, *Mechanism, Life and Personality*, London, 1913; A. N. Whitehead, *Science and the Modern World*, New York, 1925; J. Needham, *The Skeptical Biologist*, New York, 1930; van Uexküll, *Theoretical Biology*, New York, 1926; C. Lloyd-Morgan, *Emergent Evolution*, New York, 1923; and *Life, Mind and Spirit*, London, 1926; W. McDougall, *Modern Materialism and Emergent Evolution*, New York, 1929; R. F. Hoernle, *Matter, Life, Mind and God*, New York, 1923.

motion is only one, and upon different causes, of which the external or moving cause is only one.)

(3) The Aristotelian philosophy of science, furthermore, denies that mathematical physics is the supreme achievement of scientific endeavor. On the contrary, it is not even good as natural science,—except for practical purposes in engineering applications,—because its basic principles are not physical but mathematical. The biological sciences, and among these physiology, are much nearer to the ideal of investigative natural science, because the principles of physiology, for instance, are derived from general physics (the philosophy of nature). The tradition of physiology from Galen to Haldane is predominantly Aristotelian. (In other words, although all the empirical sciences deal only with the phenomenal surface of nature, those of the mathematical type are much more superficial than those which Maritain calls the empiriological type. It is their greater superficiality,—their remoteness from ontological significance,—which makes them appear "more abstract" and also enables them to be more exact.)

(4) The Aristotelian position is as much opposed to materialism of the simple-minded, atomistic-mechanistic sort as it is opposed to the dualism of Descartes, which separates matter and form as if they were independent substances.

c. This issue in the philosophy of science cannot be solved "empirically" by consulting the facts of the history of science. It is erroneous to try to use the history of science, stressing practical advances made in accordance with one or the other position, to solve the philosophical point.

d. This issue in the philosophy of science is of paramount importance for scientific psychology.[3]

(1) Either as a part of biology: reducible or not reducible to mechanics.

(2) Or as independent of biology in the same way as

[3] Cf. A. G. A. Balz, *The Metaphysical Infidelities of Modern Psychology* in the Journal of Philosophy, XXXIII, 13.

biology is independent of, and irreducible to, physics (mechanics or mathematical physics).

4. The two philosophies of science arise from radically different metaphysics. The issue between them can, therefore, be resolved only by recourse to metaphysics. It is necessary, therefore, to consider the metaphysical alternatives upon which the resolution turns. The appropriate formulation of these alternatives is in terms of cosmological propositions. We are here concerned with metaphysics only in so far as it is involved in the philosophy of nature [20].
   a. There are only four possible positions in metaphysics on the nature of existing things in change (the objects of investigative knowledge). And only one of these four positions can be right.
      (1) *Absolute materialism:* [4] best illustrated by the Greek atomists and their modern followers. (We have already seen how this metaphysical position insists upon the reducibility of all natural science to mechanics and mathematical physics, because matter has only dimensional properties.)
      (2) *Dualism:* [5] the position sometimes attributed to Plato, sometimes found in the neo-Platonic tradition, but explicitly stated by Descartes. The dualists assert that there are two independent substances: matter, the essence of which is dimensionality (extension); and mind, the essence of which is rationality (thought).
         (a) It follows, then, that there are only two sciences: physics, as mechanical and mathematical, on the one hand, and psychology, on the other. And these two sciences are independent of each other [20a].
         (b) Furthermore, just as all sciences of matter are ultimately homogeneous and mathematical, so psychology cannot be scientific at all, in the sense of being investigative knowledge, since investigative knowledge involves sense-observation. Psychology is purely philosophical knowledge and its method is entirely introspec-

[4] Vd. G. Plekhanov, *Essays in the History of Materialism*, London, 1934; A. Thalheimer, *op. cit.*; T. A. Jackson, *Dialectics*, New York, 1936: Ch. II; F. Engels, *Ludwig Feuerbach and the Outcome of Classical German Philosophy* (1888).

[5] Vd. A. O. Lovejoy, *The Revolt Against Dualism*, New York, 1930.

tive. It is the soul's knowledge of itself; it is the "science of consciousness." It was Kant's point that an *empirical science* of the "ego" could never be developed because it could not be experimental or mathematical. This further reveals Kant as Cartesian. But, curiously enough, Kant did concede an empirical science of man,—the phenomenal being whose behavior is observable,—and called this anthropology.

(c) As a result of this conception of psychology, modern psychology, which is for the most part Cartesian, is burdened with *insolubilia.* The various problems involved in the understanding of the relation of body and soul can be intelligently solved only when they are intelligibly stated. But the Cartesian misconception of form and matter as *res cogitans* and *res extensa* made insoluble riddles out of the relation of the mind and body, the problem of introspection, the problem of sensation and the passions, which seem to be connected both with the body and with the mind.

(3) *Absolute idealism:* [6] best illustrated by the philosophy of Hegel, and by other post-Kantian forms of German romantic and English epistemological idealism. This metaphysics does not occur in the ancient or mediaeval world at all, unless it can be attributed to Parmenides. (The monism of the Eleatics makes both change and plurality illusory. Only the motionless one exists.)

(a) Absolute idealism either denies matter and the plurality of individuals existing independently of Mind, or it treats them as self-contradictory appearances, as illusions due to an incomplete experience of reality. This is the familiar doctrine of Bradley's *Appearance and Reality* [20b].

(b) It makes psychology the primary, if not the only, science of reality. All the other sciences are about illusions or appearances.

(c) It makes psychology as a science non-investigative and purely dialectical, because all exist-

[6] Vd. J. Royce, *Lectures on Modern Idealism,* New Haven, 1917; R. F. Hoernle, *Idealism as a Philosophy,* New York, 1927.

ences are thoughts in an Absolute Mind which operates dialectically. In a sense, this dialectical character preserves a hierarchical structure within reality, and provides for the ordering of all the sciences, even those that deal with illusions, as subordinate to what Hegel called the pure phenomenology of spirit, which is psychology.[7]

(4) *Formal materialism:*[8] illustrated by the metaphysics of Aristotle and St. Thomas Aquinas [21].

(a) This position can best be stated by restating all the others. Absolute materialism denies substantial and qualitative forms, and faces the impossible task of having to reduce all differences and determinations to those of quantity. Absolute idealism denies matter and individuality except as illusions. Dualism insists upon both matter and form (extension and thought), but separates them as independent substances not involved in each other's existence. Formal materialism insists upon both matter and form as involved together in the nature of all existing changing things. It denies that matter exists apart from forms, and that the forms of matter exist except in matter. It denies that the only forms of matter are quantitative. It denies that matter is illusory.

(b) In terms of the analysis of matter and form, we can give an account of change as the transition from potentiality to actuality, and we can distinguish between the essential and the accidental forms by which matter is determined. (We can also give a better account than Kant

[7] Vd. Hegel, *The Phenomenology of Mind*, trans. by Baillie, New York, 1931. Cf. W. T. Stace, *The Philosophy of Hegel*, London, 1924: Part III on the Philosophy of Nature and Part IV on the Philosophy of Spirit.

[8] Vd. J. Maritain, *An Introduction to Philosophy*, London, 1930: Ch. V, VI, VII; I. Gredt, *Elementa Philosophia Aristotelico-Thomisticae*, Fribourg, 1932; R. P. Philips, *Modern Thomistic Philosophy*, London, 1934; E. Gilson, *The Spirit of Mediaeval Philosophy*, New York, 1936. For a discussion of controversial points within the doctrine of hylomorphism itself, see the account of the neo-Platonic objections in D. E. Sharp, *Franciscan Philosophy at Oxford in the Thirteenth Century*, London, 1930; also Pedro Descoqs, *Essai Critique sur l'Hylémorphisme*, Paris, 1924.

did of the distinction between the noumenal and the phenomenal orders in terms of the relation of being and operation, the properly intelligible and the properly sensible.)

(c) It clearly follows from this metaphysical position that the natural sciences (investigative knowledge of changing things) are as radically heterogeneous as there are essentially different types of formed-matter. In other words, the objects of science are different because matter is formed by irreducibly different genera of substantial forms.

(d) The picture of the sciences can be given as follows:

1.) The physical group: deals with natural things that are dead: inorganic forms. (Elemental and mixed bodies.)

2.) The biological group: deals with natural things that are alive, involving organic forms, which are called *souls*, not *minds*. (Vegetables, or plants, and animals.)

3.) With respect to psychology there are two ways in which its independent status can be conceived: in Aristotelian terms, as a separate body of knowledge dealing with the nature of the soul *as such*, considered in abstraction from plants and animals in which souls exist as material forms; or with the soul in its self-subsistence; in Thomistic terms, as the science of man, distinguished from biological science by the fact that man is rational. (In Thomistic terms, anthropology is a better name than psychology for knowledge about man, about human nature as integrally composite of body and soul, matter and form. Human psychology is in one sense a part of anthropology, dealing with the human soul as an integral part of man, and in another it belongs to natural theology since it is knowledge of a transcendent, extra-physical sort of being.) The position taken by St. Thomas is more Aristotelian than that taken by Aristotle in the *De Anima*, which shows Platonic influence in treating of soul primarily rather than of man. Vd. Note 36c *infra*.

b. The issue made by these four metaphysics is resolvable as follows. (I can merely indicate here the dialectic of the resolution. It is rationally binding. It is not a matter of opinion. There is only one right metaphysics.)

(1) Two of the four positions are at once seen to be impossible in terms of the evidence and in terms of internal contradictions. Thus:

(a) Absolute idealism arises from the simple epistemological error of identifying the *id quo* and the *id quod* of knowledge [22].

(b) Dualism has a number of inescapable internal difficulties. Its premises convert difficult but soluble problems into baffling paradoxes and impossible riddles. Thus, the problem of the unity of man throughout the neo-Platonic tradition and in modern psychology; the problem of the interaction of independent substances (body and mind), in the case of sensation, passion and volition, badly solved by recourse to the Divine providence of a pre-established harmony or left unsolved by a psychophysical parallelism which ignores the facts of vital action; the problem of change itself in a view of world which makes matter as completely actual as form; and most important of all, the impossibility of giving an account of the physical sciences, which are possessed by *minds*, but are knowledge of *bodies*.

(2) Only two of the four positions are seriously worth considering as possible, and both are materialistic, differing in that one is simple-minded and absolutistic, and the other is dialectical and relativistic.

(a) Absolute materialism ultimately reaches insuperable difficulties.[8a] On the one hand, it can-

[8a] For refutations of absolute ("natural-science") materialism, vd. Hook's account of Feuerbach's "critique of absolute materialism," and his account of Marx's criticism of "*all* materialisms from Democritus to Feuerbach" in *From Hegel to Marx*, New York, 1936: pp. 237 ff. and 274 ff.; also W. McDougall, *Modern Materialism and Emergent Evolution*, New York, 1929. The errors of "natural science materialism," —common to the atomists and the Cartesian mechanists,—are not avoided by the

not give an account of the nature of things, since it cannot reduce all forms to quantities or combinations of quantities, and it cannot give an account of all the phenomena of change, since it cannot reduce biological generation to local motion. On the other hand, it cannot give an account of knowledge itself, neither of the process by which matter knows matter sensitively, nor of the sciences of matter which seem to involve ideas as well as sensations. In short, just as absolute idealism is ultimately forced to call matter an illusion of the senses, so absolute materialism is forced to call all of our sensitive experience and all our intellectual knowledge illusory, however practical and useful it may seem to be in the world of matter.

(b) Hence, negatively, by elimination, hylomorphism or formal materialism is the only tenable metaphysics. Further, positively, it can be shown to be the only metaphysics which, without shifting its ground, without inconsistency, and without talking about fictions or illusions, can give a coherent account of physical nature, of our process of knowing it, and of the sciences which are knowledge of it. It is the only metaphysics which agrees at all points with common sense and common experience, because it is the only one which arises without error from the analysis of common experience.

c. The consequences of this metaphysical resolution are critical for the philosophy of science.

(1) It indicates the rightness of the Aristotelian account of the sciences as heterogeneous and irreducible, and the wrongness of the Cartesian or materialistic account.

(2) It leads, as we shall see, to a tripartite division of the sciences: physics, biology and psychology (or anthropology in the Thomistic sense).

(3) But, most important of all, it imposes the burden of metaphysics upon every scientist who is intelli-

addition of "historical materialism" on the level of human or social phenomena. In so far as dialectical materialism accepts atomism and mechanism as a philosophy of nature, it makes an error which such an addition does not expunge.

gent enough to consider the order and relation of the sciences. The opposition between the philosophies of science is so strictly correlated with metaphysical oppositions that any choice in the one case necessarily dictates a choice in the other, and conversely. Thus:

(a) If any one holds to homogeneity and reducibility, he must be either an absolute materialist, in which case psychology has no subject-matter; or a Cartesian dualist, in which case psychology is not an investigative science, if it is a science at all.

(b) If any one holds to heterogeneity and irreducibility, he must be either an absolute idealist or a formal materialist. In either case, psychology is separate from biology; but in the former case, it is in no sense an observational or investigative science.

(4) *Digression:* For the sake of brevity, I shall proceed upon the assumption that few scientific psychologists (certainly no experimentalists, and I doubt if any psychoanalysts) are absolute idealists.

(a) Those who are absolute materialists (such as the behaviorists) are not only wrong in metaphysics, but are involved in destroying themselves, since psychology must ultimately become mechanics and mathematical physics.[8b]

(b) And those who are dualists (as were most of the old-fashioned introspectionists or structuralists) are not only wrong in metaphysics, but are involved with such impossible problems as the relation of mind and body, the relation of psychology to physiology, etc.

(c) The only psychologists who are right in metaphysics, who can give an account of their subject-matter which properly relates it to physiology and yet preserves its independence, and

[8b] Vd. K. N. Kornilov, *Psychology in the Light of Dialectic Materialism*, in *Psychologies of 1930*, Worcester, 1930. Kornilov rejects the simple mechanism and materialism of American behaviorism and also the subjectivism of German introspective psychology. He does not see, however, as Marxists usually cannot or will not, that these denials necessarily lead to formal materialism, to the position of Aristotle and St. Thomas. Cf. Freud's comment on the dogmatic blindness of Marxism in *New Introductory Lectures on Psychoanalysis*, New York, 1933: pp. 246–7.

who have no ultimate *insolubilia* in psychology itself, are the formal materialists, of whom there are very few, if any [22a]. There are two possibilities:

1.) The *gestalters:* but they waver between dualism and hylomorphism, though they should choose the latter.

2.) The *psychoanalysts:* but they waver between materialism (complete reduction to physiology), dualism (Freud in his more neo-Platonic moments), and formal materialism, though they also should choose the last.

d. Without further demonstration, I am going to take two positions:

(1) formal materialism in metaphysics

(2) heterogeneity and irreducibility in the philosophy of science.

And in terms of these two positions I shall now discuss the subject-matter of psychology and its position among other bodies of knowledge.

III. The Position of Psychology Among the Investigative Sciences

1. Let us first consider psychology in the domain of biology.

a. Matter has various forms or perfections. Its potentialities are actualized in the existence of different kinds of bodies: elemental, mixed and living bodies. As living, matter not only has the perfection of existence but also the perfection of vital operations, such as, vegetation, sensation, locomotion and understanding [23].

b. There are no vital actions (operations) where there is no life.

(1) Soul is the actuality of an organic body having the potentiality of life. (Body besouled is body alive; the soul is the form of matter as living.)

(2) Soul is to body as form to matter. Soul and body are the *analytically* separable components in the composite nature of living things.

(3) Soul is the first act, the act of being, of a living thing. Vital operation is the second act. A living thing is not always vitally active in all the ways in which it is able to operate. It is impossible for Cartesians to make this distinction. For them, the prob-

lem of sleep is insoluble. The soul which is not thinking simply ceases to be.

(4) Biological study is of vital operations. It is concerned with the powers and operations of living things, powers and operations which are their properties because they are besouled.

(5) The different powers of vital action are related to the different organs of the body. The parts of the soul, which are these powers, are related to the parts of the body, which are endowed with these powers of vital operation because they are parts of a living (besouled) body. Thus, digestion is related to the stomach, vision to the eye, so long as these are parts of a living body.

c. The foregoing indicates the field of problems which are those of animal and human physiology.

(1) Physiology is the study of the acts of bodily organs.

(2) It is an investigation, not of the powers and operations of the body as mere matter, but of the operations of the composite: matter formed or besouled and hence alive and having powers of vital action.

(3) The question is how to distinguish the study made by the psychologist in the domain of biological phenomena, from that of the physiologist.

(a) Galen tried to make physiology the study of the operations of the vegetative organs (digestion, excretion, etc.) and of some of the organs of local motion; and to exclude, as belonging to psychology, the study of cognitive operations, such as sensation.[9] But this is untenable, because sensation is just as much the act of a bodily organ as is reproduction or local motion.

(b) The only possible distinction is one based on the distinction between the parts and the whole, the separate organs and the organism as a whole. (This must not be understood to mean that the physiologist studies organs in isolation from the organism as a whole which

[9] "Since feeling and voluntary motion are peculiar to animals, whilst growth and nutrition are common to plants as well, we may look on the former as effects of the soul (*psyche*) and the latter as effects of the nature (*physis*)" (*On the Natural Faculties*, I, 1).

is their environment; moreover he sometimes studies the organism as a whole in its physical relation to the environment.)

1.) Thus, the physiologist studies the action of the circulatory system by itself, or of the eye, or of the bladder, etc.

2.) Whereas the animal psychologist studies the behavior of the whole organism, based, of course, upon the vital action of the parts as integrated. He studies animal learning, the instincts, etc.

3.) There is no possible reduction here of animal psychology to animal physiology because the whole is not just a sum of the parts, not a collection but an integrative organization which functions integratively. Those physiologists who study the organs in relation to the organic totality recognize that the totality is not a mere summation. (It would be the same error to suppose that the whole was reducible to the sum of the organic parts, as to suppose that any of the organic parts were reducible to a mere sum or collection of atoms in their mechanical play. This is the error of the materialist and the Cartesian.)

(c) The one remaining problem is that of human psychology and human physiology.

1.) This problem depends for its solution upon the question whether man is essentially or only accidentally different from other animals.

2.) If the answer is that man differs from other animals only in degree, then psychology is a biological science, related to organ physiology, as that in turn is related to cell-physiology or cytology. In other words, the picture of the sciences of life would then be as follows:

Cytology: the life of the cell, *considered* separately, whether or not it *exists* separately.

Physiology: the life of a particular organ, *considered* separately, though it does not *exist* separately.

Psychology: the life of the organism as a whole.

3.) If this answer is given, that man does not differ radically or essentially in kind, then

a.) Psychology is only a particular natural science, and not a branch of philosophy (and it is hard to account for what appears to be a body of philosophical and non-investigative knowledge about man's nature); and furthermore

b.) Psychoanalysis is queer. There is no animal psychoanalysis, so far as the *method* of psychoanalysis is concerned. Man is at least capable of being distinguished from all other animals as able to be psychoanalyzed.

c.) Finally, though psychoanalysis may be, as speculative, only a study of human behavior, it is as practical and therapeutic more than that, and that more is intelligible only in terms of the difference between man and other animals.

2. Summary: The position of psychology seems to be peculiar among the investigative sciences. As animal psychology, it is properly located in the biological domain. But human psychology raises some difficulties.[10]

a. On the one hand, it is like animal psychology, and *in so far* is properly located in the biological domain [24].

b. But, on the other hand, it seems to be *something else*, such as psychoanalysis or philosophical psychology or introspective psychology, etc.

c. This *something else*, which human psychology seems to be, can be properly understood only *if* man is understood as essentially and radically different from other animals, and *if*, to this extent, human psychology ex-

[10] Vd. R. P. McKeon, *De Anima: Psychology and Science* in the Journal of Philosophy, XXVII, 25.

ceeds animal psychology and cannot be properly located in the biological domain.

(1) Furthermore, we have the problem whether what is peculiarly human psychology is entirely philosophical in method or whether as a body of knowledge it can be both philosophical and scientific, that is, investigative in method. (This problem does not occur with respect to animal psychology. It properly includes investigative knowledge.)

(2) We can now construct another possible picture of the allocation of psychology.

Animal psychology:
a particular natural science concerned with the behavior of animal organisms as wholes; a science in the biological domain.

Human psychology:
(a) As if it were the same as animal psychology, by ignoring what is characteristically and differently human.[11]
(b) Of man as such: but investigative in method, such as psychoanalysis, and not in the biological domain.
(c) Of man as such: but philosophical in method.

(3) The chief problem which this picture raises concerns the existence and nature of a body of psychological knowledge, relevant only to man and yet investigative in method. Psychoanalysis *seems* to be such knowledge. It is investigative in method; it is relevant only to man. If there is such a body of knowledge it is not reducible to biology, and it is not even, strictly speaking, in the biological domain.

(4) In order to solve this problem—in order to determine whether psychoanalysis is philosophical or investigative, or *both*,—we must now consider the nature of psychology as a body of philosophical knowledge.

IV. The Position of Psychology in Philosophy

1. We must, first, consider the philosophical demonstration that the human soul differs from the vegetative soul, which

[11] Vd. Note 24 *infra*.

is not cognitive, and from the animal soul, which is sensitive, by being intellective, i.e., by the power and operations of understanding (abstraction, judgment, inference).

a. It should be reiterated here that the distinction between sensation and understanding is phenomenologically unquestionable.

b. It should be emphasized, furthermore, that any account of science must acknowledge this distinction, and hence every psychologist considering himself as a scientist must admit that he has a human soul.

c. The radical difference of the human soul, that it is intellective, can be understood only in terms of a metaphysical analysis. And we must remember that whatever we say here follows from the choice we have already made in the philosophy of science. We cannot at this point give up our position that the objects of science are heterogeneous and hence that all the sciences are not reducible to one basic science, such as mechanics; and if we hold to it, we must hold to the metaphysical position upon which it is based: formal materialism or hylomorphism [25]. In terms of this position, we must give the following account of understanding.

(1) All existing physical things are composite of form and matter.

(2) But all existing physical things are individual, i.e., unique particulars, though particulars of a certain sort.

(3) Hence, the forms of individual things are individuated. The form, being in matter, is subject to material conditions which individuate it.

(4) But understanding is grasping the universal, which means separating the form from the conditions of individuation. In other words, John Smith cannot be understood as *hoc aliquid*, but only in so far as he is a man. John Smith is understood as a man when the form which in him exists individually, in *his* matter, is separated from *that* matter.

(a) The separation of the form from the matter requires two cognitive steps: first, the acts of sensation and imagination in which the form of the individual thing is separated from its matter but is apprehended under the conditions of individuality because sensation is the act of a bodily organ, and hence sensible forms as apprehended by sense are in matter (that is, sensitive apprehension is always of the particular); and second, the intellectual act of abstraction which separates the form, grasped by sense under individuating conditions, from those conditions; and thus converts *intelligibility* into something *actually understood*.

(b) Things are intelligible (potentially understood) in so far as they are composite of matter and form. They are actually understood by the separation of the form from the matter by sense, and of the form from material conditions by the intellect.

(5) Whatever is received is in the recipient according to the mode of being of the recipient.

(6) In terms of the foregoing, it can be shown now that the primary intellectual operation (the acts of abstraction and of receiving abstracted universals) cannot be the act of a bodily organ as the sensitive operation (the act of sensation) is the act of a bodily organ. For, if it were, the forms received in the intellect would be received into matter, since the act of a bodily organ is an act of matter, and forms which are acts of matter exist in matter as individuated. Hence, they would still be potentially intelligible and not actually understood. Hence, if men are able to understand,—to apprehend things in their universality (their intelligibility) as well as in their individuality (their sensibility),—intellection must be an operation that is not the act of a bodily organ. This truth is not inconsistent with the fact that intellectual operation depends upon prior sensitive operation, since the forms abstracted are abstracted from the informed matter of sensation and imagination [26].

d. This analysis of intellectual power and operation explains three things characteristic of man and no other animal.

(1) Science and philosophy, involving knowledge of universals. This does not mean that brute animals

lack knowledge, but that they have only sensitive knowledge.

(2) The practical and productive arts, involving the practical and intellectual operations of free choice, deliberate doing and intentional making [27]. Thus:

(a) In the practical sphere: men freely determine their moral characters, their social institutions, their governments, their laws. Other animals are social, but only instinctively. Animal societies are, therefore, capable of being studied entirely in the domain of biology; but not human society, which can be properly studied only in terms of a psychology that recognizes the intellect, practical reason and voluntary conduct.

(b) In the productive sphere: men make things, fine and useful productions, by conceiving and intending them. Other animals are productive, but only instinctively. Whereas man can make many different kinds of things, and by manufacturing can multiply individual instances of each kind, productive animals can build or make only one sort of thing, for the creation of which they are instinctively endowed. Birds of a given species make nests of a given kind; so in the case of ants, bees, termites. Animals cannot vary their works or multiply them by manufacturing. Animal productions are, therefore, capable of being studied entirely in the domain of biology, but not the productions of human art, fine or useful.

2. That man differs essentially and specifically from all other animals is capable of being demonstrated *a posteriori* from the observable operations of men and brutes.

a. Thus, only man manufactures. Manufacturing involves the grasp of a species of thing and its duplication by imprinting the same form upon many units of matter. To manufacture means to make according to specifications, choosing material capable of receiving such and such determinations. Only an intellectual animal could manufacture or, as Marxians say, machinofacture.

Marxian materialists, in defining man as a productive and machinofacturing animal, acknowledge his intellectuality. Unless man can comprehend universals, can separate forms from the material conditions of individuality, he cannot make things according to specifications; he cannot, in machinofacturing, impose the *same* artificial form on multiple, *different* units of matter [28].

b. Similarly, arguments could be drawn from a comparison of human and animal societies, human and animal knowledge, human and animal language [28a]. In all these cases, there is an analogy between the human and the animal mode, but the analogy also involves a specific or essential difference. The difference is not merely a matter of degree. (It should be noted here that the right use of analogy *always* includes the marking of *essential* differences. Otherwise, analogical reasoning is deceptive and illicit. Only things which are essentially different can be properly analogized, e.g., God and creatures, man and animals, art and nature.)

(1) Thus, bees live socially but not according to a political theory or in terms of moral principles; thus, birds make nests but cannot manufacture them; thus, monkeys jabber and communicate in a rudimentary way, but have no language which has syntactical structure, and without syntax there cannot be propositions or science.[12]

(2) That animals seem to think is not surprising when one remembers that most men for the most part think, not intellectually, but in terms of sense and imagination. If men can do a sort of thinking,—making comparisons, remembering, projecting, estimating, etc.,—through imagination, so can animals who have imagination because they, like men, are sensitive [29].

c. Psychoanalysis itself provides us with strong *a posteriori* evidence of an essential difference between men and brutes. The latter cannot be psychoanalyzed because

(1) They lack reason; lacking it, they have no grammatical language; and without such language, in-

[12] Even logical positivists would admit this. Vd. Carnap, *Philosophy and Logical Syntax*, London, 1935.

tellectual communication (the communication of judgments, of opinions, etc.) is impossible;

(2) They lack reason (or intellect); without intellect, free choice is impossible; without free choice and voluntary conduct, the therapeutics of psychoanalysis is impossible.

3. I have now answered all of Dr. Alexander's questions [30]. I have shown in what sense understanding has a physiological basis and in what sense it cannot have. I have shown that the difference between men and brutes is not a matter of degree. I have shown, therefore, that the type of "biological continuity" which is supposed by those who find no *essential* difference between men and brutes, does not exist. There is, of course, the type of continuity which obtains in the series of integral numbers. Such a continuity exists because *man is an animal,*—a *rational* but not a *brute* animal [31].

4. In the light of the foregoing, the nature of psychology as a body of philosophical knowledge can be understood.

   a. *In terms of its object:* the intellect is able to know reflexively as sense is not. Thus, the senses only know their proper sensible objects, but not each other or themselves (i.e., the eye cannot see, the ear cannot hear, the *eye as seeing*); but the intellect is able to understand all intelligible objects, including the senses and, most important of all, it is able to understand itself. This means that the intellect is able to know, through sensitive experience, the various organs of the human body and their several powers of operation, and such knowledge is the investigative science of physiology. But the intellect can also know directly (i.e., without investigation) its own operations, *in se* and in relation to all other human operations, and such knowledge is the branch of philosophy called psychology.[12a]

[12a] Cf. C. Alibert, *La Psychologie Thomiste et les Théories Modernes*, Paris, 1903; pp. 1–22. Alibert defines the province of philosophical psychology in terms of reflexive knowledge. It extends to all the powers of man, even to the vegetative, of which he says: "Son existence m'est révélée seulement par des inductions tirées des données physiologiques" (p. 9). It does not include, however, fields of phenomena which require investigation. "L'observation externe est encore necéssaire pour prendre connaissance des états anormaux, tels que le rêve, le somnambulisme, l'hallucination, la folie, et pour decrire la vie psychique de l'animal, délimiter la partie des facultés humaines qu'il convient de lui attribuer, et celles que nous devons tenir pour incommunicables" (p. 13).

(1) We have now solved the fundamental paradox of psychology as knowledge, which is due to its reflexivity: namely, that the psychologist as a man, as a scientist or philosopher, knows himself as a man and as a scientist or philosopher.

(2) Philosophical psychology arises from man's direct knowledge of himself as operating in a distinctively human way [31a].

b. *In term of its method:* the reflexivity of the understanding (that we know ourselves as knowing, understand ourselves as understanding) is the root of philosophical psychology and explains how psychological knowledge is possible *without investigation*. We know the nature of man *a posteriori* in terms of his operations, and these operations, in so far as they are typically human, we can know directly because the intellect is able to understand its own operations and the operations of sense and appetite as these are immediately experienced. Thus, the concept of the understanding is an abstraction from particular operations of understanding; similarly, in the case of sense, desire, passion, will, etc.

(1) This does not mean that human behavior *cannot* be investigated. It does not mean that rational operations *cannot* be investigated. The clinical studies, made by psychiatrists and psychoanalysts of the pathology of reason and will, are investigations of intellectual activity. Even behavioristic studies of human "problem-solving," devised through the analogy of rats in mazes and monkeys in boxes, are investigations of rational behavior. But all such investigations must accept the principles of philosophical psychology, or be involved in self-contradictions. When the data of such studies are properly interpreted, it is found that scientific knowledge is about the *accidents* of human, i.e., rational, behavior [32].

(2) Common experience is inadequate as a basis for knowledge of *kinds* of physical things, with the one exception of ourselves as an object of knowledge.[12b]

[12b] This statement is insufficient as an explanation. In so far as it emphasizes quantity it is wrong. The root of the matter is, as Maritain points out, that man does not know the essential natures of physical things in their ultimate specific diversity. Vd. *Degrés*

We must investigate, and these things, therefore, are exclusively the objects of the natural sciences. But, in the case of ourselves, common experience is *sufficient*, and investigation, while *possible*, is not *necessary*. Philosophical psychology is nothing more than the analysis of the immediate experience of our own operations. In short, the self is a unique object for man to know.

5. *Now, it follows from all that has preceded:*
   a. That psychology is the only branch of philosophical knowledge which is about a particular type of changing thing: namely, man in his operations [32a]. Human change consists of all sorts of learning, the formation of moral and intellectual habits, etc.
   b. That psychology, in a qualified sense, as animal psychology, is not a branch of philosophy but a particular natural science in the domain of biology, concerned with the behavior of organisms in their totality.
   c. That psychology as philosophical is concerned with the powers and operations of man and from these it seeks to learn what it can of the essence of man, the nature of the human soul, etc. It is not concerned with *human biography as such:* how a man develops. Since human development is always for better or for worse and is the result of choices freely made, the ancient and mediaeval tradition relegated developmental problems to the field of ethics [33]. This last point is, as we shall see, crucially important for the understanding of psychoanalysis.
   d. That psychology as scientific is, in large part, concerned with the behavior of animals, and with human behavior *in so far as it is animal.*
   e. One important problem remains: Can psychology as scientific be concerned with human behavior *in so far as it is distinctively human?* This is what psychoanalysis seems to be doing. Psychoanalysis seems to have the same object of knowledge as philosophical psychology,

au Savoir, Paris, 1932: p. 77. The only *infima species* man knows is human nature: man is the only physical object man can adequately define. It is in this sense that man is a unique object of human knowledge on the physical level, and this explains the distinction of psychology among all subject-matters constituted by the first-grade of abstraction.

but it seems to be proceeding by the investigative method and clearly hopes to be a body of scientific knowledge. Is this possible? If so, how? And how is it related to philosophical psychology? This last question directs us to what is, perhaps, the most difficult problem, namely, the unity of psychology as including both philosophical and scientific knowledge. We have already solved this problem in general (vd. Note 32a *infra*), but the precise nature of the scientific contribution must be determined before the problem can be more fully discussed. We shall return to it, therefore, in Lecture IV.

(1) The same questions can be asked of other types of psychological research by investigative methods, which seem to be directed to the study of man as man and not merely as an animal.

(2) Such studies as those made by psychometrics seem to be concerned with accidental features of human nature. Thus, the measurement of human intelligence, or other human abilities, is concerned with quantitative accidents; and the experimental study of human memory or perception or imagination is concerned with such accidents as are involved in time, place, number, the material, etc. We are excluding, of course, all research which is physiological in method or interpretation.

(3) It is possible for there to be a mixed science of the same sort as mathematical physics: thus, Edgeworth's *Mathematical Psychics*.[13] The two ideals of natural science,—the mathematical and the empiriological,—are to be found in psychology. In psychology, more than in physics or physiology, the mathematical type of science is superficial.

(4) Psychoanalysis is much nearer to the consideration of man as man than any of these other scientific attempts at human psychology; and it is not a mixed or mathematical science.

(5) Hence, the problem of psychoanalysis as a scientific study of man, in his peculiar character as man, is most acute.

[13] London, 1881. The subtitle is: An Essay on the Application of Mathematics to the Moral Sciences. Cf. C. Spearman, *The Abilities of Man*, New York, 1928; L. L. Thurstone, *Vectors of Mind*, Chicago, 1935.

V. Conclusion

1. We have now accounted for the peculiarities of psychology among all bodies of knowledge, philosophical and scientific. This account will also explain, as we shall see, the peculiar history of psychology.
2. What remains to be understood is the nature of knowledge which claims both to be about *man as man* and to be *scientific*. This is the claim of psychoanalysis. And it must be said here that it appears more rightfully to make this claim than any other pretender to the title of scientific psychology.[14]
3. As we have seen, these questions are most acute for psychoanalysis as a body of knowledge about man, though they can be asked about psychometrics, gestalt psychology, functional psychology, behaviorism, etc.
4. The best way to approach this general problem is through the history of psychology as the study of man by any method, philosophical or scientific.[15]

[14] Psychometrics also has ground for making this claim. It is significant that Galton who, with Fechner, was a founder of psychometrics, rightly conceived the subject-matter of psychology in his *Inquiries into Human Faculty*. Vd. Note 46 *infra* for a comparative evaluation of psychoanalysis and psychometrics.

[15] The distinction between philosophical and scientific psychology, which has been adumbrated throughout this lecture, must not be confused with the distinction, in vogue since the days of Christian Wolff, between rational and empirical psychology. Vd. Note 39c *infra*.

THE HISTORY OF PSYCHOLOGY

I. Introduction

1. I shall first summarize the points upon which we seem to agree. I shall then restate the issues raised in the last discussion, and I shall remind you of the problem with which the last lecture ended. It is for the solution of this problem that we turn today to the history of psychology.
2. The points of agreement.
   a. We are Aristotelians rather than Cartesians in our philosophy of science. That means that we view the objects of natural science as intrinsically and irreducibly heterogeneous.
      (1) There is a hierarchy of the sciences of natural things.
      (2) The biological sciences may, for instance, depend upon knowledge obtained by physical and chemical researches, but they have an independent field of inquiry. In the advance of knowledge, they will never be replaced by mechanics [33a].
      (3) Mathematical physics should not be the exclusive ideal of investigative science.
   b. We are Aristotelians in metaphysics. Negatively, this means that we are not simple-minded, absolute materialists of the atomistic sort, or dualists of the Cartesian sort, or absolute, but not quite so simple-minded, idealists of the Hegelian sort. Our unanimous negation of these positions is correlated with our rejection of what follows from each of them with respect to the philosophy of science. Positively, this means that we hold the following propositions:
      (1) The realm of natural things in change,—the subject-matter of all investigative science,—consists of things formed of matter. All natural things are material or corporeal.

(2) But the forms in which matter exists, constituting the variety of natural things, are not merely or primarily quantitative. These forms are the different perfections of matter. Thus, we find matter existing but not living, or living but not sensing, or living and sensing but not thinking. As existing but not living, matter is either elemental or mixed in form. As living, matter either merely vegetates, or senses and moves as well as vegetates.

(3) This hierarchy of perfections in existing things is the basis for the hierarchy of the natural sciences investigating them [34].

(4) The superior perfection necessarily includes inferior perfections. Thus, what is alive must also exist as a body exists; that is, living things have all the properties of inanimate bodies, and some other properties in addition; similarly, whatever is able to sense and move must also vegetate, but not conversely [35].

(5) This order of the perfections of matter indicates both the continuity in nature (the inclusion of inferior perfections) and the discontinuity (the addition of new properties).

c. The premises we have thus accepted and asserted bind us to certain conclusions.

Digression: We must avoid the error of "wishful thinking," sometimes called "rationalization."

(a) There are only two kinds of thinking: logical and illogical. "Wishful thinking" may be either. When the psychoanalyst uses the phrase "logical thinking" in a derogatory sense, he means a wishful use of logic. Thus, it is so often said that you can prove anything by logic. That is absolutely true. No one knows it better than a logician. Given a set of false premises, you can prove a conclusion which logically follows from them, and that conclusion may be either true or false in fact. If you desire to prove that conclusion, and invent the premises to that end, without any honest regard for their intrinsic truth or falsity, your thinking is only formally logical, but essentially wishful. It is rationalization. Such rationalization is the more treacherous because the wishful thinking is *formally* good by *logical* criteria.

(b) Whereas you can prove anything by logic, you cannot prove anything without it. There is, therefore, another kind of wishful thinking. The first kind is rationalization which is good logically but is based on false premises chosen wishfully. The second kind is irrational thinking. Here we assert a conclusion despite the fact that it cannot be proved logically by sound premises, or deny a conclusion even though it follows necessarily from premises which we accept as sound. This is obviously also wishful thinking, differing from the first sort, which uses logic for its purposes, by trying to avoid logic. Thus, there are two kinds of *wishful* or bad thinking: (a) logical: rationalization; (b) illogical: irrationalization.

(c) Good thinking, the thinking of a competent scientist or philosopher, must not be wishful in either sense. The premises used must be chosen and accepted, not because they prove a conclusion we desire to believe, but because by the criteria of evidence they are sound and true in fact. If they yield a conclusion, they must do so logically; and if they yield a conclusion logically, that conclusion must not be avoided even though it is contrary to our desires. Finally, no conclusion can be accepted which does not follow logically from sound premises. The two criteria of good thinking are (1) sound premises and (2) correct inference. The only *wish* must be to know the truth.

(1) In the light of this digression, let me say, first, that the analysis I presented last time was not an instance of wishful thinking of the first sort. In this connection, let me remind you that you accepted the premises,—the Aristotelian philosophy of science and formal materialism in metaphysics,[1]—*before* you saw the conclusions which followed from them. I presented these premises,

[1] Vd. Lecture II *supra*. It should be added here that the argument there explicitly determined the choice of formal materialism as against the alternatives of absolute idealism, Cartesian dualism and absolute materialism. It also implicitly determined a choice between the sound and corrupt forms of that doctrine,—the issue between Aristotle and all sorts of Platonism. Vd. Note 21 *infra*. Leibnitz, Spinoza, Whitehead are neo-Platonists, i.e. corrupt Aristotelians. For an example of neo-Platonic plural-

not because they were able to yield the conclusion I desired, but because they seemed to me to be the only sound premises and were, therefore, unavoidable.

(2) I must say, therefore, that any refusal to accept the conclusions which follow from these premises looks to me like wishful thinking of the second sort, not rationalization but irrational thinking. The remark, *that you can prove anything by logic*, is a typical defense mechanism on the part of those who wish to avoid the conclusions which do follow logically from sound premises.

(3) The only way in which to avoid a conclusion which follows logically from premises is to deny the premises as unsound and wrong in fact.

(4) Therefore, unless it can be shown that the Aristotelian philosophy of science is wrong and the Cartesian right, unless it can be shown that absolute materialism or dualism or absolute idealism is right in metaphysics, and formal materialism is wrong, the conclusions which follow logically from an Aristotelian philosophy of science and from formal materialism, must be accepted by anyone who does not do the irrational sort of wishful thinking.

3. The conclusion which some members of this group tried to reject, *without* denying the premises and *without* finding any flaw in the reasoning, was: that man is essentially different from other animals, as animals are from vegetables, and as all living things are from inanimate bodies.

a. This essential difference resides in man's intellectual power, his power of understanding as distinctly different from his power of sensing. The latter he shares in common with brute animals.

b. I shall not repeat the various proofs of this essential difference. I shall merely remind you of

(1) The phenomenological distinction between sensing and understanding discoverable by any consideration of scientific knowledge;

(2) The *a posteriori* evidence of an essential difference between men and brutes in terms of language, cul-

ism, see Whitehead's discussion of the hierarchy of "societies" as a graded continuum, in *Adventures of Ideas*, New York, 1933: pp. 260–267.

tural history, social institutions, the arts and sciences.

(3) The metaphysical proof that understanding is not the act of a corporeal organ, such as the brain; but that understanding is an act which depends upon the act of a corporeal organ such as the brain. The latter activity is imagination. If I were to use Dr. Alexander's language, I would make this point as follows: Understanding is a function of imagination; imagination is a function of the brain. The word "function" is ambiguous. It has two meanings in the foregoing statement. A secondary function, a function of a function, is not the same as a primary function; only the latter is the act of a corporeal organ. Furthermore, this point holds if brute animals understand as well as men. If they do, understanding in them, as in man, must be a secondary function [36]. It should be added that when it is said here that understanding depends on, or is a function of, imagination, imagination is being regarded as a *necessary* but not a *sufficient* condition of intellection.

c. I shall accept Dr. Alexander's formulation as adequate. The only point of disagreement which remains, then, is whether men are essentially different from brute animals with respect to their exclusive possession of this so-called secondary function, understanding.

(1) As against the strong *a posteriori* evidence in favor of the difference, Dr. Alexander offered the case of the cretin idiot. The Mongolian idiot can be added, and also the dementia praecox patient in the later stages of dementia and catatonic stupor.

(2) The objection raises only a question of verbal usage. If by the word "man" we mean an offspring of human parents, then aments and dements are men. In which case, the class of men would include individuals who perform only as animals do, differing from animals only to the extent that they are curable, as the cretin idiot is known to be by thyroid.

(3) But what does curable here mean? It indicates at once another meaning of the word "man." We cure a cretin in order to make him able to perform as a man can. This second meaning of "man" does not define man as an offspring of human parents, but as a creature able to be an artist or a scientist or a statesman,

a creature able to be psychoanalyzed by verbal methods.

(4) When I say that man is essentially different from brutes, I mean a class of individuals defined by the second meaning of the word "man." I will now give you three criteria for telling whether a creature is *actually* a man, or actually but *incompletely* a man as the cretin is, or *merely* a brute.

(a) The ancient criterion: *rationality*, which means the ability to learn or be taught science and philosophy, the ability to govern other men by laws or to be governed by them, the ability to communicate by grammatical language, etc.

(b) The Marxian criterion: *productivity*, which means the ability to manufacture things according to specifications and plans.

(c) The Freudian criterion: *psychoanalyzability*, which means the ability to be changed in moral character by a technique dependent on the use of language and grammatical communication; or, more generally, *psychological curability*, i.e., the potentiality for becoming more fully a man, whether the efficient cause of therapy be the administration of thyroid, psychiatric devices, or psychoanalysis. These three criteria exclude all brutes absolutely. They also exclude the Mongolian idiot and the dementia praecox patient *for the time being*, that is, until we learn how to cure them, where curing them means making them actually men [36a].

d. I wish to add here only one other point, with which you have not so far, and I think cannot ever, disagree. If the statement, man is a rational animal, means that man is able to be a scientist, and if being a scientist means asserting as true only those propositions which are based upon sound evidence in a logical manner (i.e., doing non-wishful thinking), then the psychoanalyst, who claims to be a scientist, cannot say that *all* human thinking or knowing is wishful, whether the wishful thinking be rationalization or the sort we have called irrationalization. In other words, a psychoanalyst cannot claim to be a scientist and at the same time deny that man is a rational animal.

4. I now turn to the problem of to-day's lecture, which is to

discover the subject-matter and scope of psychology as a body of scientific or investigative knowledge.

a. There is no problem about psychology as a body of philosophical or non-investigative knowledge. I have already indicated the subject-matter of psychology, as developed by philosophical analysis, namely, the powers, operations and essence of man.[1a] This analysis man is able to make through self-knowledge, without any research of the investigative sort. I shall make this clearer in the course of reporting the history of psychology.

b. With respect to scientific psychology, we have seen
   (1) That it must be different from physiology, which studies the powers and operations of particular bodily organs;
   (2) That it achieves this difference by studying the operations of the organism as a whole.
   (3) But the problem still remains whether there is a specifically human psychology, different from animal psychology, and related to human physiology as animal psychology is related to animal physiology.

c. In short, we are here trying to understand the subject-matter of psychoanalysis. It is not, at least in its present formulation, an animal psychology. It deals specifically with man. Its method seems to be primarily investigative rather than philosophical. The primary question is whether psychoanalysis is *the* science of human psychology. If so, there are three further questions:
   (1) What are its investigative methods and problems?
   (2) Is it aetiological, physionomic or taxonomic? (or any two or three?)
   (3) How is it related to philosophical psychology?

5. I suggested that these questions could best be answered by a brief survey of the history of psychology. I proceed now to that history. It divides, first, into two periods: from the beginning until the 19th century, and from the 19th century to the present day; and the first of these two periods divides further into the period from the beginning until the 17th century, and from the 17th century to the 19th century. Thus:

a. The first division into periods is based on the distinction between philosophical and scientific method. Prior to the 19th century, psychology was non-investigative. The science of psychology has a fairly recent history [36b].

[1a] Vd. Note 32a *infra*.

b. The second division, of the first period, is based on the discrimination of what is sound from what is unsound in philosophy. From the 17th to the 19th centuries, psychology as a branch of philosophy is for the most part unsound, filled with errors, confused as to subject-matter, etc.

c. Psychology is the most recent of the natural sciences. It became autonomous as a branch of investigative knowledge by revolting from philosophy. To the extent that there can be a scientific psychology, the revolt was fortunate and justified; it was only extremely unfortunate that scientific psychology arose at a time when its basic concepts were derived from the bad philosophical psychology of the 17th and 18th centuries, and when the prevalent positivism made it difficult, if not impossible, for psychologists to understand the relation of their science to the philosophy of man. If it had been born earlier, it would have had a less tainted heritage and we would have less trouble getting it over its present feeble-mindedness.

d. In general, it is a misfortune to be born in modern times, a period in which each thinker commits the sin of pride, acknowledges no ancestors, rests in no tradition, but insists with consummate egotism, upon his complete originality and his complete independence of all prior human learning. (This is peculiarly true of psychoanalysis, and particularly of its great founder, Freud, who is curiously unaware of the tradition to which he belongs as a thinker and a student.)

II. From the Beginning to the 17th Century: Philosophical Psychology

1. So far as the literary tradition goes, the beginning of psychology, as of all other bodies of knowledge except mathematics, is in the work of Aristotle. His method required him to define separate subject-matters and to develop separate bodies of knowledge, both philosophical and investigative. Thus, his *Metaphysics* and *Physics*, unlike his treatises in astronomy and zoology, were entirely non-investigative, entirely philosophical. His psychology (*De Anima* and *Parva Naturalia*) was partly investigative and partly philosophical. Thus, the double status of psychology is indicated at the beginning of its history. It would have been clearer had Aristotle written a treatise on man [36c].

2. But, first, as an initial digression, we must consider Plato. (Freud is most indebted to Plato and Schopenhauer among philosophers, even though he seldom cites Schopenhauer, and his references to Plato are peculiarly trivial, considering his debt to Plato.)
   a. We shall ignore the metaphysical error which Plato seems to make in separating soul and body as if they were independently existing things. We shall also ignore the errors which follow in Platonic psychology. All these are repeated by Descartes [37].
   b. Here we are only concerned to state Plato's true insights about the nature of man:
      (1) That he is a rational animal, and is, therefore, subject to the fundamental conflicts between animality and rationality. (Thus, the myth of the charioteer in the *Phaedrus*, which is devoted to speeches about love.[2]) Here Plato anticipates Freud in great detail concerning sexuality, and love as its proper sublimation. I am referring to the three papers by Freud on the psychology of love in 1910, 1912 and 1918.[3] Here, furthermore, Plato describes in detail the conflicts in man between his lower and higher nature, between his animality and his rationality, between his id and his ego and super-ego.[4]
      (2) That he is a loving animal. This means that in all his activities, whether they be sexual or artistic or philosophical, man acts through love. The Platonic insistence upon Eros as a fundamental trait of the psyche is the Freudian insistence that all human activities are an expression of libido. Libido, desire, love—all name the same fundamental root of activity. In the *Symposium*, and elsewhere, Plato enumerates and orders the various objects of love. His distinction between sensual and intellectual love is the Freudian distinction between sexuality and its various sublimations.
      (3) That man can be rational without ceasing to love, and love without ceasing to be rational. Here the

[2] Vd. especially the second speech which Socrates makes: *Phaedrus*, 244–257.
[3] In *Collected Papers*, London, 1925: Vol. IV, Papers XI–XIII, three contributions to the psychology of love.
[4] Vd. *Republic*, IX, 588 C–590 B, in which Plato employs the image of a three-headed beast to describe the soul.

Platonic points are that reason is not reason unless it rules the irrational parts of man, his animality; that love is not human love unless it is ruled by reason (*sexuality* sublimated into *eros*.)

(4) Finally, that health is a harmony in the body and that happiness is a harmony in the soul. The important principle here is the insight that human well-being requires integration to resolve conflicts and dissociations; that dissociation is basic to all psychopathology, and that dissociation can be cured or prevented only by the harmony or integration which results from an ordering of the parts. This is achieved only when reason rules, when man is a rational lover.

c. It is important to note, in passing, that the Platonic discussion does not separate psychological analysis from medical and moral precepts. The close relation in the practical application of psychology, between the medical and the moral aspects, should also be noted.

3. Aristotle sharply separates his psychological analysis from its various practical applications.

a. In the first place, Aristotle corrects the metaphysical error of Plato with regard to the relation of soul to body. They are not related as two separate existences, but as the form and matter of the same existence. In short, man exists and operates as he does, by virtue of the composition in him of form and matter. (The form of any living matter is called "soul"; hence, the form of man is the human soul. All of the powers and operations of man are functions of the composite of form and matter, except one, understanding, which is only secondarily a function of the composite.)

b. The *De Anima* [4a] is concerned with the powers and operations of all living things (all things having souls).

(1) Here we learn the distinction of three grades of soul in terms of distinctive operations: *vegetable*, *animal*, *human*.

(2) Here also we learn the hierarchy of living powers, the kinds of vital action: the vegetative (nutritive, augmentative, generative), the sensitive (the various

[4a] To this should be added, of course, the short treatises of the *Parva Naturalia*, especially the *De Sensu et Sensibili*, *De Memoria et Reminiscentia*, *De Somno et Vigilia* and *De Somniis*. The last should be of particular interest to psychoanalysts.

senses), the locomotive, the appetitive, and the intellectual or rational.

c. In the case of man, the following points are made:

(1) The distinction between the cognitive and non-cognitive powers. Only men and animals are cognitive, and hence only they have an appetitive power (i.e., can be said to desire) because desire depends upon objects known, either by sense or by intellect.

(2) The distinction between the rational and the non-rational parts of man, the rational part being both cognitive and appetitive. Will is rational desire (intellectual appetite), what Plato would have called rational as opposed to animal love.

(3) The various dependencies: of sense and locomotion upon vegetative operations; of intellect upon sense; of appetite upon both sense and intellect; and of appetite also upon locomotion. Yet appetite, in a sense, rules all the other powers, in that whatever we do, we do from desire, either sensual or rational.[5]

(4) The analysis of the senses: the division of exterior and interior senses; the enumeration and description of the various exterior senses; the interior sense as perception, imagination, memory. (Exterior and interior sensitivity can be regarded as functions of the sense-organs and brain respectively.)

(5) The analysis of the intellect: the distinction of the active and the possible intellect; and the separation of the three intellectual acts of abstraction or understanding, judgment or forming propositions, and reasoning or inference. (Also, the order of abstraction, the grades of abstraction, and the distinction between the speculative and practical dimensions of intellectual operation.)

(6) The analysis of desire (appetite): first into the sensual and the rational (or will); then, the sensual into the concupiscible and irascible (with the dominance

[5] There are two aspects of appetite, the affective or emotional side, the conative or impulsive side. The states of the appetite are, therefore, both passions and sources of activity. This, of course, must be qualified by the distinction between the sensitive and the intellectual appetite. The same names are often given to the passions and the states of will, but they are used analogically. Thus, sensual and intellectual *love* are not the same, any more than brutal *anger* and righteous *indignation*.

of love as the root of all the passions). The nature of the passions: as sensual appetites or desires able to control action *without* or *in spite of* reason, though also to obey reason.

d. The basic terms of this psychological analysis are power and act: the capacity to operate or perform actions, and the actions which express those capacities.
   (1) Powers are either active or passive; thus, vegetation is active, and sense is passive.
   (2) To the basic terms must be added the notion of habit or disposition, as a mean between power and act; [6] thus, habits of locomotion; sensitive habit, known as memory; habits of action and passion (now spoken of as sentiments, attitudes or complexes); habits of intellect, the knowledge we possess but are not at the moment considering.

e. Psychology is concerned with acts, habits and powers. It is concerned with acts in order to learn about habits and powers. It studies acts in relation to their objects. It is *not* concerned with human behavior as such, or with the development of human character as the result of habit-formation of different sorts.

4. The fuller account of human life (of behavior, of character, of development and biography and the types of men) is not, according to the Aristotelian mode of treatment, the province of psychology, but the application of psychology in the practical order in which we are interested in controlling other men, or in directing our own lives well [38].

[6] A habit is a developed power, a determinate potentiality. It is a mean between the power as pure operative capacity and actual operation. Habits thus participate in both potentiality and actuality; with respect to the powers they determine, they are as acts; with respect to the operations they incline toward, they are as powers. Habits are both the results of operation and the causes of operation. A habit is formed by specific acts within a given power, and the habit of that power thus formed enables us better to perform further acts of the same sort. What we are able to do at first with difficulty, by virtue of an undeveloped power, we are able to do after repeated acts with ease and celerity, because a habit has been formed. Habitual operation is pleasant because unimpeded. It approaches the perfection of instinct and it is for this reason that habit is rightly regarded as second nature. Traditionally, the word "habit" is restricted to those formations in which rational power is directly the subject or indirectly involved, and the word "disposition" is used for what we would call "bodily habits." The concept of habit and disposition is indispensable in psychological analysis. It is of crucial importance for understanding what Freudians mean by an "active unconscious." Vd. Note 55 *infra*.

a. The control of others: the practical field of politics, with its subordinate fields of education and rhetoric. Here we have a fuller discussion of the emotions (appetites, desires, passions) and of types of men; the techniques to be used by the orator, the educator and the statesman to control behavior.[6a]

b. The direction of one's own life: the practical field of ethics.

(1) The practical aim of ethics is human well-being, happiness.

(2) But human well-being depends upon the nature of man, and hence ethics as practical is applied psychology.[6b]

(3) The basic points of theoretical ethics are psychological:

(a) The distinction between voluntary, involuntary, and non-voluntary conduct by reference to the way in which reason is involved, and knowledge is used.

(b) The analysis of the virtues as habits of action, passion and cognition (moral and intellectual virtues). The moral virtues are good habits of man's animal nature, good in the sense of habits formed rationally, and good because means to happiness. (The intellectual virtues are good habits of the rational powers; the moral virtues are good habits of those powers which are rational *only by participation*, through submitting to the regulation of reason.)

(c) The fundamental conflict between reason and the passions (what, in Freudian terms, is the conflict between the reality principle and the pleasure principle).

(d) The types of human life: sensual and practical lives (life-instinct dominance) and contemplative activity (death-instinct dominance).

[6a] Vd. *Rhetoric*, Bk. II, Ch. 2–11.

[6b] "The student of politics,"—or ethics,—"must know somehow the facts about the soul, as the man who is to heal the eyes or the body as a whole must know about the eyes or the body" (*Ethics*, I, 13, 1102a18–22). In other words, psychology is to ethics and politics, as physiology is to medicine. The *Ethics* introduces psychological discussions at various relevant points; thus, for instance, the analysis of wish and volition in Bk. III, Ch. 1–4; and the analysis of intellectual power and operation in Bk. VI devoted to the intellectual virtues.

(4) The various practical treatises (*Ethics*, *Politics*, *Rhetoric*) also contain classifications of types of men, descriptions of types of characters, and accounts of human biography in terms of the aetiology of character. None of this material is scientific in the sense of being the result of deliberate, special investigations or researches.

5. This Aristotelian distinction between theoretical and practical psychology (the application of psychology in ethics and politics) is significant in the history of psychology.
   a. In the Hellenistic period and in the Renaissance, men wrote books about the classification of characters and about the types of lives (biographies). Theophrastus's *Book of Characters* and Plutarch's *Comparative Lives* are examples of such taxonomic and physionomic knowledge of men.[7] This knowledge was not thought to be part of theoretical psychology. The subject-matter of human psychology was rather, according to the *De Anima*, the powers and acts of man. Furthermore, such knowledge was not the result of what we would call scientific research.
   b. This interest in the types of men and the types of lives was predominantly practical, that is, moral, even when the author was merely a biographer or a classifier of characters.
   c. This separation of the theoretical and the practical in psychology did not deny the dependence of the practical upon the theoretical.
6. The mediaeval development in psychology was primarily Platonic from St. Augustine to the beginning of the 13th century.[8] In the 13th century, the works of Aristotle were in the possession of Jews, Moors and Christians, and the issue between Plato and Aristotle was finally resolved by St. Thomas, who purified the Jewish and Arabic, as well as earlier Christian, Aristotelians of their Platonic misreading of the Aristotelian texts. Aquinas's work was an enlargement and a perfection of Aristotle's analysis [38a.]

[7] Vd. La Bruyère, *Les Caractères*, 1688; and also the contemporaneous work of Sir Thomas Overbury and Bishop Earle.

[8] Cf. A. Pegis, *St. Thomas and the Problem of the Soul in the Thirteenth Century*, Toronto, 1934; E. Gilson, *The Spirit of Mediaeval Philosophy*, New York, 1936; Ch. IX, XII–XV; D. E. Sharp, *Franciscan Philosophy at Oxford in the Thirteenth Century*, London, 1930.

a. In the *Treatise on Man*,[9] the *De Anima* was amplified. Here we have theoretical psychology: the analysis of human nature, its powers and operations. (It should be noted that St. Thomas points out that the acts of the appetitive part of the soul are reserved for later consideration in the subsequent moral treatises.[10] It should be noted also that although this treatise pays great attention to cognitive operations, there is no "epistemology" in the modern sense of that word, no analysis of the "content and validity of knowledge.")

b. In the *Moral Treatises*,[11] the *Ethics* and *Politics* were amplified. Here, in addition to an analysis of the will, the passions and desires, we have strictly practical psychology: the analysis of habits or virtues and vices; the analysis of the conditions of human well-being, of the ends and means of a good life.

c. But there is little or no taxonomy or physionomy, such as was started by Theophrastus and Plutarch. Their work is not continued in the mediaeval tradition, and when it is taken up again in the later renaissance, it is the work of literary men primarily and not moralists.[12]

III. From the 17th to the 19th Centuries: Philosophical Psychology

1. Philosophical psychology during this period can be summarized under a number of heads: (a) the resurrection of old errors and confusions, (b) the misunderstanding of, and attack upon, the doctrine of faculties, and (c) the misconception of the subject-matter of psychology. There is a sequence and relation of these points which will become apparent.

[9] *Summa Theologica*, I, QQ. 75–88. For other parts of psychological doctrine, one must go to the moral treatises: *Summa Theologica*, I-II, QQ. 6–17 (on will); QQ. 22–48 (on acts and passions); QQ. 49–54 (on habit). Cf. *Summa Contra Gentiles*, II, Ch. 56–78; also *De Veritate* and *De Anima* among the Disputed Questions; and *De Unitate Intellectus* among the Philosophical Opuscula.

[10] Vd. Notes 33 and 38 *infra*.

[11] Vd. fn. 9 *supra*. The following references may be added here: *Summa Theologica*, I-II, QQ. 1–5 (on the ends of life); II-II, QQ. 171–189 (on types and states of life).

[12] That this was the case can be explained by the great influence of Aristotle's *Poetics* during these centuries, an influence complicated unfortunately by misunderstandings of the text.

2. *The resurrection of old errors and confusions: materialism and Platonism.*
   a. Hobbes[13] revived once more the ancient error of the atomists: that there is only matter in motion, the matter being reducible to small particles differing only in quantity, the motion being entirely local. Although Hobbes used an Aristotelian vocabulary, even to the extent of distinguishing faculties, his treatment of psychological phenomena as results of atomic motions in sense-organs and brain, had the familiar consequences of materialism: sensationalism in the analysis of cognition, and the denial of intellect; the dominance of the passions in the analysis of motivation, and the denial of free-will. Hobbes was the first behaviorist. (To his credit it must be said that he was inconsistent with his principles. Despite his analysis, Hobbes recognized that man is rational both in his account of knowledge and of political behavior.)
   b. Descartes[14] revived once more the Platonic error of dualism, and exaggerated that error, making a sharper separation between body and soul by identifying soul with mind or intellect [39]. As a result:
      (1) The substantial unity of man was destroyed, and psychology became burdened with the impossible riddles of the mind-body relation, of sensation and free-will as interactions between incommunicable substances, etc. (Where Hobbes had written *Of Man*, Descartes wrote of the soul.)
      (2) The basic terms of psychological analysis (power, habit, act) were obscured or lost because the soul was viewed as a complete substance rather than as the formal principle of the composite and the proximate source of its powers. Furthermore, since its essence was identified with the operation of thought, the soul could have no variety of parts or powers. (It became impossible, therefore, for Descartes properly to distinguish cognition and appetite, the spheres of intellect and will. Psychology became almost exclusively an analysis of cognition and ignored or distorted the non-cognitive and non-rational

[13] *Human Nature* (1650); *Leviathan* (1651), Pt. I, Ch. I–II.
[14] *Rules for the Direction of the Mind* (1628); *Meditations* (1641), especially I and VI; *Principles of Philosophy* (1644), especially Pt. I; *The Passions of the Soul* (1645–6) in *Philosophical Works*, ed. by Haldane and Ross, Cambridge, 1931: v. I.

aspects of human nature. This ultimately led to the confusion of psychology with epistemology.)

(3) As sensationalism was the error of Hobbes' materialism, so intellectualism or intuitionalism was the characteristic error of Cartesian Platonism. Ideas are both innate and directly known, rather than acquired by abstraction from sense, the instruments not the objects of knowledge. (A materialism consistently carried out reduces man to the grade of brutes; the Platonic error goes to the opposite extreme of elevating the soul to the substantial and cognitive level of angels. The Aristotelian conception of man as a rational animal is the mean between these errors; as St. Thomas so frequently says, man is on the boundary between the material and the spiritual worlds.)

(4) Physiology, animal and human, became the science of mechanical automata.[14a]

c. Locke, Berkeley and Hume [15] followed Hobbes in his sensationalism, but also made the Platonic error of treating "ideas," i.e., sensations or impressions, as the objects of knowledge.

(1) In these three writers, the confusion of psychology with epistemology reached its height. They tried to give a genetic account, an inventory, and a critical evaluation of the contents of the mind. Thus, Locke stated his problem to be "the original, certainty and extent of human knowledge." [16] As a result of the simple error of treating sensations or ideas as *that which* (*id quod*) is known instead of as *that by which* (*id quo*) man knows *what* (*quid*) he knows of *that which* he knows (physical things), the development of psychological doctrine from Locke to Hume ended in subjectivism, phenomenalism and positivism.

(2) In all three, it is not man but the mind, cognition, or

[14a] La Mettrie in *L'Homme Machine* (1748) showed how readily Cartesianism became mechanistic materialism. Vd. also Holbach and Helvetius.

[15] Locke, *An Essay Concerning Human Understanding* (1690); Berkeley, *A Treatise Concerning the Principles of Human Knowledge* (1710); Hume, *Treatise of Human Nature* (1739–40); *Enquiry Concerning Human Understanding* (1748).

[16] *Op. cit.*, I, 1, ¶ 2.

experience, which is made the subject-matter of psychology.

(3) Apart from its obvious errors, Locke's *Essay* is the best work in the British tradition, largely because its author, like Hobbes, was not always consistent with his principles. Thus, Locke was a realist despite his definition of an idea as the *id quod* of knowledge. He is to be praised for his basic distinction between ideas of sensation and reflection, the latter being the understanding's reflexive knowledge of its own operations. His analysis of sensation is sound although it made no advance on the Aristotelian tradition. Furthermore, both in Book II and Book IV, Locke retains the distinction of power and act, and that between active and passive powers.[16a] Locke is a faculty psychologist despite the fact that he objected to the doctrine of faculties because he misconceived faculties as separate agents rather than diverse channels through which the vital energy of the soul expresses itself. (The best that can be said for Locke is that his *Essay* was in the best tradition of philosophical psychology, although neither adequate nor clear analytically. The worst that must be said of him is that his many errors and inconsistencies permitted Berkeley and Hume completely to nullify all the sound insights of his analysis.)

(4) Hume, following Hobbes, emphasized the passive association of ideas as the only principle of mental life, or experience.[17] Hume's positivism, itself the result of psychological errors, discarding the concepts of substance and cause, not only denied soul, either as a substance or as a principle, but also made nonsense of such basic terms as power and operation. Thus, we see how psychological error (of a Platonic variety) is a cause of positivism, and how positivism is in turn the source of even more egregious psychological error (pure phenomenalism). Hume is the

[16a] Locke's chief defect is with respect to the act of abstraction. As a result of his failure to distinguish sensation and intellection, the having of "simple ideas" is entirely a matter of passive reception, though the mind actively compounds and divides, judges and reasons. Cf. Books II and IV of the *Essay*. Vd. Lecture I, fn. 3, *supra*.

[17] *Enquiry Concerning Human Understanding*: Section III.

fountain-head of British associationism from Hartley, Brown and Reid to James Mill, Bain and Spencer.[18]

(5) The French psychologists of the 18th century, such as Condillac,[19] were followers of the English school, and were, therefore, associationists and sensationalists.

3. *The misunderstanding of, and attack upon, the doctrine of faculties.*

a. The traditional analysis of Aristotle and St. Thomas can be called "faculty psychology" only if the concept of faculty is rightly formulated and is not the ridiculous notion it has come to be in modern usage.[19a] Briefly stated, it involves the following points:

(1) That the faculties are powers of operation, i.e., abilities, capacities. (The Wolffian distinction between faculty and power, related to the distinction between habit and disposition, is a misleading confusion of the distinction between the intellect as an incorporeal power and the powers of bodily organs, with the distinction between those powers which are rational or submissive to reason and those which are not. I shall ignore Wolffian terminology in what follows; faculty and power are synonyms.)

(2) That the faculties or powers are neither parts of the essence of soul nor separate from the soul as independent agents, but rather distinctions within the total power of the soul. They are its potestative parts. The faculties are related to the soul as the properties of a substance to its essence.

(3) That the distinction of the faculties from each other and from the soul, which is their principle, is real rather than formal. It is a real distinction of a modal sort. Faculties, being accidents, cannot exist inde-

[18] Hartley, *Observations on Man* (1749); Thomas Reid, *Inquiry into the Human Mind* (1764); Thomas Brown, *Lectures on the Philosophy of Mind* (1820); James Mill, *Analysis of the Phenomena of the Human Mind* (1829); Alexander Bain, *The Senses and the Intellect* (1855), *The Emotions and the Will* (1859); Herbert Spencer, *The Principles of Psychology* (1870–2).

[19] Condillac, *Treatise on the Sensations* (1754), trans. by H. W. Carr, London, 1930. Cf. N. Malebranche, *Recherche de la Verité* (1674); vd. also Maine de Biran, *Essai Sur Les Fondements de la Psychologie* (1812). Malebranche and Maine de Biran are, in contrast to Condillac, the best examples of French Augustinism.

[19a] Vd. C. A. Hart, *The Thomistic Concept of Mental Faculty*, Washington, 1930.

pendently of their subject, man, but they are really distinct from their principle, the soul, as is clear from their independent variability. Such modal distinction of the faculties from each other and from the soul does not violate the unity of the soul or of human behavior, in which the powers *cooperate*.

(4) That the faculties are not *that which* act but *that in virtue of which* man acts. The soul is the principle but man is the subject of operation, and hence of the operative powers. In other words, the powers are of the composite, of man, and not of the soul. (It is important to remember this since it is almost impossible for any writer, even St. Thomas, to avoid such inaccurate phrasing as "the intellect knows" or "the will commands" when what is meant is that man by his intellectual power knows, etc. St. Thomas would agree with Locke that it is not will which is free, but man through the will. The misreading of St. Thomas on this point is extraordinary, since knowledge of his philosophy would make it impossible to suppose that he could be treating a power as if it were a substance, a subject of operation.)

b. We have already seen how Descartes mistakenly supposed the distinction of the faculties to be inconsistent with the soul's unity. In this he was followed by Spinoza. We have also seen how Locke employed the concept of powers, but attacked the false notion of faculties as independent agents. Unfortunately, Locke made the understanding (i.e., soul) itself the subject of the powers he distinguished rather than man, so that Hume denying the soul as substance made an end of faculty analysis in the tradition of British psychology.

c. Leibnitz [20] reduced the faculties to "mere empty dispositions which are the remains or traces of earlier impressions." This was tantamount to denying their existence entirely. Leibnitz, like Descartes, was a neo-Platonist; following the Augustinian concept of the seminal reasons, he accounted for psychological phenomena in terms of the awakening of slumbering, innate ideas rather than as the activation of native powers.

[20] *Monadology* (1714); vd. also *New Essays on the Human Understanding* (1704), an answer to Locke.

d. Kant, influenced by Locke and Hume, on the one hand, and by Wolff,[21] on the other, presents a confused picture. Kant is a faculty psychologist; his philosophy, in all three critiques, but especially in the *Critique of Pure Reason*,[22] depends largely on his analysis of the soul, its powers and operations. Viewed positively, Kant is important as an antidote to British associationism. Unfortunately there is the negative side: his erroneous analysis of the relations of sense, understanding and reason, his Rousseauian addition of feeling as a separate faculty, his failure to see that man and not the transcendental ego is the subject of the powers,—these are blemishes which give Kant, in psychology as in everything else, the pathetic status of being almost right [39a].

e. Herbart[23] took the position of Leibnitz, rejecting the faculties as mere fictions, and returning to a modified form of associationism,—a dynamic sort of "mental chemistry," —in which Wundt followed him,[24] though not always consistently.

f. Brentano[25] is the only outstanding exception in modern times to the denial or misconception of faculty psychology. His "act-psychology" is clearly in the Aristotelian tradition. He is followed by Husserl and others[26] who expanded his analysis in some respects but, because of characteristically modern deviations concerning metaphysics, muddled its clarity and simplicity.

[21] The word "psychology" as the proper name for a subject-matter is probably due to the influence of Christian Wolff (1679–1754), though its invention is attributed to Melancthon (1497–1560). Thus, Wolff, in this as in many other things, obscured the clarity of the scholastic tradition which had made man rather than the soul the central object of analysis.

[22] First ed., 1781.

[23] Vd. *Lehrbuch zur Psychologie* (1816), trans. by M. K. Smith (1891); *Psychologische Untersuchungen* (1839–40); *Psychologie als Wissenschaft* (1824–25). For a succinct comment on Herbart's relation to Kant, on the one hand, and to experimental psychology, on the other, vd. Boring, *A History of Experimental Psychology*, New York, 1929: pp. 237–250.

[24] Vd. Note 39a *infra*.

[25] *Psychologie von empirischen Standpunkte* (1874).

[26] Husserl, *Logische Untersuchungen* (1900–1); Meinong, *Untersuchungen zur Gegenstandtheorie und Psychologie* (1904); Witasek, *Grundlinien der Psychologie* (1908); Lipps, *Die Grundtatsachen des Seelenlebens* (1883); Stumpf, *Erscheinungen und psychische Functionen* (1907). Vd. Titchener, *Experimental Psychology of the Thought Processes*, New York, 1909.

4. *The misconception of the subject-matter of psychology.*

a. The proper subject-matter of psychology, as we have seen, is man *qua* man, his powers, operations and nature. It is neither the soul *per se*, nor the body, nor immediate experience (consciousness or psychological phenomena, i.e., the content of cognitive operation). But as a consequence of the errors of materialism and Platonism, and of the denial or misunderstanding of the doctrine of faculties, modern philosophical psychology has chosen one or another inappropriate subject-matter.

(1) Thus, Hobbesian materialism, consistently carried out, must lead to behaviorism and the reduction of psychology to physiology or animal psychology.

(2) Cartesian dualism made the soul the subject-matter of psychology, and since the soul in operation is thinking or knowing, psychology became the study of consciousness (cognitive content).

(3) The Cartesian influence upon more recent developments must be understood as modified by the positivism of Hume and Kant, for it is in terms of their phenomenalism that the experimental enterprise, beginning in the 19th century, discarded soul and mind, as well as the distinction of power and act, and conceived itself as the investigation of consciousness, or the phenomena of mental life [39b].

b. The influence of Hume and Kant on the subject-matter of modern psychology is twofold:

(1) Locke's error of making ideas the object of knowledge ultimately led to Hume's denial of substance and cause, and hence of the soul as a substantial principle and as a cause of powers and operations. Psychology necessarily became the report of the content of immediate experience. All psychological phenomena, even those of the emotions, desire and will, were reduced to elements in the stream of consciousness, governed by the laws of association. William James' chapter on the Stream of Thought is representative of this tradition in philosophical psychology.[26a]

(2) Following Wolff's distinction between rational and empirical psychology, Kant's denial, on positivistic grounds, of rational psychology, led to the errone-

[26a] *The Principles of Psychology* (1890): I, 9.

ous supposition that psychology must be restricted to the study of phenomena. This is shared by post-Kantian idealists,[26b] as well as by those who began experimental psychology in the 19th century. The experimentalists also misinterpreted Kant's attack on rational psychology as a denial of the possibility of philosophical psychology. The absurdity of this is obvious when it is realized that Kant's own philosophy was in large part psychological [39c].

c. Thus we can see how psychological errors of Platonic lineage led to positivism and how positivism in turn led to the circumscription of psychological subject-matter, on the one hand, and to the attempt to develop a scientific psychology apart from, or in lieu of, a philosophical analysis of man's nature, on the other. Yet, paradoxically, it is only with the development of scientific psychology that we return to a proper definition of subject-matter. Both psychoanalysis and psychometrics study man *qua* man.

5. *Summary:*
   a. There is no investigative or scientific psychology in this period (from the beginning through the middle of the 19th century).
   b. *The works in philosophical psychology during this period add nothing except error and confusion to Aristotelian psychology as that was perfected by St. Thomas Aquinas.* Even most of the errors are ancient ones, to be found in the atomistic or Platonic traditions. Only positivism, with its consequent denial of philosophical psychology itself, is new in modern times.
   c. If one were writing the history of psychology as a branch of philosophy and were concerned only to report genuine advances in analysis, everything from the 17th to the 19th centuries could be ignored, *without exception.* Even the best writers need not be mentioned because at their best they are only poor statements of what is better found in Aristotle or St. Thomas.[26c]
   d. But in writing the history of psychology, as both philosophical and scientific, it is necessary to mention these

[26b] Vd. F. H. Bradley, *A Defense of Phenomenalism in Psychology*, Mind, N. S. IX (1900).

[26c] Vd. C. Alibert, *La Psychologie Thomiste et les Théories Modernes*, Paris, 1903.

writers because of their influence upon those who tried to be scientific psychologists in the 19th and 20th centuries.[27] Thus, the influence of Locke and Kant on Wundt; the influence of Hume and British associationism on William James and American behaviorists; the influence of Brentano and Wundt on gestalt psychology, etc.

e. The classification of types of character (types of personality) and the interest in human development, in biography, as an account of the ways in which men develop, is largely lost during this period, except what is left of it in the hands of literary men.

IV. From the 19th Century to the Present Day: Scientific Psychology

1. The rise of scientific psychology cannot be understood apart from the development of the biological sciences in the 19th century. Three different fields of biological research exerted an influence: (1) physiology and neurology, particularly of the sense-organs and brain; (2) natural history, particularly accounts of animal behavior and the mythological part of the doctrine of evolution; (3) medical researches, and particularly the development of general pathology. I shall reserve the third of these until the end.

2. The influence of physiology is to be seen in the development of the Wundtian type of experimental psychology and in the development of psycho-physics.

a. Wundt, the father of experimental psychology, was influenced by such physiologists as Weber, Müller, Helmholtz, who were primarily concerned with physiology of sense-organs and nervous system.[28]

(1) But Wundt's work was a curious mixture of philosophical and scientific psychology. So far as his great works were "systematic," they were philosophical psychology.[29] His basic analysis did not

[27] Cf. G. Murphy, *An Historical Introduction to Modern Psychology*, New York, 1929; E. G. Boring, *A History of Experimental Psychology*, New York, 1929; G. S. Brett, *A History of Psychology*, New York, 1921. Vd. Note 36b *infra.*

[28] J. Müller, *Handbuch der Physiologie des Menschen* (1833–40); E. H. Weber, *Der Tastsinn und das Gemeingefühl* (1846); H. von Helmholtz, *Handbuch der physiologischen Optik* (1856–66), *Tonempfindungen* (1863).

[29] *Physiological Psychology*, 6th ed., 1911; *Outlines of Psychology* (trans. by Judd) 3rd ed., 1907; *System der Philosophie* (1889).

depend at all upon his experimental findings [40].

(2) As a philosophical psychologist, he did not have a consistent doctrine. He followed Descartes in the substantial dualism of mind and body.[29a] (He is not, however, an interactionist, but a parallelist. In his *Physiological Psychology*, he tried to treat psychic phenomena as mere correlates of brain processes.) He also followed Locke and Hume in being a sensationalist and an associationist; yet he followed Kant and Herbart in retaining some mental activity, e.g., the act of apperception.

(3) His experimental work on reaction time, on association, on attention, had no bearing whatsoever on his analysis.

(4) It must be said in his favor that he broadened psychological subject-matter to include the affects and will, but these he treated as if they were *mental phenomena*, i.e., elements of consciousness.

(5) Psychology, instead of being an analysis of man's powers and acts, became in Wundt's hands an analysis of mental elements and their combinations. This is characteristic of all of Wundt's followers, whether they are structuralists or functionalists.[30] It should be noted that this was not the result of research. It was not an investigative finding. It was the result of bad philosophical analysis.[30a] (The differences between Wundt and Kulpe are of little importance, except, perhaps, in so far as the Wurzburg school helped to further the beginnings of *gestalt* psychology.)

[29a] Father Brennan (*General Psychology*, New York, 1937: p. 14) quotes Wundt as saying in his *Physiological Psychology*: "The products of my labors do not square with the materialistic hypothesis nor with the dualistic theories of Plato and Descartes. It is only the animism of Aristotle, in which psychology is combined with biology, that issues as a plausible metaphysical conclusion from experimental psychology" (Bk. II, Ch. 23). However gratifying this declaration by the great experimentalist may be, his work, as well as this very statement itself, betrays little or no understanding of the principles of hylomorphism as a philosophy of nature or in psychology. He is as much an Aristotelian as Descartes is.

[30] Thus, for example, H. Ebbinghaus, *Grundzüge der Psychologie* (1897–1908); Külpe, *Outlines of Psychology* (trans. by Titchener), 1909; E. B. Titchener, *A Text-Book of Psychology* (1909), *Systematic Psychology*, 1929.

[30a] Vd. Note 39a *infra*.

b. Psycho-physics (the work of Weber, Fechner,[31] etc.) also resulted from researches in sense-physiology. It was the beginning of a mathematical psychology, imitating mathematical physics in applying mathematics to the measurement of "psychical" phenomena (e.g., acts of the power of sense). This developed into what has come to be called psychometrics, including not only the measurement of judgments in the field of sensation but all kinds of mental tests and measurements (the work of Spearman, Thorndike, Thurstone,[32] etc.)

(1) This type of research contributed nothing to general psychological theory.

(2) It was, nevertheless, a body of investigative knowledge, much more precise in its methods and findings than any other part of scientific psychology.

(3) But it was neither an analysis of man's powers and operations, nor a science of human behavior. It was at best a science of the quantitative accidents of human operations, particularly the operations of perception and judgment; just as mathematical physics is a science of the quantitative accidents of physical things, particularly their local motions.

3. The influence of natural history, 19th century studies of animal behavior and, in general, the doctrine of evolution, is best seen in the contributions of William James to a science of psychology.[33]

a. James was not himself an experimenter; nor, for the most part, even an investigator except in such fields as telepathy, psychical research, etc.

b. Like Wundt, he was primarily a philosophical psychologist, but one who tried to incorporate into his exposition of psychology everything that seemed relevant to the study of man. As a result, his *Principles* are not in any sense a system; but rather a collection of chapters that do not hang together.

(1) On the one hand, his chapters on the stream of

[31] G. T. Fechner, *Elemente der Psychophysik* (1860); also *Vorschule der Aesthetik* (1876).

[32] C. Spearman, *Nature of Intelligence and the Principles of Cognition* (1923), *The Abilities of Man* (1927); E. L. Thorndike, *The Measurement of Intelligence* (1927); L. L. Thurstone, *Vectors of Mind* (1935). Cf. R. J. Slavin, *The Philosophical Basis for Individual Differences, According to St. Thomas Aquinas*, Washington, 1936: esp. pp. 115–140.

[33] *The Principles of Psychology* (1890).

consciousness, conception, imagination, reasoning, are a confused mixture of Aristotle and Hume. They are bad philosophical psychology.

(2) On the other hand, his chapters on instinct, habit, emotion, hypnosis, personality, draw largely from the results of investigative work in physiology, biology and medicine. They expanded the subject-matter of psychology to include much more than cognition and immediate experience. They created an interest in animal psychology and pointed to its significance for human psychology. (The influence of evolution is apparent here. Man like any other animal lives by adjusting himself to his environment.)

(3) James lacked an analysis whereby to organize all this knowledge about man, and failed to distinguish psychology and ethics. Thus, his chapter on habit is a confusion of psychology and morals [41].

4. We can now trace the way these various influences mix and converge to constitute the currently existing schools of psychology.[33a] These schools differ from one another either philosophically or in terms of some limitation of field of research [42]. The amazing thing is the way in which they combine a positivistic attitude toward philosophy with the espousal of some form of Platonism or materialism in philosophical psychology. The results of materialism and Platonism are errors in philosophical psychology. The result of positivism is the attempt to construct psychology as purely scientific and as independent of philosophy. This is impossible. But, in addition, the two results are inconsistent with each other. Either by itself would produce bad psychology. Together, they make the scandal of this academic subject in the 20th century.

a. *The introspective or structural school: followers of Wundt.*[34] As philosophical psychologists, they are concerned with the elements of consciousness and their

[33a] This enumeration omits psychometrics and psychoanalysis because they can be treated as bodies of scientific knowledge rather than "schools of thought." Vd. Note 46 *infra*. Except for verbal differences and negligible shades of meaning, this enumeration is otherwise as exhaustive as those made by Murchison, Woodworth, and Heidbreder. Vd. Note 1 *infra*.

[34] *E.g.*, Titchener, Judd, Warren, Witmer, Weld, to mention only some Americans.

combinations. As investigators, they do work in sensation, perception, memory, association, imagination, attention, feeling, reaction time, etc.

b. *The functionalists: followers of James.*[35] They are broadly interested in anything having to do with man, his mind, his knowledge, his personality, his life, etc. Primarily, however, they are interested in the facts of human behavior and in its physiological basis. Man can be studied both in the way animals are studied and by introspective techniques. They do any kind of research. Theirs is the broadest conception of psychological subject-matter and the one nearest to the entire ancient tradition.

c. *The behaviorists: radical functionalists who ceased compromising with structuralism.* (Thus, Angell, the functionalist, is followed by Watson, the behaviorist.[36]) They are concerned only with behavior, human or animal. Their methods are those of the physiologist and the animal psychologist. Their only concepts are physiological. They deny any real distinction between man and other animals, and as "philosophers" they are ultimately materialists and sensationalists, following Hobbes and Hume.

d. *The gestalt school: originally followers of Brentano and Husserl, von Ehrenfels, Meinong and Witasek.*[37] They started as critics of both structuralism in human psychology and behaviorism in animal psychology.[38] In one sense, their philosophical analysis is in the tradition of Aristotle; it is an analysis in terms of powers and acts and in terms of form and matter.[38a] But, in another

[35] *E.g.*, Dewey, Angell, Woodworth, Thorndike, Carr. Vd. J. R. Angell, *The Relations of Structural and Functional Psychology to Philosophy*, Dec. Public of Univ. of Chicago, 1903. Cf. T. J. Ragusa, *The Substance Theory of Mind and Contemporary Functionalism*, Washington, 1937.

[36] J. B. Watson studied under J. R. Angell at the University of Chicago. *Psychology from the Standpoint of a Behaviorist* appeared in 1919. Other behaviorists are Weiss, Hunter, Tolman, Lashley.

[37] M. Wertheimer, *Ueber Gestalttheorie* (1925); W. Köhler, *Gestalt Psychology* (1929); K. Koffka, *Principles of Gestalt Psychology* (1935); K. Lewin, *A Dynamic Theory of Personality* (1935).

[38] Vd. Köhler, *Gestalt Psychology*, New York, 1929: Ch. 1–3.

[38a] Vd. R. Allers, *The New Psychologies*, New York, 1933; T. V. Moore, *Gestalt Psychology and Scholastic Philosophy* in The New Scholasticism, VII, 1.

sense, they are sensationalists and physiologists of the same sort as the behaviorists, denying any essential difference between man and brute animals. Their experimental work is narrow, being mainly concerned with cognition and animal learning. In so far as they are concerned with the behavior of the organism as a whole, they cannot be distinguished from the behaviorists, although they use a different language and a more sophisticated neurology [43].

5. *Summary: Where is the science of psychology?*

a. In the first place, the continuing existence of "schools" of psychology during the investigative period indicates that psychology did not become purely scientific when it started to experiment at the end of the 19th century. From its beginning until the present day, experimental or investigative psychology has neither mastered philosophy nor left it alone.[39] In the philosophical dimension, the variety of doctrines in the post-Wundtian schools is constituted by new combinations of earlier errors and confusions in analysis. They add as little to philosophical psychology as did their predecessors from the 17th to the 19th century. If we ignore the differences among the schools as nothing more than bad philosophical polemic, consisting of ungenuine issues and wrong solutions, what have we left? We do have, it must be admitted, a body of knowledge resulting from research and investigation.

(1) This can be summarized under the following heads: sensation, perception, imagination, problem-solving, emotion, feeling, learning, habit, memory, reaction time, association, fatigue, movement, attention, distraction, drug-effects, psychophysics, mental tests and measurements, genetics, individual differences, etc. [44].

(2) This body of investigative findings cannot be denied by any "school of psychology." It is a tremendous mass of scientific data, data discovered by research. But, for the most part, there are no outstanding generalizations, no clear formulae, nothing that resembles the scientific facts of physiology or chemistry. Psychometrics and, as we shall see,

[39] Vd. E. G. Boring, *History of Experimental Psychology*, New York, 1929: p. 660. Cf. pp. 249–50. Vd. also Note 42 *infra.*

psychoanalysis are the only exceptions to the inductive sterility of psychological research [45].

b. In the second place, if one examines all the results of research and investigation done by experimental psychologists, one finds that it can be classified as follows: [40]
   (1) As physiology: all the materials on sensation, reaction time, memory, emotion, fatigue, etc.
   (2) As animal psychology (including studies of human beings *as if* they were animals essentially): all the material on instinct, learning, behavior, development, etc.
   (3) As psychometrics: all the results of tests, measurements, psychophysics, etc. (This can be made to include all experimental data which are metrical.)
c. There is no question that we have acquired much knowledge as a result of the attempt to make psychology a science, but these additions to knowledge:
   (1) *Negatively:* do not alter or expand the traditional philosophical psychology, which is the analysis of human powers and acts.
   (2) *Positively:* are contributions to physiology, animal psychology, or psychometrics (mathematics applied to psychological measurements).
d. Our problem was to find a subject-matter, studied investigatively, which was neither physiology nor animal psychology. The history of so-called experimental psychology, with one exception, reveals none. That exception is psychometrics. Otherwise, experimental psychologists do physiological research or study the behavior of animals and the behavior of men as if they were animals [45a].
e. The only other exception, psychoanalysis, is not in the tradition of experimental psychology. It arose as a result of the third way in which biology influenced psychology in the 19th century.[41]
   (1) Medical researches and the science of pathology are responsible for the rise of psychiatry and psychopathology.[42] The early psychiatrists were not

[40] Vd. *The Foundations of Experimental Psychology*, ed. by C. Murchison, Worcester, 1929. Cf. *Psychology, a Factual Textbook* (New York, 1935) by Boring, Langfeld, Weld and others.

[41] Vd. Section IV, 1 of this lecture, *supra*.

[42] Vd. B. Hart, *Psychopathology, Its Development and Its Place in Medicine*,

experimenters or testers. As physicians, they employed a clinical method, a method which involved the classification of types of cases (the diagnostic determination of syndromes) and the study of case histories for the sake of diagnosis and prognosis [45b].

(2) Psychiatry, from the beginning, was a taxonomic and physionomic study of men as men, and not in the manner of the behaviorists, a study of men as brutes.

(3) A basic divergence arose with respect to aetiology. On the one hand, right-wing psychiatry looked to neurology for explanations of pathology; on the other hand, psychoanalysis attempted to give a psychogenesis of the disorders of men.

(4) Ordinary psychiatry is in unstable position between neurology, on the one hand, and psychoanalysis, on the other. It is psychoanalysis which is truly a science of psychology; that is, an investigative study of man as man, and not of man as an animal.

f. The historical significance of this fact can easily be shown. We saw that in the ancient and mediaeval period, psychology had both a theoretical and practical dimension. Its theoretical dimension was the analysis of human powers and acts. Its practical dimension was ethics, concerned with the problem of the formation of habits and the development of character, and, in general, with the conditions of human well-being. We must also remember the tradition of Theophrastus and Plutarch: the classification of the types of character, and human biography.

(1) Psychoanalysis, originating in medicine as practical, as concerned with the health of man in the fullest sense, his complete well-being,—happiness is equivalent to health in this sense,—is naturally in the tradition of ethics. We shall find that the doctrine of psychoanalysis is in part ethical. This is quite proper, to the extent that psychoanalysis is applied psychology. (To the extent that the psy-

New York, 1927; R. S. Woodworth, *Dynamic Psychology*, New York, 1922: Ch. I; S. Freud, *The History of the Psychoanalytic Movement* in *Collected Papers*, London, 1924: I, pp. 287–359; also in the same volume a paper on Charcot: pp. 9–23.

choanalyst is merely a therapist, his practical interest is much narrower than that of the moralist, who is primarily concerned with prevention rather than cure.)

(2) But psychoanalysis is not merely practical. It does not merely apply knowledge. It seeks knowledge; it is investigative. As investigative, it is a body of research that is primarily taxonomic and physionomic, achieved by the appropriate clinical methods of diagnosis, case-history, etc.

(3) In other words, the classification of the types of men and the formulation of the types of development in human biography is the proper subject-matter for a science of psychology. We had knowledge of these matters before psychoanalysis, but until psychoanalysis we did not have scientific or investigative knowledge in this field. Furthermore, the investigative method of psychoanalysis, being clinical, is properly adapted to such subject-matter.

g. In the next lecture, I shall more fully substantiate the point that I have made in this one, namely, that psychoanalysis is the only *non-mathematical* science of psychology, the only body of investigative knowledge about man as man,—as essentially different from other animals,—knowledge achieved by a method of investigation that could not be used in studying animal life [46]. In the course of the final lecture, I shall attempt to establish this point.

h. In so far as I shall find it necessary to criticize psychoanalysis and to suggest corrections of its errors, the faults and errors will all be due to its misfortune of having been born in the 19th century.[43] But I shall try to

[43] As is so often the case, Freud is both a positivist and given to "speculations" which are his unacknowledged philosophy. He is a positivist in so far as he holds that, other than science, "there are no sources of knowledge or methods of research" (*New Introductory Lectures on Psychoanalysis*, New York, 1933: p. 218). He rejects the notion that science is only one field of inquiry and that philosophy and religion are others with equal claims to truth. "The bare fact is that truth cannot be tolerant and cannot admit compromise or limitations, that scientific research looks on the whole field of human activity as its own" (*op. cit.*, p. 219). Yet Freudian metapsychology cannot be purified of "philosophy." Vd. Note 51 *infra*. The task is not one of freeing psychoanalysis from all philosophical presuppositions, but rather of correcting the mixture of materialism, dualism and evolutionism which is the Freudian philosophy. Cf. R. Allers, *The New Psychologies*, New York, 1933: pp. 5–24.

show that psychoanalysis can be cured of its heritage of bad philosophy,—the currents of error which dominated its 19th century origin. *Upon such corrections, its future depends.*

PSYCHOANALYSIS AS PSYCHOLOGY

I. Introduction

1. This lecture is devoted to the status of psychoanalysis as psychology, both theoretically as a body of knowledge and practically as a moral doctrine. To state the problem of this lecture, it is necessary here briefly to reiterate:
   a. The distinction between philosophical and scientific knowledge. (Generalizations which are neither are *opinion*. The opinions of scientists are often confused with philosophical knowledge, because scientists think that philosophy is "speculation," in the sense of guessing about what they do not know.)
   b. The distinction in kind between man and brute animals, established *a posteriori* in terms of the absolute difference between what man can do and brutes can do.
   c. The thesis that the proper subject-matter of human psychology is man as man, and not merely as an animal.
      (1) Human psychology must, therefore, be differentiated from animal psychology.
      (2) Furthermore, man is a unity, and psychology is the study of that unity, both in being and in operation, whereas anatomy and physiology are studies of the nature and operation of the parts, considered separately. (Psychology is distinguished from physiology in two respects: first, in studying the cooperation of the parts in the activity of the whole; and second, in studying certain operations which can be best known reflexively because they are not acts of bodily organs.)
   d. The thesis that psychology is the only branch of philosophical knowledge about a particular type of physical being. Thus, with respect to nature in general, there is philosophical knowledge, which we have called general

physics, or the philosophy of nature; with respect to different types of natural things and different types of change, there are the particular natural sciences, all of them bodies of investigative knowledge. *Psychology is distinguished from all these by the fact that, in part, it is philosophical in method, though particular in subject-matter.*[1] The reason for this exception is that psychology is man's knowledge of himself, and because of this reflexivity investigation is not necessary, although it is possible; not only possible, but desirable as providing supplementation and detail. In the case of other particular subject-matters, investigation is necessary.

e. The thesis that a sound philosophical psychology exists.[1a] It is the analysis of the unity of man as body and soul, and the analysis of man's powers and operations in relation to each other and as cooperating in human life.

f. The thesis that psychology unites both philosophical analysis and scientific findings in one continuous doctrine, in which philosophy, answering the basic questions, necessarily subordinates, as well as interprets and regulates, scientific research.[1b]

2. As a result of these distinctions and theses, we then faced the following problem: what is the nature and scope of scientific psychology, that is, a body of knowledge about man as such, which is neither physiology nor animal psychology, and yet is obtained by investigative methods? To answer this question, we surveyed the history of psychology, and discovered:

a. That until the 19th century, there was no attempt at a scientific (investigative) study of man;

b. That the history of psychology from the beginning until the 19th century is a history of philosophical psychology, in which can be found:

(1) The correct analysis, made by Aristotle and St.

[1] In other words, there is both a philosophical and a scientific psychology, but not both a philosophical and a scientific chemistry, botany, hydrodynamics, histology, etc. The philosopher must not give psychology up to the scientist, nor can the scientist ever dispossess him from this field. Vd. Note 32a *infra.*

[1a] It has existed in a continuous tradition since the Greeks, obscured somewhat by the interruptions of modern philosophy. Those who ignore or neglect this tradition are led to suppose that knowledge of man is a modern or even a recent achievement, or to place it in the future, still to be achieved.

[1b] Vd. Notes 32a and 39c *infra.*

Thomas, of the union of soul and body as a composition of form and matter. It follows that the basic terms of psychological analysis are power, habit and act. This analysis distinguishes the various powers, habits and operations, formulates the order and relation of these powers and operations, etc.

(2) The three errors of dualism (or Platonism), materialism and idealism (another form of Platonism). Each of these errors is in metaphysics, but each metaphysical error has psychological consequences. Thus, dualism in separating soul and body as existing independently, assigns to the soul powers and operations it does not have, and improperly orders and relates the various powers of man. This error is the source of the overemphasis on cognition, the confusion of psychology and epistemology, and, worst of all, the misconception of the subject-matter of psychology as immediate experience or consciousness. Similarly, materialism, denying the immateriality of the soul, is unable to distinguish sense and intellect and reduces psychology to physiology and animal behaviorism; and idealism, denying matter, is forced to the absurd extremes of phenomenalism, solipsism and skepticism, or, what is worse, pantheism (objective idealism).

(3) The way in which these errors entailed a misunderstanding of the doctrine of faculties and hence the loss of the basic principles and concepts of philosophical psychology. It is interesting to observe that both positivism and idealism converge upon, and reinforce each other in making, a purely phenomenalistic construction of the subject-matter of psychology.

Note: The four metaphysics thus have four psychologies correlated with them. The three metaphysical errors generate errors in psychology. The history of modern philosophical psychology (usually without an explicit metaphysics) is a history of these errors, two of which are the consequences of Platonism. If we are Aristotelians in the philosophy of science and in metaphysics, we must be Aristotelians in psychology.[2] These issues cannot be avoided

[2] Vd. Lecture II *supra*.

by psychologists, because scientific work in psychology depends upon philosophical analysis. Other natural scientists can be positivists without impairing their research, but positivism either blinds scientific psychologists to the scope and nature of their field of investigation, or encourages them to continue unwitting and incompetent "philosophizing."

c. That the various "schools" of psychology since the 19th century do not differ "scientifically," but only as one bad philosophy from another,[2a] and this polemic is perpetuated by the fact that most scientific psychologists are at once positivists and also philosophically doctrinaire.

d. That an examination of all the *experimental* work done in the name of psychology shows it to fall under the following heads:

(1) *Animal psychology:* the work of the behaviorists and gestalters.

(2) *Physiology:* the work of the behaviorists and gestalters, as well as work done by introspective psychologists in the field of sensation.

(3) *Psychometrics:* measurement of the quantitative accidents of human performances.

e. That psychometrics,—the analogue of mathematical physics,—satisfies all the requirements of a science of psychology. (Psychometrics can be extended to include all the experimental work on perception, judgment, memory, association, etc., in so far as it is metrical. In so far as such work is not metrical,—i.e., qualitative introspective research,—it is a description of the field of consciousness or the flow of immediate experience, and belongs to what Santayana called "literary psychology.") Furthermore, psychometrics as a scientific psychology employs, as it should, the basic conceptual schema of philosophical psychology,—the analysis of the faculties.[3]

[2a] Vd. Note 42 *infra.* All those who have recently surveyed "schools of psychology" concur in Boring's judgment that the varieties of doctrine present only philosophical issues. This is the meaning of Woodworth's statement that "the contentions of each school seem to me not of the nature of hypotheses that are susceptible to proof or disproof by the weight of evidence" (*Contemporary Schools of Psychology*, New York, 1931: p. 217). Cf. E. Heidbreder, *Seven Psychologies*, New York, 1935: Ch. XI.

[3] The relation between psychometrics and faculty analysis as Spearman formulates it, nicely exemplifies the proper ordering of scientific and philosophical knowledge in psychology. Vd. Notes 39a and 45 *infra.*

f. That psychometrics as the only science of man in the experimental tradition does not exclude psychoanalysis, which is also a science of man, but non-metrical and non-experimental. In the sense that any non-mathematical science of a subject-matter is more obviously an account of that subject-matter than a science applying mathematics, psychoanalysis is more obviously knowledge of man than psychometrics.[3a] But, unlike psychometrics, psychoanalysis obscures, or even denies, its dependence upon a philosophical analysis of human nature. As a consequence, psychoanalytic doctrine is in large part a confusion of science and philosophy.[3b]

3. In order to clarify the scope and content of psychoanalysis, we must answer the following questions:
   a. What are the methods and problems of psychoanalysis as a non-mathematical science of psychology?
      (1) With respect to method: the distinction between clinical and experimental procedures.
      (2) With respect to problems: the distinctions of taxonomy,—including morphology,—physionomy, and aetiology [47].
   b. What is the relation between psychoanalysis and philosophical psychology? What, in general, is its relation to philosophy?
   c. What is the relation between psychoanalysis as theoretical (as a body of knowledge) and as practical (as medicine and morals)?

II. The Strictly Scientific Contribution of Psychoanalysis

1. The traits of scientific knowledge can be briefly summarized as follows: [4]
   a. Scientific propositions, describing the phenomenal order by characterizations and correlations, are inductive gen-

[3a] Vd. Notes 46 and 47 *infra.*

[3b] Freud would hardly say of traditional philosophical psychology what Professor Spearman does when he points to the fact that modern efforts in this field never render "the older fine works in any way obsolete. Thus we moderns (in physics) can afford to look at Archimedes patronizingly, as down at a brilliant child; but (in psychology) Plato, Aristotle, Aquinas, not to mention many others, even yet oblige us to look upward as at our masters" (*The Nature of Intelligence*, New York, 1923: pp. 27–28). *Parentheses mine.*

[4] Vd. Lecture I; also my *Analysis of the Kinds of Knowledge* (privately issued, Chicago, 1935): pp. 21–32.

eralizations from observations made under special circumstances and by special methods.

b. Such generalizations are a contribution to knowledge only if men are not able to make them from common experience, or if men are not able to make them as well, that is, with as much precision or in as much detail. We must remember, of course, that precision and detail are in some matters gratuitous. Thus, many of the generalizations of social research are in no sense a contribution, because they are common knowledge. The precision supposed to be added by investigation is, for the most part, pretentious.[5]

c. A scientific fact is a general proposition inductively achieved from scientific evidence. Scientific evidence consists of the data obtained by special investigation.

(1) Scientific facts are the basic inductions. What are called scientific laws are usually inductions from these inductions; i.e., higher generalizations. Both scientific facts and scientific laws are descriptions of what is the case in the phenomenal order. The law does not "explain" the facts, except in the sense in which the less general is made intelligible by subsumption under the more general.

(2) The words "hypothesis," "theory" and "explanation" have two quite distinct meanings in relation to science. Thus, an hypothesis means either a supposed entity (a fictive hypostasis), or a proposition to be proved (a problem); a theory means either an imaginative description of the properties and behavior of hypothetical entities or a systematic organization of the facts and laws which constitute a body of scientific knowledge; an explanation means either a statement of the causes or the demonstration of a conclusion by premises.

(3) A scientist should not make "hypotheses" in the first sense, and should not have a "theory" in the first sense. If he does, the result is merely guessing; it is neither scientific knowledge nor philosophy [48].

(4) A scientist may attempt explanation by turning to descriptions of phenomenal systems of lower order, as the biologist turns to chemistry; [5a] but as a scientist he

[5] Cf. *Art and Prudence*, New York, 1937: Ch. 9 on Knowledge and Opinion.
[5a] Vd. Notes 33a and 47 *infra*.

must not employ fictitious entities whose behavior he imagines. (If he seek explanations in the sense of genuine aetiology, he is in danger of becoming either a guesser or a philosopher.) A scientist need not explain; explanation is not a necessary part of scientific knowledge. Thus, taxonomies and physionomies are bodies of scientific knowledge and do not treat of causes; so also mathematical physics is descriptive and not explanatory [49].

2. The scientific contribution of psychoanalysis must be limited to taxonomic and physionomic problems. (These, with the addition of morphology, are the only problems proper to a non-mathematical natural science and capable of being solved by investigation. But, as we shall see, "psycho-morphology" is primarily philosophical rather than scientific.)
   a. *Human taxonomy:* the classification of the types of men.
      (1) At this point, psychoanalysis is in the tradition of the study of man, following Theophrastus, la Bruyère, and the characterologists, who classified types of characters.[5b] This kind of knowledge has always been the possession of moralists and novelists, and of men in general, but psychoanalysis has made a contribution in precision and detail, by means of scientific method.
      (2) Psychoanalysis has made a number of basic classifications. Thus:
         (a) The infantile, the neurotic, the adult.
         (b) The abnormal types: the various neuroses.
         (c) The normal types: the neurotic characters: the analerotic, the narcissistic, the anacilitic, etc.
      (3) The classifications are, of course, developed by detailed characterizations of each type.

      Note: It was Freud's brilliant insight that the normal and the abnormal are continuous; that every character is a neurosis, although we call a character a neurosis only when its typifying characteristics become unduly predominant.
   b. *Human physionomy:* the formulation of the pattern of human development as a uniform secular trend. There is a universal invariancy here, as in the functional statements of covariation in mathematical physics; the invariancy differs with regard to the time dimension. Human physi-

[5b] For the history of these writings, vd. A. A. Roback, *The Psychology of Character*, New York, 1927: Ch. II.

onomy is analogous to the embryological series, the growth curves and life-histories in biology.

(1) Here, too, psychoanalysis is in the tradition of the study of man, following Plutarch and other biographers, whether moralists or novelists. This kind of knowledge has always been the possession of moralists and novelists, but here even more than in taxonomy, psychoanalysis has made a contribution to knowledge of the pattern of human development, by means of scientific research.

(2) This contribution is of two sorts:

(a) *The general physionomy:* the life-history of any man, the elements of which are such episodes as the intra-uterine period, birth trauma, infancy, weaning, the Oedipus crisis, latency, adolescence, adulthood, either neurotic or complete.

(b) *The special physionomies:* typically different life-histories for different types of characters. (Here taxonomy and physionomy are related.)

c. These two sorts of knowledge about man are scientific. They consist of generalizations based on scientific evidence. This evidence is gathered by a method which I shall call "clinical" to distinguish it from experimental procedures.

(1) The clinical method in the study of human beings is merely a special case of a method commonly employed in the biological sciences, the method of the natural historian. That we call this special case of the method of natural history "clinical" is due to the understandable accident that a clinic affords excellent opportunities for taxonomic and physionomic research with regard to human beings.

(2) The biological sciences are in good part taxonomic and physionomic, concerned with the classification of plants and animals and the formulation of life-histories. As such, they are not experimental and could not be. In distinction, such biological sciences as pathology, physiology, genetics, are experimental.

(3) The method of psychoanalysis extends the clinical procedures of medicine.

(a) Diagnosis is rudimentary classification; clinical pictures are typologies, characteristic sets of symptoms. Psychoanalytic diagnosis is much more elaborate; its syndromes are detailed formulations of character types.

(b) Ordinary medical procedure is satisfied with a case-history reported by the patient, whereas psychoanalysis has invented a technique for getting a case-history in detail far beyond what is obtainable by the ordinary exercise of memory. *The psychoanalytic couch is an instrument of case-history research which has discovered many details of human biography hitherto unknown. It stands to biography as the microscope to anatomy or the telescope to astronomy.*

d. To the extent that psychoanalysis is purely taxonomic and physionomic, its original method,—an extraordinarily ingenious modification of clinical procedure—is the only proper method of investigation. (This explains why the condemnation of psychoanalysis as not scientific because not experimental, or mathematical, or statistical, is so absurd and irrelevant.)

e. But for the most part, psychoanalysts will not be satisfied with this appraisal of their scientific accomplishment. They claim that by the use of scientific methods they have contributed two other sorts of knowledge: (1) a morphology, or analysis of the structure of the psyche, which they call "topography"; and (2) an aetiology, or an account of the causes of psychic action and development, and this includes what they call "dynamics" and "genetics." It remains to show, therefore, that this claim is not justified. I do not mean that topography, dynamics and genetics are not a part of psychoanalytical doctrine; in fact, they comprise a large part of the theoretical literature written by psychoanalysts. I mean, rather, that to the extent that this group of problems is capable of solution, they belong properly to philosophical psychology and, for the most part, have been already solved. If psychoanalysis has made any contribution here, it has been made by psychoanalysts, not in their capacity as scientists drawing inductions from clinical data, but as philosophers. Even a psychoanalyst cannot repress his reflective and analytical powers. In spite of his emotional reaction against the name and tradition of philosophy, Freud has had a number of insights which genuinely enrich philosophical psychology.

f. I shall devote the next section of this lecture to Freudian topography, dynamics and genetics, in an attempt to separate that part of it which is sound philosophical analysis from that part which, unfortunately, is the kind of bad "philosophizing", of the sort current in the late 19th century, which consists of *guesses* (hypotheses, theories, explanations, all in the bad sense) *beyond the evidence*. In that part which is good analysis, I shall try to distinguish what is an original contribution from what is merely a translation of the Aristotelian tradition into the conceptual vocabulary of psychoanalysis. But, before turning to that discussion, there are a number of preliminary observations.

(1) The morphological problem may belong either to scientific investigation or to philosophical analysis. Thus, anatomy is a natural science dealing with this problem. But the parts of the soul are not observable as the parts of the body are. The parts of the soul are the powers of man. They are not phenomenal entities, but belong rather to the ontological order, since they are founded in the essence or specific nature of man. They are known only by inference from operation or activity. The data, on which such inferences rest, are facts of immediate experience. They fall within man's reflexive knowledge of himself. The analysis of the powers of the soul is the best established part of philosophical psychology throughout its long ancient and mediaeval tradition. It remains only to show that the scientific evidence, assembled by psychoanalysis, can do no more than exemplify distinctions already and better known; and that the topographical analysis which psychoanalysts have made of the structural parts, the layers or levels, of the psyche, is at best a repetition of traditional points, and at worst a confused or inadequate statement.

(2) The aetiological problem, strictly, does not belong at all to theoretic science. In so far as psychoanalysis is intimately related to therapeutic medicine, it must of course be concerned with causes. To the extent that the reading of psychoanalytical doctrine is colored by practical considerations, it may appear to be aetiological. That is not inconsistent with what is here being said, namely, that as a body of theoretic knowledge, obtained by the methods of science and

therefore restricted to the phenomenal order, psychoanalysis does not treat of the causes of human behavior or psychic development or, in the broadest sense, the changes of which man specifically is the subject [47].

(a) Psychoanalysts may attempt to explain the phenomena they describe by reference to physiology, which is the study of phenomenal systems of lower order. But this sort of explanation must always be incomplete, because human reason, which is the essential and distinguishing cause of human activity, is not the act of a bodily organ. Hence, the reduction to physiological terms can at best explain man as an animal, but not man as man.

(b) Psychoanalysts may unwittingly convert their physionomies into aetiologies. This type of interpretation is justifiable in the practical dimensions of diagnosis and therapy, but it is not, in any sense, an addition of new theoretic knowledge [50]. Furthermore, if the interpretation be regarded as theoretic rather than practical, it transgresses the positivistic restrictions of science, as well as commits the fallacy of *post hoc ergo propter hoc*.

(c) This is not to deny that an aetiology of human activity is possible, but only to assert that it belongs properly to philosophical psychology which, being knowledge of a distinctly different type from science, can achieve real causal insights. (As the principle and determinations of causality in general belong to the philosophy of nature and not to natural science, so human causation belongs to philosophical and not scientific psychology.) Even so, there is a limitation of our knowledge of human causation, because reason is a principal and essential cause, and it is different from every other natural cause in that it is free.[6] With this qualification, philosophical psychology treats of the causes of human operation by formulating the dynamic and cooperative relation of the various powers, the tendencies

[6] Vd. *Art and Prudence*, New York, 1937: Ch. 8 and 9.

of their habits, and the determination of their acts by objects. Psychoanalytical theory, in that part of it which is called "dynamics", is aetiological in the same way; but here it is philosophy rather than science, and furthermore it is here, for the most part, a repetition of the traditional analysis. There are two exceptions to this statement: on the one hand, psychoanalysis makes the crucial error of misconceiving the dynamic and special role of reason as a cause; on the other hand, psychoanalysis makes a number of genuine philosophical contributions to dynamics, especially the concept of repression. We shall discuss this later [55].

(d) The remaining part of what the psychoanalyst thinks is an aetiology,—his genetics,—is neither scientific nor philosophical knowledge. We shall deal with this after the dynamics.

III. Psychoanalysis as Philosophical Psychology and as Guessing:

1. I repeat: only the taxonomic and physionomic knowledge which psychoanalysts have contributed is scientific psychology. Everything else in psychoanalytic literature is either *physiology* or *metapsychology*. I shall use Freud's word "metapsychology" to name two quite different sorts of thing: on the one hand, philosophical analysis; on the other hand, opinions of a speculative sort (neither scientific nor philosophical knowledge, but guesses, conjectures,—"theories" in the sense in which a scientist should not have theories).
   a. In using the word "metapsychology" Freud recognized that the doctrine advanced under that head was not strictly scientific knowledge [51].
   b. In so far as the metapsychology is philosophical psychology, its chief defect arises from the fact that it is based too much on special, or clinical, experience. (This may explain why the originality of the metapsychology, to the extent that it is philosophical, is largely its peculiar terminology.)
   c. It should be remembered that the criteria for judging the goodness or badness of the metapsychology are not the same as those before used to judge the contribution of psychoanalysis to science. *The part of the metapsychol-*

ogy that is philosophy must be judged by the criteria of philosophical knowledge. The part that is opinion or wild speculation can, of course, be dismissed as such. Our task, therefore, is to separate the metapsychological doctrine into these two parts.

2. But first we must distinguish three sorts of problems dealt with in the metapsychology.
   a. *The topographical problem:* Here the concern is with the structure of the psyche. Psycho-topography is the analogue of anatomy, as psycho-physionomy is the analogue of embryology [52].
      (1) The topographical problem is the basic philosophical problem of distinguishing the various powers of the soul.
      (2) Topography is related to taxonomy (the parts of the psyche in different types of characters) and to physionomy (the parts of the psyche at different stages of development).
   b. *The dynamic problem:* Here the concern is with the cooperation, dependence and interdependence of the various parts of the psyche.[6a]
      (1) The dynamic problem is also a basic philosophical problem, that of ordering the various powers of the soul in terms of their dependence and cooperation with each other.
      (2) To the extent that the dynamic problem involves the consideration of the conditions under which the powers become operative, it leads to an aetiology: either the sort of scientific explanation accomplished by turning to physiology, or a philosophical analysis of causes.
      (3) Dynamics is related to taxonomy (the order of the parts in different types of characters) and to physionomy (the order of the parts at different stages of development).
   c. *The genetic problem:* This is concerned with the origins of the psyche itself: how the individual man comes to have the psyche that he has: or how man as a kind of animal comes to have his psychological nature.

[6a] It is interesting to note that Alibert conceives the empirical province of Thomistic psychology as *la dynamologie*. This is the province both of philosophical analysis and scientific inquiry. Vd. Note 39c *infra*.

(1) This is neither a scientific nor a philosophical problem [53].

(2) It is at this point that the metapsychology becomes speculative in the bad sense of unfounded "theory" about unobservable events.

3. I shall survey the metapsychology, first by considering its topography and dynamics in the light of the traditional philosophical psychology [53a]; and then by showing why the genetics has no status either as scientific or philosophical knowledge.

4. The Freudian topography is for the most part sound as philosophical psychology. It is, however, analytically inadequate. This can be shown by indicating briefly the translation of the Freudian and Aristotelian analyses.[7]

a. The structures of the psyche ≡ the parts or powers of the soul. (In neither case is the psyche or soul supposed to exist apart from the body. The Freudian correlates psychic structures with bodily parts; the Aristotelian correlates psychic powers with bodily organs, except in the case of understanding. This difference is, of course, crucial and is the source of all the Freudian errors.[7a])

b. The basic distinction of ego and id ≡ the basic distinction between the rational and the non-rational parts of the soul.

(1) Here the Aristotelian analysis is better because more complete. It distinguishes between the cognitive and the appetitive powers; in the case of the cognitive power, between sense and intellect; in the case of the appetitive power, between the natural or vegeta-

[7] The translation which follows does not aim to be exhaustive but illustrative. Moreover, it will not be understood unless it is read as a statement of formal equivalence between the conceptual schema of two doctrines which, though the same, are expressed in different vocabularies. I have used the sign ≡ to signify such formal equivalence. In making this translation between Freudian and Aristotelian doctrines, I have not distinguished between the contributions to the latter which were made by St. Thomas and by Aristotle.

[7a] The problem in natural theology of the self-subsistence of the soul turns on the proposition that understanding is not the act of a bodily organ. Vd. Note 26 *infra*. There is no inconsistency between the fact that the soul is the substantial form of the composite and the fact that its one incorporeal power (intellect) is a mark of its capacity to subsist apart from the body upon the corruption of the composite. From the point of view of psychology rather than natural theology, it is important to stress here that the soul is a formal principle, the proximate source of all the vital powers of which man is the subject, only one of which is a power of the soul *per se*.

tive appetite,[7b] the sensitive appetite and the intellectual appetite. The rational part of man includes intellect as cognitive and as appetitive; the non-rational part of man includes the senses as cognitive and as appetitive, as well as the vegetative and the locomotive powers.

(2) The incompleteness of the Freudian analysis here is confusing because the id is non-rational *both* as non-cognitive *and* as appetitive only in the vegetative or sensitive way. In other words, the Freudian distinction of ego and id is partly in terms of the cognitive vs. the appetitive powers (knowledge and desire), and partly in terms of that which is rational and that which is not (reality vs. pleasure principle).

(3) Furthermore, the Freudian analysis of the ego in terms of its cognitive functions and in terms of its rationality is very inadequate. The Freudian analysis is adequate only with respect to the id.

c. The distinction between the pure id and the organized id (complexes, erotic organizations, etc.) ≡ the natural appetites (non-cognitive, vegetative) and the cognitive appetites, which are specific desires based on the determination of the appetite by objects known sensitively or intellectually [54].

(1) The Freudian analysis fails to make a clear distinction between need and desire in terms of the cognitive determination of appetite.

(2) The analysis of object-fixations, erotic organizations, complex formation, can be improved by a better understanding of the relation of cognition to appetite.

(3) The Freudian theory of instincts is the analysis of the vegetative powers (natural appetites, needs).

d. The differentiations of the conscious, the preconscious, the unconscious and the repressed unconscious. Here the translation is as follows:

(1) Conscious ≡ any knowledge or desire in act or operation as such.

(2) Preconscious ≡ any knowledge or desire in habit.

[7b] The natural appetite is not identical with the vegetative appetite. What is here meant is only that the appetitive inclinations of the vegetative powers are natural in the sense of not being cognitively determined to a particular object. Vd. Note 54 *infra*.

The habit may be either sensitive or intellectual. But the Freudian analysis fails to distinguish between the sensitive and the intellectual preconscious (sensitive and intellectual habit).

(3) Unconscious = the vegetative needs which have not yet become cognitively determined. (The unconscious is the pure id. The organized id may consist either of preconscious desires or repressed complexes, etc.) In a broader conception of the instinctive, the unconscious includes all the powers of the soul as undetermined by habit and as naturally appetitive, i.e., as tending to their appropriate acts. Habits belong either to the preconscious or the repressed unconscious.

(4) Repressed unconscious = habitual desires which achieve motility without ideational representation and issue in all forms of overt conduct without the control of reason. The repressed tendencies may be temporarily barred from motility by the opposition of reason, but such interference is never permanent, nor does it abolish the tendency [55].

e. The ego and the super-ego = the distinction between the speculative and the practical reason, between reason as knowing the truth and reason as using the truth for the purposes of action.

(1) Here, as we shall later see, the Freudian analysis is poorest, because it fails to understand the identity of reason as knowing and reason as prescribing, or directing or commanding, action. As a result of its questionable genetics, the Freudian account of the super-ego separates it from the ego, and makes it a secondary function of ego and id.

(2) In one important point here the Freudian analysis is correct. The super-ego is related to the id as the practical reason (the reason as moralistic) is to the appetitive part of the soul. The Freudian, however, fails to distinguish the rational appetite from sensuality, the will from the passions.

(3) And the Freudian analysis is bad in so far as it makes the super-ego a function of the id in relation to prevailing social conventions as these are learned by the ego. This reduces morality to mere conformity to the tribal *mores*. From the point of view of Freud-

ian therapy and moral doctrine, this is the worst error in psychological analysis.

f. The various complexes and erotic organizations of the id ═ the various passions and determinations of the sensitive appetite.[8]

g. *Summary and criticism* [56].

(1) In regard to the ego: the Aristotelian analysis is much more adequate, not only because it distinguishes between sense and intellect and between intellect and will, but because it analyzes their operations and relationship.

(2) In regard to the ego and super-ego: the Aristotelian analysis is much more adequate with respect to the distinction between speculative and practical intellect, and between the practical intellect and the intellectual appetite or will.

(3) In regard to the id: here the Aristotelian and Freudian analyses are about the same, but the Aristotelian is clearer because it more sharply distinguishes needs (vegetative appetite) from desires (appetite cognitively determined to an object). There are minor differences in the account of the various passions (or complexes, erotic organizations, object-fixations).

(4) In general, the recognition of the bifurcation of the human psyche into ego and id is the recognition, however unclear, of man's dual nature, i.e., his rationality and animality. Furthermore, both Freud and Aristotle agree on the physionomic point: man is born with an actual id (at least with regard to instincts or vegetative needs), but not with an actual ego. The ego develops in the course of human life as man learns from his environment. So the Aristotelian would say with the Freudian that the ego (or the rational part of the soul) is potential, or merely a power, in the infant and only becomes actual, i.e., operative and habituated, in the course

[8] This translation can be carried out in great detail for the various passions, which are determined as different according to object or tendential mode. The analysis of the passions is scattered throughout Freud's writings. The Thomistic analysis can be found in the *Summa Theologica,* I–II, QQ. 22–48. The Aristotelian analysis is in the *Rhetoric,* II, 2–12. Cf. H. I. Smith *The Classification of Desires in St. Thomas,* Washington, 1915.

of development. This is the difference between an infant and a man.

5. The Freudian dynamics is, to a lesser degree, sound philosophical psychology. Here the Freudian analysis makes one original contribution (the concept of repression), but in other respects, it is inadequate and even in error. As before, this can again be shown by a brief translation of the Freudian and Aristotelian analyses.
   a. The relation of ego and id. Freud recognizes, as Aristotle recognizes *more fully*, (1) the reciprocity of intellect and will, (2) the subordination of the will to both reason and the passions, and (3) the subordination of the sensitive appetite to both reason and vegetative needs.
      (1) According to Freud, the id is able to influence the ego, to determine its processes, and the ego is able to influence the id, in repression, censorship, etc. So in Aristotelian psychology, desire is the source of all activity, the acts of all the powers of the soul, on the one hand; and on the other hand, the acts of one of these powers, the cognitive power, determines desires. Not only does the intellect move the will and the will move the intellect, but the passions move the will and the will is able to control the passions. In short, there is a very complicated reciprocal interdependence of the rational and non-rational parts of the soul, as well as between the cognitive and the appetitive functions. This is because reason rules the non-rational part not as an absolute despot but only as a ruler suffered by free subjects, who can disobey and even usurp his power and subject him to their will [57].
      (2) Reason is able to operate independently of the passions, and the passions independently of reason. Freudian psychology must also recognize some independence of ego and id; that is, the ego can function to some extent apart from the id, and conversely. If this were not the case, their reciprocal subordination would be impossible [58].
   b. Types of dominance by the ego of the id (conflict and harmony, repression and discipline) = reason ruling the passions by counteracting their motions, or ruling them

by moderating or perfecting them through prudence (the moral virtues).[8a]

(1) Here, although the two types of dominance are recognized by both Aristotle and Freud, the Aristotelian analysis is better because it more explicitly recognizes that the non-rational part of the soul is not anti-rational, but is rational to the extent that it is able to participate in reason, to be governed by reason.

(2) The Aristotelian analysis of the way in which reason positively rules the passions (by prudence in the formation of the moral virtues) is much more adequate. But the Freudian account of the way in which reason negatively rules the passions,—the account of the conflict between ego and id, in terms of censorship and repression,—is a notable addition to the Aristotelian analysis at this point.[9]

c. Types of dominance by the id of the ego (either determining its processes as in dreams, wishful thinking, etc. or in completely submerging it) = the influence which the passions exert upon reason and the complete obstruction of reason by temporary excesses of passion.[9a] The Freudian analysis here is much more detailed, and adds positively and definitely to the Aristotelian account.

d. The sources of conflict in the soul, i.e., causes of schizophrenia.[10]

(1) The basic conflict is due to the fact that desire is subject to two determinations, by the pure id (or instincts) on the one hand, and by the ego, on the other. The ego conflicts with the instincts (or pure id) in the control or determination of desires. So the Aristotelian analysis speaks of the appetitive power as subject to determination by the vegetative power in so far as sensitive operations serve vegetative needs, and also as subject to determination by the cognitive power of reason.[10a] The source of the conflict is the same in both cases.

[8a] Vd. Note 57 *infra.*

[9] This is the Freudian's chief claim to originality. Vd. Note 55 *infra.*

[9a] Vd. Note 57 *infra.*

[10] I am using the word "schizophrenia" very generally in its etymological meaning of "split soul," and not as a synonym for the psychosis *dementia praecox.*

[10a] Cf. St. Thomas Aquinas, *Summa Theologica,* I–II, Q. 9, AA. 1, 2; Q. 10, A. 3; Q. 17, AA. 7, 8, 9.

(2) Subordinate conflicts are described in the two analyses: between the ego and the fixated or organized id ≡ between reason and the particular passions (between will and sensitive appetite); between the various fixations or libidinous organizations themselves ≡ the conflict of the passions *inter se*.

e. The focal point of conflict: in the Freudian analysis, the focal point may either be in exterior actions or in thought; so in the Aristotelian analysis, the conflict may focus either upon the control of exterior motility or upon the interior actions of the imagination or intellect (as in dreaming or wishful thinking).

f. Sublimation ≡ the determination of the passions by intellectual objects. Thus, for Aristotle, the transformation of sensuality into intellectual love; for Freud, the transformation of sexuality into love for any idealized (which is the same as an intellectualized) object.

g. Degradation ≡ the determination of the will by sensible objects. (The transformation of love into sexuality.)

h. Abreaction ≡ the catharsis or purgation of the passions.

i. The basic principles of human behavior, as they occur in the two analyses:

(1) Instincts ≡ vegetative needs and natural appetite.

(2) Pleasure principle ≡ sensitive appetite, i.e., the passions as moving toward sensual gratifications.

(3) Reality principle ≡ intellectual appetite, i.e., the will as moving according to reason commanding through knowledge.

(I have omitted the repetition compulsion and the death instinct. Vd. Note 60 *infra*.)

k. *Summary and Criticism* [56]

(1) The chief inadequacy of Freudian dynamics arises from its incomplete analysis of intellect and appetite (ego and id).

(2) But, as we have seen, the Freudian dynamics in a number of important respects is a contribution to the philosophical analysis of the relation of the powers of the soul.[11]

(3) The chief error is due to the supposition that the ego is a function of the id in relation to physical reality, and that the super-ego is a function of the id

[11] *E.g.*, repression, censorship, sublimation, degradation.

and the ego in relation to social reality. The ego cannot be merely a function of the id, if it is able to control the id or to oppose it in conflict. In short, to be consistent with itself Freudian dynamics cannot assert that the ego is a function of the id, and also admit that the ego can function independently of the id and can subordinate the id [58].

(4) This error is really not an error in dynamics. It occurs often in Freudian dynamic accounts because the Freudian permits his genetics to color all his other thinking. This, as I shall now show, is his great misfortune. Freudian topography and dynamics are, to some extent, sound; against the background of modern academic psychology, these parts of the Freudian analysis are a great original contribution, although in fact they add only a few significant points to the older tradition of philosophical psychology. (The genius of Freud must be differently estimated if it is measured against the modern or the ancient achievement.) They are erroneous in part because of the Freudian genetics they involve. We must now turn to this third part of the metapsychology.

6. The Freudian genetics is of two sorts: (a) the origin of the different parts of the psyche in the development of the individual (ontogenetics); and (b) the origin of the whole psychic structure in the development of animal life (phylogenetics).

a. In both of these genetic accounts, the leading points made are:

(1) That all psychic organizations or functions are determined by the needs of animals in their adjustment to environment;

(2) That man is merely a stage in the evolutionary development of animal life;

(3) That there is continuity throughout the animal series, the basic functions of life being present in the single-cell organism;

Note: This proposition fails to take account of the obvious discontinuities. Those who hold it are forced to say not only that human sensitivity is essentially the same as unicellular irritability, but that reasoning, if it is a vital function, is also present in the unicellular life.

(4) That in the life of the individual, the phylogeny is repeated: the ego (or theoretical reason) is a function of the id in its adjustment to the *physical* environment; the super-ego (or practical, moral reason) is a function of the id in its adjustment to the *social* environment.[11a]

b. These propositions are not philosophical truths. They are not analyses of common experience. They are not propositions in metaphysics, mathematics or general physics. They are not propositions in philosophical psychology. In fact, the Freudian ontogenetics is directly inconsistent with the philosophical truth that one generic power is not derived from another in any way. Now, either sense and understanding (the ego) are not powers at all or they cannot be developmentally derived from the vegetative powers (the id).

c. These propositions are not scientific truths. They are not inductions from scientific evidence. They are not propositions in any biological science, not in anatomy, physiology, zoology, genetics, etc.

d. They are propositions in what is called "the theory of evolution." This "theory" is not a theory in the sense of a systematic organization of scientific facts and laws, in the sense in which Newton's *Principia* is a theory. It is a theory in the sense in which there is an attempt to explain certain facts, which have been scientifically established in the biological sciences, by making *hypotheses* which are not propositions to be proved, but are merely imaginative guesses about unobservable processes or events. This is the sense of hypothesis in which Newton said no scientist should make them.

e. This "theory" is the kind of wild speculation which, in modern times and particularly in the 19th century, is confused with philosophy. Darwin himself is partly responsible for much of this speculation. *The Origin of Species* is full of guesses which are clearly unsupported by the evidence. (To the extent that *The Origin of Species* contains scientifically established facts, these facts are not organized into any coherent system.) Fur-

[11a] Vd. Note 53 *infra*.

thermore, these guesses, which constitute the theory of evolution, are not in the field of scientific knowledge anyway. They are historical. This conjectural history, begun by Darwin, was even more fancifully elaborated by the 19th century evolutionary "philosophers" [59].

(1) On the one hand, the post-Darwinian "scientific cosmologies": Spencer, Haeckel.[12]

(2) On the other hand, the post-Darwinian "evolutionary philosophies": e.g., Bergson.[13]

Note: The genetics to be found in Freud's metapsychology has its best expression in Bergson's *Creative Evolution,* in which all the forms of life are the result of the life-force,—the *élan vital* or cosmic id,—struggling against the inorganic environment.[13a]

f. The criticism can be briefly made.[14]

(1) In the first place, "evolution" is not a scientific fact, but at best a probable history, a history for which the evidence is insufficient and conflicting.

(2) The relevant facts are facts in embryology, genetics, palaeontology, comparative anatomy. These facts establish only one historical probability: that types of animals which once existed no longer exist, and that types of animals now existing at one time did not exist. They do not establish the elaborate story

[12] H. Spencer, *First Principles*, London, 1862; 4th American ed., 1880; E. Haeckel, *The Riddle of the Universe at the Close of the Nineteenth Century* (trans. by McCabe), New York, 1900.

[13] H. Bergson, *Creative Evolution*, London, 1911. Although Schopenhauer antedates Darwin, his influence upon "evolutionary philosophy" is tremendous. It is clearly reflected in Bergson. Vd. *The World as Will and Idea,* 1st ed. in 1818; trans. by Haldane and Kemp.

[13a] The theories of Schopenhauer and Bergson have a bearing on the form which the doctrine of the unconscious takes in Jung. Vd. *Contributions to Analytical Psychology*, New York, 1928. For a general discussion of Jung and other variants of psychoanalysis, vd. Woodworth, *Contemporary Schools of Psychology*, New York, 1931: Ch. 5; also Allers, *The New Psychologies*, New York, 1933: pp. 25–51; Crichton-Miller, *Psycho-Analysis and its Derivatives*, New York, 1933.

[14] Vd. L. T. More, *The Dogma of Evolution*, Princeton, 1925; T. H. Morgan, *Evolution and Genetics*, Princeton, 1925. The latter is a revision of Professor Morgan's Vanuxem Lectures for 1915–16, entitled *A Critique of the Theory of Evolution.* Vd. also *Evolution in Modern Thought* by Weismann, Bateson, Lloyd-Morgan and others.

which is the myth of evolution; nor do they establish any of the aetiological guesses about the way in which species originated or became extinct, such as natural selection, adaptation to environment, struggle for existence, transmission of acquired characteristics, etc.

(3) If the grand myth of evolution, as a history of the development of the forms of life, and the grand theory of evolution, as an explanation of how it all happened, are not scientific knowledge, how much less are they philosophical knowledge. (This type of speculation, peculiar to the 19th century, did much to bring discredit upon the name of philosophy which it so wrongly arrogated to itself.)

(4) For the most part, the wild speculations of Spencer, Haeckel, Schopenhauer and Bergson are now generally discredited both by scientists and philosophers.[15] Yet this is all that Freudian genetics amounts to,–a repetition of these speculations in a form even wilder, if that is possible, than in Spencer, Schopenhauer, Bergson [60].

7. *Conclusion so far*

a. Psychoanalysis as a scientific psychology is taxonomic and physionomic but not aetiological. Here we have a contribution by psychoanalysis to the knowledge of man.

b. Psychoanalysis is aetiological in that part of the metapsychology which we have called dynamics. Here it contributes the concept of repression. Otherwise it is a reworking of the traditional philosophical analysis of the order and interdependence of the powers of the soul.

c. Where the dynamics *appears* to be most original, in attempting to account genetically for the origin of the ego, it is most in error. The error is demonstrable. The genetic account is inconsistent with the analysis of the relation of ego and id. This error occurs in the metapsychology as a result of the uncritical acceptance or espousal of the "evolutionary speculations" of the 19th

[15] Cf. H. Höffding, *The Influence of the Conception of Evolution on Modern Philosophy* in *Evolution and Modern Thought;* John Dewey, *The Influence of Darwin on Philosophy and Other Essays in Contemporary Thought*, New York, 1910.

century, which are neither scientific nor philosophical knowledge, but have only the status of unsupported opinion.

d. Psychoanalysis as scientific knowledge would be totally unaffected by the complete elimination of this genetics. Psychoanalysis as philosophical knowledge (the topography and dynamics of the metapsychology) would be greatly improved by its elimination.

e. In any case, it is perfectly clear that the genetic fictions have absolutely nothing to do with psychoanalysis as scientific psychology.

f. The argument that I have with psychoanalysts at this point is not with them as psychologists or even as scientists, but with them as uncritical speculators, as bad philosophers. This is the misfortune of their 19th century heritage. To cure them of their superstitions would, of course, take more time than is proper at this place. It could be done by showing them how little there is in the way of strictly scientific evidence to support the popular myth of evolution.

IV. Psychoanalysis as Practical Psychology: Medicine and Morals

1. I wish to consider psychoanalysis as practical for two reasons: first, to make the point that the genetics has no practical significance, whereas the topography and dynamics are significant in psychoanalytic therapy and morals; and second, to show the correlation between Freudian and Aristotelian ethics, a correlation which could occur only through their sharing the same analysis of man's nature. To the extent that the Freudian analysis is inadequate, the ethics will be so also.

2. The end of ordinary medical therapy is the health of the body, considered with respect to the functioning of its various organs. The end of psychoanalytic therapy is health in a more general sense, i.e., the health of the whole man, of body and soul together. Health in this sense is what Aristotle means by happiness: an activity of man in accordance with the perfection of all parts of his nature. The end of the psychoanalyst as a practitioner is the same as the end of the moralist as a teacher. Both are practical psychologists. They use psychological knowledge for the sake

of making men happy, so far as one man can help another to become happy.[16]

3. In general we can make a translation between Aristotelian and Freudian ethics. I shall briefly indicate it as follows:
   a. The moral virtues ═ the socialized id, i.e., the id as it is governed by the ego and super-ego.[16a] (Here there is an important difference. The moral virtues are the passions and social actions moderated by reason in the light of knowledge. The id is socialized by the ego and super-ego merely in the direction of conformity to the prevailing conventions or customs of the tribe.)
   b. The intellectual virtues ═ insight or self-understanding. (Here also there is a difference. The Freudian does not understand the intellectual virtues because his psychological analysis is inadequate with respect to the intellect and the cognitive process. He does not know what it means to say that the good of the intellect is the truth. He does not fully admit,[16b] because of his genetic superstitions, that the ego (reason) is the measure of goodness in the id, as reality in turn is the measure of goodness in the ego.)
   c. The aim of psychoanalysis: to cure mental disorder, that is, to reduce the conflict in the psyche between ego and id; not to destroy the id, but by relieving repression to make a man understand himself, and through understanding his desires to adjust them to reality, which is another way of saying, to make a man reasonable; to sublimate the libido so far as this is conformable to a proper satisfaction of the vegetative needs.
   d. The aim of morality: to reduce the conflict between reason and the passions; not to destroy the passions, but to make them participate in reason through submitting

[16] The essential difference in aim between the moralist and the psychotherapist is that the former is primarily concerned with positive training, the latter with the elimination of defects. Their difference is analogous to that between preventive medicine and surgery.

[16a] This translation could be carried out in great detail by comparing the Freudian account of the genesis of neurosis with the Thomistic account of unhappiness in terms of sin and vice, especially the relation of capital to superficial sins which corresponds to the relation between complex and symptom in the Freudian analysis.

[16b] Yet, on the question of truth, Freud is opposed to skepticism and relativism, as on the question of the contribution of the intellect, he is opposed to materialism. Vd. *New Introductory Lectures on Psychoanalysis*, New York, 1933: pp. 240 ff.

to prudent government; to subordinate the sensitive appetite to the intellectual appetite; so to order all the goods desired by man that he is able to achieve all of them in a proper measure and in a proper subordination of lesser to greater goods.

e. Both the psychoanalyst and the moralist recognize the same basic difficulty in human life: the conflict or disorder in the soul due to the imperfect rule of the passions by reason, either because of the weakness of reason or because of the strength of the passions. The difference between them is with respect to what they do about this difficulty. The moralist appeals directly to reason; he hopes by giving the reason the knowledge it needs, to strengthen it; but he knows that this is not enough, that the virtues are moral habits, and that the virtues cannot be simply taught as geometry is. The sound moralist knows that his analysis of what a good man is does not enable him to make men good. Aristotle said that it was almost impossible to teach ethics to young men because of their subjection to the passions. The psychoanalyst seems to recognize this difficulty, and so approaches the problem, not from the side of reason but from the side of the passions. He tries to relieve the pressure of the passions; he tries to help reason without using it directly. And he knows, when he is honest, that he cannot succeed any more than the moralist in making men good; and ultimately for the same reason. His knowledge is not sufficient. He does not know how.

f. Yet the moralist succeeds better than the psychoanalyst *to the extent that* the psychoanalyst proceeds as if the goodness of a man did not depend essentially upon the cultivation of his reason.

(1) Freud's criticism of hypnosis as therapy was that it only cured the symptoms of hysteria and did not cure the disease. It removed the symptoms by a trick without attacking their causes.

(2) My criticism of psychoanalysis as therapy is similar. It only relieves or alters one of the conditions of the moral problem. By an extraordinary trick,—much more ingenious and extraordinary than hypnosis,—it influences the passions which are involved in the disorder of the soul. But this is negative. So is the cure of repression. The problem is fully

solved only if the individual acquires sound moral principles and then is able to form habits and direct his life according to these principles by the rule of reason [61].

(3) To the extent, then, that the psychoanalyst is not competent as a moralist,—to the extent that his philosophy is incomplete or erroneous,—he cannot achieve the end he sets himself: to make men happy [62]. At best, he can give them a little help by a kind of purgation of the passions through understanding them objectively. (In other words, psychoanalysis works in the same way that art, particularly the drama, does. It makes a man a spectator of his own passions by a process of identification, transference, etc.)

(4) What a good friend who is a wise man and a competent moralist can do in some cases, the psychoanalyst who is a wise man and a competent moralist can do in other cases. The difference in the cases is the difference between the normal and the neurotic, a difference in the degree to which the passions are disordered and reason is weak.

g. Unfortunately, the psychoanalyst is seldom a wise man and a competent moralist, because he is seldom if ever a philosopher. The Freudian conception of a good man as a complete adult is inadequate because all that this ideal involves is normal biological functioning, primarily on the vegetative and social level. The crucial error in his moral insight arises from his crucial error in psychology: his failure to understand the nature of intellect and will. (As a result of his analysis of the super-ego the Freudian thinks that morality is nothing more than conformity to the prevailing *mores*. He does not recognize that moral principles are based upon speculative truths, that they hold for all men, that they are not relative and changing.)

V. Conclusions

1. I have tried to show positively that psychoanalysis has a place in the European tradition, both among the sciences and in relation to philosophy. It is due to the great genius of Freud in rediscovering man as the subject-matter of psychology that the vitality and significance of the ancient tradition

has been at last infused into psychology as a scientific enterprise.

2. But psychoanalysts do not understand their place in this tradition, and as a result they do not understand their own doctrine. This may account for their failure to make an intelligible presentation of it to those who are not psychoanalysts and who employ critical standards to judge what is presented.
   a. Psychoanalysts fail to understand what part of their contribution is scientific, and what part of their doctrine is philosophical.
   b. They do not understand the relation between the theoretical and the practical aspects of their undertaking.
   c. These failures of understanding may account for the failure so far of any psychoanalyst to make a clear, systematic statement of psychoanalysis in terms of its basic concepts, its principles, its evidences, its facts.[17]
3. To what are these failures of understanding due? To lack of philosophical training, on the one hand; and to the influence of the 19th century,—its bad philosophy, its prejudices and superstitions,—on the other. The only cure that I know of for the influence of the 19th century is education in the European tradition which was almost completely obscured in that century.
4. But education is not enough. To suppose that it is is to make the error of assuming that men, psychoanalysts among them, are completely rational and are capable of being moved by the truth. Prejudices are like passions. May I borrow the technique of the psychoanalyst for a moment, and analyze his prejudices in the hope that he may get the insight that will work as a cure.
   a. If you were to psychoanalyze me,—and you will probably start as soon as I leave the room,—you would say that I have the prejudices and the passions of an anal-erotic. I am trying to be completely submissive to objective truth and order. I am masochistic toward reason.
   b. If I were to psychoanalyze psychoanalysts, I would say that as a group they have the prejudices and passions of the narcissist. They are trying to be original; they are trying to swallow everything in psychoanalysis. To be orig-

[17] Vd. the not quite successful attempt made for psychoanalysis by W. Healy, A. F. Bronner and A. M. Bowers, *The Structure and Meaning of Psychoanalysis*, New York, 1930.

inal in this way, they must ignore their sources in the European tradition, and they must be sadistic toward order and reason. In other words, psychoanalysts commit the sin of pride. They are unwilling to recognize their place in the great intellectual tradition of western Europe, and to make what contribution they can to its science and wisdom, however slight that may be.

c. I have added this little psychoanalytical ending for the sake of warning you that you cannot dismiss what I have said in these lectures by psychoanalyzing me. That defense can be used against you as readily as against me. Psychoanalysis is irrelevant to the merits of any intellectual position. The truths of science and philosophy, resting on evidence and demonstration, are not challenged by the *ad hominem* of calling their proponents narcissists or anal-erotics. A man becomes an authority by speaking the truth; the truth does not rest on the authority of its human source and is thus unaffected by states of personality.

NOTES

1. In the history of physics and chemistry there have been, of course, many instances of theoretical controversy. The opposition between the corpuscular and the wave theory of light, the issue concerning phlogiston in the science of heat, the war between the Neptunists and the Vulcanists in geology, the argument about the hypostatical or veridical character of molecules in the kinetic theory of gases,—these and many others constitute interesting chapters in the modern history of the natural sciences. But in every case, the polemic is between alternative theories within the area of a science, the fundamental data and principles of which the controversialists commonly share. The controversy has usually, if not always, been as to which of two competing theories gives a more adequate account of all the facts. The acknowledged facts, the observational data and basic inductions, constitute the unity of a science within which there may be two or more opposing theories. The situation in psychology, from the beginning of its history as an empirical science to the present day, is different. The "schools of psychology" are not rival theories within a single science, defined by common principles and given unity by common data. The schools of psychology do not even agree about the subject-matter of their "science." The phenomenal area which behaviorists investigate is not the same as that explored by introspective structuralists; structuralists and psychoanalysts do not seek their data in the same quarter. Not only do the different schools of psychology,—however they be named and enumerated,—not have the same subject-matter, but they do not acknowledge each other's methods as "scientific"; they share neither common principles nor common data. This is not an opposition of theories within a science. It is rather an opposition of rival pretenders to the title of being *the* science of psychology. So long as this situation persists, may one not wonder justifiably whether there is *any* science of psychology? The nearest analogue to psychological controversy is the polemic between vitalists and mechanists in biology, but even this is much more like an opposition of theories than like the civil war which makes the field of psychology anarchic.

   Vd. *Psychologies of 1930*, Worcester, 1930; R. S. Woodworth, *Contemporary Schools of Psychology*, New York, 1931; and E. M.

Heidbreder, *Seven Psychologies*, New York, 1935. In what other field of natural science could such books be published? Consider the varieties assembled by Professor Murchison in his 1930 circus of psychologies: hormic psychology, associationism and act psychology, functionalism, motor psychology, structural psychology, configurational psychology, Russian (i.c., Marxist) psychology, behaviorism, reaction psychology, dynamic psychology, factor school of psychology, analytical psychologies. Professor Woodworth devotes his attention only to five: introspective psychology, behaviorism, gestalt psychology, psychoanalysis and related schools, purposivism or hormic psychology. In his introductory chapter Professor Woodworth writes: "With all these divergent movements going on, contemporary psychology might be expected to show no coherence at all, but curiously enough the psychologists of the day enjoy meeting and discussing the problems of psychology, and still treat one another with respect. . . . The mutual respect of psychologists reflects the obvious zeal shown by members of all schools for the continued progress of the science. Some schools are more concerned to make psychology scientific and others to make it more human and adequate. One would like to see it both scientific and adequate, and the psychologists keep together in the hope that such results can be achieved" (*Op cit.*, pp. 15–16; by permission of The Ronald Press Company). That divergent psychologists still respect each other in their common aim to establish a science which will be adequate may be regarded as a hopeful sign; but it can hardly be regarded as indicating that a science of psychology now exists.

Professor Woodworth admits that "schools such as we have been considering seem almost peculiar to psychology. It may be there are some in the social sciences, but at least in the natural sciences at the present time they are hard to find" (*Op. cit.*, pp. 214–215). And he is forced to conclude that this looks "like an indication that all is not well and that psychology does not yet know where it stands or what it has to do" (*Op. cit.*, p. 215). In the face of this situation the forced optimism which current commentators, such as Woodworth and Heidbreder, try to summon up in their concluding chapters seems ever so much like whistling in the dark. Cf. E. G. Boring, *A History of Experimental Psychology*, New York, 1929: Ch. 24. Vd. Note 42 *infra.*

2. The way in which formal logic is presupposed by material logic is clearly illustrated by the relation between the prior and posterior analytics in Aristotle's *Organon.* In the *Prior Analytics* we find the formal principles of inference. The account of syllogisms considers only the formal characteristics of the nexus of terms and propositions which constitute reasoning. But all syllogisms are not scientific, nor is the formal structure of a science fully stated by the analysis of syllogisms. The account of science depends upon this prior analysis,

but requires also a consideration of the relation between definition and demonstration, of both to causal analysis, and of the ordering of the syllogisms of a science by its ultimate principles, those primary definitions and indemonstrable or assumed propositions which generate the science. To say that these considerations are material is not to deny the formality which everywhere rules the posterior analysis; it is merely to say that the account of science is an application of the forms to particular types of matter. The difference between the *Prior* and the *Posterior Analytics* can be seen in another way. There is little or no psychology needed for the analysis of syllogisms. But the analysis of science requires an account of induction, an account of the origin of its first principles. Any attempt to give a formal account of induction reduces it to syllogisms, and the search for the grounds of demonstration, its first premises, must continue. That is why the exposition of induction with which the *Posterior Analytics* concludes (Bk. II, Ch. 19) is necessarily and unavoidably psychological.

The relation between these two parts of Aristotle's *Organon* is found in modern treatises which try to be as comprehensive analytically. Thus, Book I of Jevons' *Principles of Science* (1874) is devoted to what he calls "formal logic." The concluding chapter of this part deals with induction, but attempts to reduce it to syllogisms. The rest of the treatise is concerned with induction genuinely; Book II considers number, variety and probability, Book III, the methods of measurement, Book IV, inductive investigation, and Book V, generalization, analogy and classification. In these books we find the exposition of scientific method and it is inextricably interwoven with material considerations, on the one hand, and psychological analysis, on the other. The same relation obtains between Books I and II of J. S. Mill's *System of Logic* (1843), and Books III to VI. The three parts of Johnson's monumental work on *Logic* (1921–1924) are similarly divided: the first and second parts are formal, even in their consideration of induction; the third part is concerned with "the logical foundations of science." In some instances, modern logicians have devoted special treatises to the application of formal logic to the matter and method of scientific knowledge, as in the case of Venn's *Empirical Logic* (1889). But, generally, the structure of Aristotle's *Organon* is imitated both by original treatises and by text-books. Vd. Cohen and Nagel, *An Introduction to Logic and Scientific Method* (1934); Stebbing, *A Modern Introduction to Logic* (1930). In their material portions, the modern treatises differ from Aristotle in the extent to which they are methodological. This is due obviously to the crucial difference in the meaning of "science" in ancient and modern times. Aristotle was not concerned with the procedures of research: measurement, experimentation, etc.

There is one further point of difference between Aristotelian logic and those modern treatments which are sensitive to the nature and methods of science. The formal logic of Aristotle is predicational.

The distinctions of subject and predicate, the analysis of the predicaments, the post-predicaments, and the predicables, the division of the kinds of predication, the concern with real definitions and the role they play in syllogisms,—these are essential to Aristotelian logic. In modern times, what is called a non-Aristotelian logic has been developed. It is relational rather than predicational. It reduces all subjects and predicates to classes and distinguishes classes as belonging to different orders according to the way in which they are related. Its basic distinctions are among types of relation and relational order. It is not concerned with real definitions, and treats the syllogism as a special case of substitutional operation in linear inference. The point that logic and mathematics are continuous is true for this relational logic; it could not be maintained for predicational logic.

It has been held by some that relational logic is the general case, and by others that relational logic can be translated into the logic of predication. Whether such subsumptions or translations can be achieved seems to me only a matter of grammatical subtlety. There is a real difference between these two logics. Aristotelian logic is the logic of philosophical knowledge in so far as it is concerned with ontological problems. It is the logic appropriate to an inquiry into substance and causes. Relational logic is the logic of modern mathematics and investigative science. Science does not treat of substance and causes; it investigates the phenomena with a view to classification, order, correlation, measurement, systematization. The operational character of relational (or mathematical) logic is appropriate to the operational principles of scientific method. Aristotelian "science" is bad as science because it attempts to apply a predicational logic to the study of phenomena. Modern "philosophy" is bad as philosophy to the extent that it makes the opposite error. Vd. Notes 9, 10a, 16a and 47 *infra.*

3. In Book IV of the *De Rerum Natura*, Lucretius expounds the psychology of cognition. In this context, he states the basic canon of scientific method in terms of the relation of sensation and reasoning. "You will find that the concept of the true is begotten first from the senses, and that the senses cannot be gainsaid. For something must be found with a greater surety, which can of its own authority refute the false by the true. Next then, what must be held of greater surety than sense? Will reason, sprung from false sensation, avail to speak against the senses, when it is wholly sprung from the senses? For unless they are true, all reason too becomes false" (trans. by C. Bailey, Oxford, 1921: p. 159). "And if reason is unable to unravel the cause, why those things which close at hand were square, are seen round from a distance, still it is better through lack of reasoning to be at fault in accounting for the causes of either shape, rather than to let things clear seen slip abroad from your grasp, and to assail the grounds of belief and to pluck up the whole foundations on which life and

existence rest" (*Ibid.*, p. 160). Yet the atomic philosophy which Lucretius espouses is an attempt to explain away by reasoning the immediate sensitive experiences we have of the qualitative variety which exists among physical things. Sensible qualities are not really *in* things, though they are apparently there, because the atomistic materialist claims to know, not by sense but through reasoning, that the atoms have only quantitative properties and that composite bodies are arrangements of atoms, differing *inter se* only in geometrical properties. Lucretius' account of scientific method is thus inconsistent with what he claims to know as a scientist. The inconsistency is even more devastating when Lucretius attempts, at the end of Book II and in Books III and IV, to give an analysis of the soul and of the psychological processes of sensation and reasoning in terms of the size, shape and motion of atoms. Atomism, or what is the same, simple-minded absolute materialism, is always thus self-refuting. It claims to be knowledge gained in a certain way, and this "knowledge" makes it impossible to give a tenable account of knowledge itself and violates the procedure by which it is said valid knowledge must be obtained. The *reductio ad absurdum* which can easily be made of Lucretius applies as readily to the materialism of Hobbes in the 17th century and to that of Büchner, Moleschott, Vogt and Feuerbach, in the 19th century. (Vd. The account of Feuerbach's refutation of "absolute materialism" in Hook, *From Hegel to Marx*, New York, 1936: pp. 237–242. This refutation, made in 1838 when Feuerbach was still an idealist, applies to the materialism he himself later adopted as well as to that of Marx.) Materialism does not escape its insoluble dilemmas by becoming dialectical in the post-Hegelian sense of that word, but only by becoming dialectical in the Greek manner. It then ceases to be an absolute materialism and becomes the materialism of hylomorphism, or formal materialism, which sees that being, becoming and knowing require a formal as well as a material principle for a consistent and adequate account both of the nature of things and of our knowledge of them. Vd. Notes 21 and 28 *infra*.

4. The ancient error of the materialistic philosophy is nicely illustrated in the *reductio ad absurdum* which Professor Lovejoy makes of behaviorism, which is distinguished as a contemporary "school of psychology" not only by its restricted methods but by its bad metaphysics. Vd. A. O. Lovejoy, *The Paradox of the Thinking Behaviorist*, in the Philosophical Review, XXXI, pp. 135–147 (1922). It is not only that the behaviorist is a philosopher while at the same time denying the validity of any knowledge not obtained by scientific methods (vd. J. B. Watson, *Psychology From the Standpoint of a Behaviorist*, Philadelphia, 1919: Ch. I). That is an error which most scientific psychologists share. In addition, the behaviorist presents the conclusions of his research *as if* they were rationally founded in his data, yet at the same time reduces all "reasoning" to conditioned reflexes in the

sphere of the laryngeal musculature. His scientific work indicates plainly *that* he thinks, though not always well, as is clear from the fact that *what* he thinks makes it impossible for him to explain, without contradiction, *how* he thinks. Cf. Scott Buchanan, *An Aeolian Theory* in Psyche, April, 1927: pp. 100–101.

What Lovejoy and Buchanan have done humorously to the behaviorist, F. H. Bradley did to the British associationist psychologists with dialectical severity. The error is strictly the same. The attempt to reduce all rational operations to the mechanical association of ideas, —an "idea" being nothing more than a sensation or a sense-image,— is the prototype of the more recent attempt to reduce thinking to the mechanical conditioning of reflexes. Bradley not only shows the impossibility of all such reductions, but exhibits the crucial error of sensationalism. If ideas are purely the particulars of sense, if they are not actually universals in the mind, thinking of any sort is impossible, even the thinking which comes to the conclusions of sensationalistic psychology. Any psychology which denies the distinction between sense and intellect, between perceiving and understanding, is thus self-annihilating. Vd. *The Principles of Logic*, London, 1883: Bk. II, Pt. II, Ch. I on the theory of the association of ideas.

The point here being made is not that the mind cannot know itself as it knows other things. Quite the contrary! The fact of reflexivity is not itself the stumbling block in the path of a scientific psychology. All that is here being insisted is that the mind which is the object of psychological science be described in a way that is consistent with the characteristics of the mind which the psychologist reveals himself as having in his operations as a scientist.

5. The distinction between common and special experience can be illuminated by an understanding of the nature of experience. Experience is usually identified with sense-experience, although it can be extended to include the immediate but non-sensitive awareness we have of our rational operations. But, taking experience in the more restricted meaning of the word, it must be further observed that sense-experience is not identical with, and hence not reducible to, sensations. While it is true that all sense-experience arises from the activity of the senses,—the sensations which result from their activation by sensible objects,—experience goes beyond sensation in that it does not refer exclusively to particular objects here and now present, as all sensations do. Experience involves memory and imagination and this explains the kind of generality it has. It is a product of sensation, not simply but in consequence of the summation and composition of sensations, which is the work of memory and imagination. Aristotle makes this point in his account of induction. "Out of sense-perception comes to be what we call memory, and out of frequently repeated memories of the same thing develops experience; for a number of memories constitute a single experience" (*Posterior Analytics*, II,

100a4–5). An experience thus contains the "rudimentary universals" to be made explicit and genuine universals by the act of abstraction which is essential to the process of induction or generalization. Cf. *Metaphysics*, I, 1. What Aristotle called "a single experience" is treated by modern psychologists as a "generic image," an image which has quasi-universality because it lacks the individual intention of the perceptual image. Vd. Wundt, *Outlines of Psychology*, III, 16; Kulpe, *Outlines of Psychology*, IV, 27; Galton, *Inquiries into Human Faculty*, Appendix A.

The notion of common experience must not be interpreted to mean that all men have the same experiences. That is plainly not the case. I have used the phrase "common experience" to denote the whole set of experiences which men have naturally through the ordinary operation of their senses, their memories and imaginations. Though the experiences of two men are not in all details the same, they both have common experience to the extent that they share experiences which have thus arisen naturally in the course of their lives. That men share experiences follows from the fact that they live, for the most part, in the same world of objects and from the fact that as sensitive animals they have the same specific powers and operations. The negative definition of common experience is that it does not result from investigation. This does not mean that ordinary men, men who are not scientists, never investigate. It means only that their common experience is not the result of any deliberate research or inquisitive effort on their part. (Ordinary men investigate whenever they make a deliberate use of their powers of observation in order to answer definite questions. Such investigation differs from scientific inquiry, however, in that the latter is directed by problems formulated in terms of technical concepts. It is only scientific investigation which creates a new order of experience.)

Special experience is positively defined as being the result of deliberate research and specially contrived inquisitive efforts. An experiment can be defined as an artistically devised experience. Instead of waiting for the multiplication of sensations and memories to do their work toward the production of an experience, the scientist performs operations and manipulations which create for the senses at once what the imagination might never produce naturally. The experiment as an artificial experience has the same quasi-universality that a natural experience has. It is this quasi-universality which makes both the natural experience and the experiment the proximate matter from which an induction can be made. The experiment is the ideal of scientific method, not only because it so readily yields an induction, but because it differs so radically from the natural manner of experiencing. Scientific procedures which consist in the collection of huge amounts of data which must be statistically refined before they are anything like an experience that is pregnant with inductions, are not only usually infertile but lack the artistry which distinguishes scientific from ordinary experiencing.

The distinction between common and special experience is thus seen to be a distinction between natural and artificial experience. Scientific method, from its best experimental to its crudest empirical forms, is the art of creating experiences which men do not naturally have. The value of experience, whether common or special, whether natural or artificial, is the same: it is the immediate source of inductions, of generalized knowledge of the world of experienceable objects. The maxims of common sense, the axioms or principles of philosophy, the general facts and laws of science, all arise from experience, but not the same kind of experience, because the method of ordinary and philosophical knowing is thoroughly natural, whereas the method of scientific knowing involves operations of art in the production of special experiences.

6. The conception of scientific knowledge as based on special experience is generally accepted in modern times, i.e., it is generally said that the data of science result from investigation. But the conception of philosophical knowledge as based on common experience seems scarcely to be understood at all in modern times. The history of the modern degradation of philosophy to the status of being handmaiden to the sciences is a long and complicated one. But it is clear that, in the course of the last three centuries, philosophy has gradually lost the status of a body of knowledge having independent validity in its own right. Nineteenth and twentieth century positivism was the inevitable result of a development which at first looked upon scientific method as a way of correcting the "unchecked speculations" of the philosopher and then came to regard scientific knowledge as the type of all valid knowledge of a generalized sort. Positivism expresses itself in many ways, but all of them reduce to a denial of philosophy as knowledge of the world of experienceable objects. The conception of the philosopher as working on the periphery of the scientific domain, trying but failing to solve problems which the scientist will later succeed in solving as science advances (vd. William James, *Some Problems of Philosophy*); the conception of the philosopher as endlessly trying but failing to answer unanswerable questions (vd. M. W. Calkins, *The Persistent Problems of Philosophy* and John Dewey, *The Quest for Certainty*); the conception of the philosopher as "fusing religion and science into one rational scheme of thought," as tentatively formulating "ultimate generalities" in the light of science, and therefore compelled to change his philosophy from time to time as science advances (vd. A. N. Whitehead, *Process and Reality*); the reduction of the philosopher to the role of a logician, nay a grammarian, whose chief task is to keep scientific language in order and undefiled (vd. R. Carnap, *Philosophy and Logical Syntax* and *The Unity of Science*)—these are all expressions of positivism which holds that the

only questions genuinely answerable by knowledge are those which can be answered by the investigative procedures of science. What is most amazing is that so few recent philosophers have seen the absurdity, if they have not resented the indignity, of a role which makes their work entirely subordinate to and dependent on the contingencies of changing scientific knowledge. No self-respecting man should want to be a philosopher according to this conception of his task.

There are a few exceptions, of course. I am not thinking here of those who work in the tradition of the perennial philosophy, such as Jacques Maritain and Étienne Gilson; but rather of those others among contemporary thinkers who, though somewhat more divergent from the ancient and mediaeval tradition, nevertheless share in its conception of philosophy as knowledge; thus, E. Husserl, who as a philosopher refers the truth of his analysis directly to common experience in utter disregard of the content of changing science; and similarly George Santayana, from whom I quote the following passage. "There is one point, indeed, in which I am truly sorry not to be able to profit by the guidance of my contemporaries. There is now a great ferment in natural and mathematical philosophy, and the times seem ripe for a new system of nature, at once ingenious and comprehensive, such as has not appeared since the earlier days of Greece. . . . But what exists today is so tentative, obscure and confused by bad philosophy, that there is no knowing what parts may be sound and what parts merely personal and scatter-brained. If I were a mathematician I should no doubt regale myself, if not the reader, with an electric or logistic system of the universe expressed in algebraic symbols. For good or ill, I am an ignorant man, almost a poet, and I can only spread a feast of what everybody knows. Fortunately exact science and the books of the learned are not necessary to establish my essential doctrine, nor can any of them claim a higher warrant than it has in itself: for it rests on public experience. It needs, to prove it, only the stars, the seasons, the swarm of animals, the spectacle of birth and death, of cities and wars. My philosophy is justified, and has been justified in all ages and countries, by the facts before every man's eyes; and no great wit is required to discover it, only (what is rarer than wit) candour and courage. Learning does not liberate men from superstition when their souls are cowed or perplexed; and, without learning, clear eyes and honest reflection can discern the hang of the world and distinguish the edge of truth from the might of imagination. In the past or in the future, my language and my borrowed knowledge would have been different, but under whatever sky I had been born, since it is the same sky, I should have had the same philosophy" (*Skepticism and Animal Faith*, New York, 1923: pp. ix–x; by permission of Charles Scribner's Sons).

This statement by Santayana epitomizes the points involved in the methodological distinction of philosophy from science. The distinction turns, in the first place, on the fact that philosophy appeals only to what Santayana here calls "public experience",–the common experience of men, essentially the same at any time because under the same sky. From this fact it follows, in the second place, that philosophical doctrine must ultimately agree with the well-tested opinions of common sense because both arise by induction from the same common experience. Philosophical knowledge differs from common sense in the subtlety of reflection by which it discovers the implications of the obvious first truths,–"the facts before every man's eyes." Common sense is the beginning of wisdom and philosophy is its fruit. The relation of scientific knowledge to common sense is different. Philosophy deepens common sense into wisdom by performing the dialectical task, which Socrates rightly called intellectual midwifery, of making common sense deliver the truths it implicitly contains. Science merely makes up for the inadequacy of common sense by obtaining knowledge of the detailed operations of particular sorts of things, knowledge which cannot be gained from common experience. Investigation is required to know such details. But the knowledge of such details is not necessary for wisdom. As Santayana said, "exact science and the books of the learned are not necessary to establish" a philosophical doctrine. The changing content of the positive sciences can never alter a single philosophical truth. The works of Aristotle and St. Thomas Aquinas contain many statements which science has taught us are wrong as a matter of fact; but those statements were not in the first instance philosophical truths. The modern reader of such ancient books must remember that they contain both philosophical and scientific knowledge, without distinguishing labels attached to the different sorts of propositions.

This leads to the next point. We can find scientific errors in the works of Aristotle because scientific knowledge is essentially contingent. Its conclusions are only hypothetically necessary. The contingency of their truth is due to the fact that their truth is always relative to the data of special experience, and these data change from time to time, as scientists work ingeniously at contriving new and better special experiences. The essential contingency of scientific knowledge is based upon the same fact which properly leads us to expect interminable progress in the accomplishment of more and better scientific knowledge. But the data of philosophy are the facts of common experience. Errors in philosophy are due to failures of analysis, inconsistencies, inadequacies, etc.; they are not due to the inadequacy of the data. When a philosophical work is well-done, it is finished, though the work of philosophy to refine analyses and follow implications may itself never be finished. We should not hope for the same sort of progress in philosophy that we expect in science; in fact, we can do very little to improve upon ancient wisdom, because the limits of wisdom are not set by the limits of our ingenuity or industry in doing research, but by the natural limits of our reflective powers, our powers of understanding and judgment. For the same reason that progress in philosophy is accidental, whereas it is essential in science, philosophical truths are necessary and not contingent. I would go further than Santayana's statement that scientific knowledge cannot claim a higher warrant than philosophy has in itself; I would say that the warrant which philosophy has in common experience establishes it with a necessity and a permanence which makes it superior to science. I do not mean that philosophy can replace science or make science gratuitous. It is not as if in the same sphere philosophy were better knowledge than science. Their spheres are different, complementary rather than competitive, as science is complementary to common sense, as special experience completes common experience. (Vd. Dr. G. Phelan's discussion of the difference between progress in the sciences and in philosophy,—"progress by substitution and progress by deepening insight,"—in his essay on *Jacques Maritain*, New York, 1937. The first intellectual duty is "to defend thought against false progress;" the second is "to defend perpetual novelty against immobilists.")

The superiority of philosophical knowledge is not merely the necessity and permanence due to its source and method. The practical value of philosophy is greater. The modern world does not understand this because it thinks of utility narrowly. Knowledge is useful to the extent that it enables us to control and direct the operations of things. In this sense of utility, scientific knowledge is highly useful and philosophy is useless. But man operates on things as means to ends. The determination of the ultimate ends of human conduct and the ordination thereto of all means, cannot be accomplished by scientific knowledge. This is the work of philosophy in the practical sphere. Wisdom in the speculative sphere becomes practical when it is used for solving the problems of action. In the same sense that philosophy is superior to science in the speculative sphere because the principles which constitute its knowledge have greater generality and belong to higher orders of abstraction, so ethics and politics, which are practical philosophy, are superior to engineering and medicine, which are applied science, because they are concerned with the ends and the ordering of means, whereas the applied sciences give us at best a mastery of the means. But the means can be directed to the right or the wrong ends. It is, therefore, clear that scientific knowledge has the kind of utility which enables it to be used or misused, used for good or evil; whereas philosophy as practical wisdom cannot be misused. At worst, we can fail to use it. This is the unfortunate plight of the modern world which, denying philosophy in the speculative order, fails to use it practically. The danger of vast scientific knowledge unaccompanied and undirected by wisdom is obviously enormous. As Santayana said, learning, —of the scientific sort,—does not liberate men from superstition which, practically, is the confusion of means and ends.

The denial that philosophy is a body of knowledge, utterly independent of the results of scientific investigation, is currently due, as we have seen, to the curious fallacy of supposing that common experience, the existence of which cannot be denied, is unable to yield inductions and to validate generalizations in exactly the same way that special experience does. (Historically, of course, it is due to the psychological errors which underlie the positivism of Hume and Kant. Vd. Note 16a *infra.*) Those who hold this position must deny that, prior to science, men knew general truths, the significance and validity of which have remained unchanged despite all the results of research. They can do this only at the expense of denying truths which lie at the foundation of science, which science did not itself achieve and without which science cannot interpret its own findings. Those who claim that all valid knowledge, having generality, is the product of scientific research must, furthermore, be made to consider the nature of mathematics, which certainly has generality and which is certainly not the result of special investigations or based on special experience. (When we talk about "mathematical research," we do not mean any sort of observational inquiry, but a purely reflective process. Mathematics is arm-chair knowledge. Scientific research creates new experiences; mathematical research discovers new implications, new conclusions, new orders of propositions.)

Confronted by mathematics, the positivists are forced to admit that it is not the same sort of knowledge that science is; but instead of recognizing in mathematics knowledge that is typically philosophical, they take the characteristic modern alternative of treating mathematics as not knowledge at all, but rather as a sort of fictional logistic. All mathematical truths are *merely* conventional; they are not knowledge of the real world; they are nothing but the deceitful rules of a complicated grammar of symbolic operations. I say "deceitful" because mathematics appears to be knowledge of the real world of physical things, among the properties of which quantity and order are primary. The difference between mathematics and physics in subject-matter is that the former abstracts from the matter and motion of physical things, but it deals nevertheless with the properties of physical things. The ultimate criterion of truth is the same in mathematics and in physics. Unless mathematics is not knowledge of reality *in any sense* (i.e. not even from the point of view that its object is a certain grade of abstraction from reality), then the existence of mathematics establishes the existence of knowledge which does not depend upon the investigative methods of science. That mathematics is philosophical knowledge can be tested by applying to it all the criteria employed in differentiating philosophy from science. But mathematics is not *the type* of philosophical knowledge, particularly not modern mathematics which tries to be faithful to the positivistic ideal of being conventional and employing assumptions. Metaphysics is the type of philosophical knowledge; it proceeds from first principles and makes no assumptions; its concepts clearly refer to the real world and not to fictive entities. In the sense in which the word "metaphysics" is currently used by positivists, this statement is, of course, unintelligible or ridiculous. Vd. *Art and Prudence*, New York, 1937: Ch. 9; cf. P. Descoqs, *Essai Critique sur l'Hylémorphisme*, Paris, 1924: Appendice I.

I conclude this discussion by stating one dilemma: *either* philosophy is not genuinely valid knowledge, which rests directly on experience and is independent of scientific research, *or* philosophy is knowledge which is superior, both speculatively and practically, to science. The modern world, in its violent repugnance to the second horn of this dilemma, has gradually torn itself free from wisdom by embracing the first. Cf. J. Maritain, *Les Degrés du Savoir*, Paris, 1932: Ch. 2.

6a. In his introduction to this book Dr. Alexander speaks of my contempt for "practical" accomplishments and my failure to evaluate scientific concepts "according to the degree to which they increase our ability to control and influence natural phenomena." But, as we have seen, there are two meanings of utility applicable to knowledge: (1) the use of knowledge to control and influence natural phenomena, and in this sense science is magnificently useful whereas philosophy is totally useless; (2) the use of knowledge to determine the ultimate ends of human conduct and the ordination thereto of all proximate and remote means, and in this sense philosophy is practically indispensable whereas science can be disregarded. Scientific knowledge, at its best, provides us with a mastery over natural means or enables us to devise new means where nature fails us. The simplest rule of wisdom in the practical order of human life requires us to choose means according to the ends they serve, and if these ends be not ultimate they must, in turn, be ordered to a final end. The practical utility of science is, therefore, dependent upon a determination of the order of all human goods according as they are means and ends. It is clear that science itself does not make this determination; in fact, since such an ordering of goods is normative and involves what is currently called "value judgments", the scientist would be the first to admit, nay to insist, that the question of the order of goods is beyond him. If he dare to say that there is no objective order of goods, no ultimate end, no right determination of means,–as the psychoanalyst does in his claim that all moral standards are conventional or relative,–then he speaks as a philosopher and not as a scientist. And if he were right in his moral relativism, then how could he consistently defend his own dogmatic assertion of the unquestionable *value* of scientific knowledge because it enables us to control nature? Is such control good really or is it only a matter of our western European opinion? And if really, why?

I do not deny the utility of science, but I hold that the utility of philosophy is paramount. Ethics is architectonic in the practical order; all the applied sciences and the practical arts, all forms of engineering and medicine, are subordinate. All the scientific knowledge which has been accumulated since the Renaissance does not change, in one essential detail, the analysis of man's moral problem, the problem of virtue and happiness, as that is set forth in Aristotle's *Ethics* or the moral treatises of the *Summa Theologica*. Nor will any further accretions of scientific knowledge make any difference. If this can be called contempt for the scientific achievement, then the opposite position is an idolatry of science. Both contempt and idolatry are avoided by a just appraisal of the goodness of science in relation to the goodness of wisdom. Science unquestionably increases human power to achieve the ends of human life. But the goodness of this gift of power depends upon whether or not it is properly used; and since the power is entirely a mastery of means, that, in turn, depends upon wisdom about means and ends. Science without wisdom is dangerously ambivalent; the greater the power, the more ominous is its improper use. The hazards of human welfare in modern times can be understood in the light of the ever increasing disproportion between science and wisdom, between the operative power of men in an age of science and that clarity of direction which guides men only in so far as philosophy rules in the practical order. Even if philosophy were not attenuated in modern times, its directive task would be made more difficult by the augmented utilities which scientific advances confer.

This analysis of the practical importance of philosophy and science applies to the relation of ethics and psychotherapeutics. Psychoanalysis may be useful medically when it is subordinated to sound morals; it is full of danger to human well-being when it is substituted for morality. Vd. Notes 61 and 62 *infra*.

6b. Fully to understand that philosophy is independent of the changing content of scientific knowledge requires an understanding of the difference of their formal objects. It is not sufficient to define philosophy *negatively*, as we have so far done, by saying that it is non-investigative. For contemporary readers, the negative approach has pedagogic advantages. Science is knowledge and it is based upon empirical research. To those who hold this it is important to say philosophy is knowledge, though it is *not* based on empirical research. This negative point is essential to the distinction between science and philosophy, but it does not adequately define philosophical knowledge. We turn, therefore, to a positive distinction in terms of different formal objects of knowledge.

The material object,—the thing which is known,—is the same for science and philosophy. (For the time being, we shall disregard natural theology which has a different material object. Vd. Notes 8 and 9 *infra*.) Let us call that object the physical order: that which exists sensibly and under conditions of change. But of *that which* is known, *what* is known may be different, according to distinctions in the manner of knowing. Thus, sensitive and intellectual modes of apprehension are different, and we speak of the physical thing in its particularity and in its universality as different formal objects of knowledge according to this difference in the mode of considering it. Thus, the formal object of history is distinguished from the formal object of science and philosophy, but both sorts of knowledge are relevant to the same reality, the same material object.

This first distinction in formal objects depends upon the primary intellectual act of total abstraction. Further distinctions depend upon the difference between total, or extensive, abstraction, and formal, or intensive, abstraction. (Vd. St. Thomas Aquinas, *In Librum Boetii de Trinitate*, Q.V., A.3; J. Maritain, *Les Degrés du Savoir*, Paris, 1932: pp. 74–75; J. T. Casey, *The Primacy of Metaphysics*, Washington, 1936: pp. 81–82.) Within the sphere constituted by an abstract mode of consideration, the scientist is concerned with the phenomenal order, i.e., the sensible accidents or properties and their correlation, and the philosopher is concerned with the ontological order, the intelligible conditions of being and the essential nature of physical things. As Maritain says, the scientist goes from the observable to the observable, while the philosopher goes from the observable to the purely intelligible. The proper domains of science and philosophy do not overlap. Though they may have the same material object,–the world of bodies,–they do not have the same formal object. A scientific account of the phenomena can never displace or replace a philosophical understanding of the existences involved, or vice versa. Scientific descriptions, or even explanations, do not give us the intimate being of things. Philosophy is thus formally independent of science. The sciences by their proper means "will never suffice adequately to decide a philosophical question, for these questions depend on principles and on a light which are not within the range of science." (Vd. Maritain, *op. cit.*, pp. 93–95, 100–102.)

Further distinctions within the sphere of intensive abstraction,–what are called the grades of abstraction,–make the difference between science and philosophy clearer. Thus, all the natural sciences are of the same grade of abstraction, whereas within philosophy, there are mathematics and metaphysics, which differ from the philosophy of nature by being higher grades of abstraction. No one can doubt that the formal objects of mathematics and metaphysics are different from the formal object of the natural sciences. It is only the philosophy of nature which has a formal object constituted by the same grade of abstraction as that of the natural sciences. The problem of the independence of philosophy is, therefore, difficult, if at all, only with regard to the philosophy of nature. (For a discussion of this problem, vd. Note 10a *infra;* for a discussion of the three grades of abstraction, vd. Note 9 *infra.*)

That a difference in the formal objects of two bodies of knowledge is the sufficient formal condition of their independence can, perhaps, be most readily seen in the case of science and history. The general truths of natural science are unaffected by the changing content of historical knowledge; and scientific advances do not modify the facts established as probable by historical research. Here, then, are two bodies of knowledge, having the same material object, which are formally independent of each other because they are different modes of considering that identical object. (The exceptions to this independence are accidental; thus, the scientific generalization employed in an historical inference may be subject to alteration in such a way that the probability of the historical conclusion is affected; or an historical fact may be used as a singular datum in scientific research, e.g., the historical fact of an eclipse in astronomy.) The formal independence of mathematics and natural science will also be readily acknowledged. (Vd. Note 10 *infra.*) All that is here being said is that philosophy, comprising metaphysics and the philosophy of nature as well as mathematics, is related to investigative science as mathematics is, or as the whole field of science is to history.

The independence of philosophy and science can finally be understood in terms of the difference between common and special experience. Special experience does not alter common experience, though it adds a multitude of particular details in regard to which common experience is silent. Since philosophical facts are derived from common or vulgar experience, as scientific facts are inductions from experiment, the inadequacy of common experience with respect to details is indifferent, and the birth of science through special experience does not displace philosophy in the household of human knowledge. Two misunderstandings must be prevented here. (1) The facts of philosophy, its general truths, are not the facts of vulgar experience, any more than the facts of science, its inductive generalizations, are the same as its experimental data. The facts of ordinary experience,—what can be called the facts of common-sense knowledge,—play the same role in philosophical thought that experimental data do in scientific thought. They are the starting point for reflection and analysis. (2) Ordinary experience is more, rather than less, certain than scientific experience. Maritain quotes Duhem as saying: "The layman believes that the result of a scientific experiment is distinguished from vulgar observation by a higher degree of certainty; he is deceived, for the description of a physical experiment has not the immediate and relatively easy to control certainty of the common and non-scientific account. Less sure than the latter, it is of greater value by the number and precision of the details it makes known to us; there is its veritable and essential superiority." But, as Maritain says, the addition of these details is irrevelant to such properly philosophical facts as "there exists something, there exists a multiplicity, there exists change and becoming, there exists knowledge and thought, there exists desire" (*Op cit.*, p. 114).

7. The conflict between science and philosophy in modern times is strictly a conflict between scientists and philosophers. The fault is on both sides. Philosophers who have exceeded their domain, who have "speculated" in the bad sense of that word, who have guessed at

conclusions which could properly result only from painstaking research, have been justly rebuked by scientists as "arm-chair thinkers". Philosophers have been guilty of such disorder almost to the extent that they have not recognized their true vocation, i.e., reflection about the data of common experience. In the 17th century Descartes is the example of a philosopher attempting to answer scientific questions without recourse to scientific method; in the 19th century, Herbert Spencer is the much more distressing example of a thinker who did little else but "speculate" in scientific fields. He is one of the causes of philosophy's bad name at present. Hegel and Schopenhauer are, for different reasons, equally subject to the charge of fomenting a conflict between philosophy and science by transgressing the line which distinguishes scientific from philosophical questions. The charge, in other words, is that they are bad philosophers; only when they are bad in this sense of lacking their proper discipline, of failing to recognize the limits of their data and the character of the questions they can answer, do philosophers come into conflict with science.

Modern scientists, on the other hand, have been equally guilty of such transgressions, moving, of course, in the opposite direction. Newton, for instance, great scientist that he was, did not seem to recognize the difference between questions which could be answered by experiment or research and those which could not. He pretended to speak about philosophical matters with the same assurance that characterizes his well-founded scientific conclusions, although he exhibited little or no competence in the learning and discipline of philosophy. The concluding sections of the *Principia* and the *Optics* illustrate the unwarranted and incompetent dogmatism of a scientist trying to do arm-chair thinking without realizing that it has a technique just as rigorous as, and much less obvious than, the manipulations of the laboratory and the observatory. It is true that philosophical questions can be answered in an arm-chair, but success in scientific work is neither preparation for, nor a mark of ability to perform, the philosophical task. Darwin is another example of a scientist who concerned himself with questions his evidence could not possibly answer. The concluding chapter of *The Origin of Species* so confused scientific with philosophical and theological questions that the 19th century never fully recovered from the vertigo it suffered in trying to separate them. As a result we are all heirs to the myth, the religion, of evolution. If Darwin had had any competence in philosophy or theology or if, lacking it, he had contented himself with reporting the data and conclusions of his research, the conflicts about "evolution" which embroiled science with religion and generated the elaborate guess-work of 19th century thought, could never have occurred. In more recent years, the Gifford lectureship is the source of similar confusions and transgressions. Successful scientists are called to the platform to discourse on the problems of natural theology, which is a branch of metaphysics, in the light of scientific findings. They suppose, in the first place, that the scientific findings are relevant; they proceed, in the second place, as if it required years of training to become a scientist but only moments of leisure to indulge in the "idle speculation" which they take to be the understanding and solution of philosophical problems.

Formally, the chief sources of conflict between science and philosophy are two: (1) both general physics, i.e., the philosophy of nature, and the particular natural sciences, are knowledge of natural things, from the point of view of the same grade of abstraction; (2) metaphysics, though it is of a different grade of abstraction than the philosophy of nature, supplies the latter with its fundamental principles and concepts. (Vd. Note 9 *infra* for a discussion of the grades of abstraction.) If, in the first instance, the difference in method between natural philosophy and natural science is not carefully observed, the kind of question which can be answered by philosophical thought will not be distinguished from the kind of question which can be answered about the same subject-matter only by scientific method. The difference provides a clear, formal criterion. Philosophy can answer questions only about the mode of existence and the kinds of change to which all physical things are subject; it cannot answer questions about particular types of physical existence or particular causes of change. Such questions, as Aristotle pointed out, require investigation involving "intimate association with nature" (*De Generatione et Corruptione*, I, 316ª6). By this criterion it must be said that when Aristotle concludes that the heavenly bodies are imperishable and suffer only local motion, he is doing so as a scientist because the object of his knowledge is a particular kind of physical body, and not natural things or change in general. He may have been right in terms of his observations, but we have other and undoubtedly better observations. In his day, the observations of an astronomer were not radically different from the common experience of men. Under such circumstances the distinction between philosophy and science is not so readily made. But in our day, the experience of an astronomer, implemented by telescopes and spectroscopes, is radically different from "public experience." We can, therefore, easily make the distinction. But the formal principle of it is the same in the 4th century B.C. and today. To understand it is to read the works of those ancient and mediaeval authors who were at once philosophers and scientists, more intelligently. As Maritain points out, "on the side of the human subject, one must recognize that too great a confidence in the intelligibility of things and in the procedure of reason, in a domain which precisely is not that of philosophy but of experience, and where essences are not revealed to us, had its part (and perhaps a predominant part) in the errors of ancient science." From this point of view, he would declare that "modern science has rendered philosophy the immense service of delivering it from the foreign care, which has oppressed it so long, of describing phenomena." But, on the side of the object, "there is no necessary connexion between ancient mechanics and physics and astronomy, on the one hand, and the metaphysics or natural philosophy of the scholastic tradition, on the other. The whole edifice of the experimental sciences of the ancients could fall, and this immense ruin could appear to hurried minds as the ruin of all that the ancients had thought, whereas in reality their metaphysics and their philosophy of nature, in the essential principles" would not have been touched (*Les Degrés du Savoir*, Paris, 1932: pp. 118–119).

In the second instance, if the difference between metaphysics and natural philosophy in grade of abstraction, is ignored, the metaphysical principles which are involved in natural philosophy will be subjected to the same type of exemplification to which the conclusions of natural philosophy are susceptible. But this is not possible without confusion or distortion. All the details of scientific knowledge about nature can be interpreted so as to exemplify the general propositions of the philosophy of nature because both are knowledge having the same grade of abstraction. But to require that metaphysical propositions be similarly exemplified is to mistake their grade of abstraction and hence their true signification. The process of interpreting the results of scientific research in terms of metaphysical propositions can be accomplished only through the mediation of the philosophy of nature, and not directly. It follows, therefore, that when the formal difference between metaphysics and the philosophy of nature is ignored, or when the relation of these two is not understood, *apparent conflicts* are likely to occur between metaphysical truths and scientific facts. This has happened many times in the history of modern philosophy, from Descartes to the present day.

8. The individual thing, in its individuality, is infra-intelligible in the sense that it cannot be defined or comprehended by abstractions of any sort. This does not mean that the individual thing is unintelligible in the strict and absolute sense. Only prime matter, matter totally without form and hence purely potential, is strictly unintelligible. The individual thing, as an object of aesthetic intuition or of personal acquaintance, is not grasped by the senses alone, but by the senses and the intellect in that mode of cooperation which constitutes what the middle ages called "the knowledge of vision". God's knowledge is vision; the beatific vision of the blessed approaches it in type; the aesthetic intuition is a remote analogue in natural human knowledge. Although the intellect cooperates in the aesthetic intuition, it does so defectively because of its inadequate comprehension of individuals. As Kant said, it is knowledge without concept, and yet it is not subject to the blindness of pure perception. The Thomistic statement of the beautiful object as *id quod visum placet*, suggests the relation between aesthetic intuition and knowledge of vision. Vd. *Summa Theologica*, I, Q.5, A.4, ad.1. *Visum* does not refer to the operation of the sense of sight. Cf. *Summa Theologica*, I, Q.12, A.13; Q.14, A.7; Q.58, A.7, ad.3. Professor A. E. Taylor's essay on Knowing and Believing

provides an interesting commentary on these points. Vd. *Philosophical Studies*, London, 1934: pp. 386–394.

A word must be added about supra-sensible objects of knowledge. Just as the intellect cooperates in the knowledge of infra-intelligible objects, so the senses cooperate in the knowledge of the supra-sensible. In the former case, the cooperation is by conjunction; in the latter, sensitive apprehension is ordered instrumentally to the knowledge of transcendent objects, since all natural knowledge arises from sense-experience. Supra-sensible objects are the concern of that branch of metaphysics which is natural theology. Within the scope of natural knowledge, it is possible for men to know only that such objects are, but not what such objects are, except negatively and analogically. In a sense, such objects, whose mode of being transcends the physical order, are not only supra-sensible but also eminently intelligible. They are more intelligible in themselves than they are for us, because they transcend the physical order and thus exceed our intellectual capacity, rooted as it is in sense and imagination. The natural knowledge of transcendent beings must not be confused with that supernatural knowledge of them, which is proposed by the dogmatic theology of a revealed religion. The greater adequacy of the latter is due to the supplementation of reason by faith; the former is inadequate because it is merely rational and rational in a way that is limited by its dependence on sense.

8a. We have seen that the historian, unlike the scientist, is frequently concerned with questions of existence. In fact that is his primary interest; it is only after he has established the existence of some historical particular, a person, an event, etc., that he proceeds to questions of characterization and relationship. The scientist is concerned primarily with the characteristics and relational patterns of the phenomenal world. He never asks, because he need not, whether that world exists. If he sometimes seems to be asking the existential question, viz., whether atoms exist, he has unwittingly turned philosopher. The proper philosophical question is, of course, about the divisibility of matter, and not about the existence of real beings corresponding to the constructions of mathematical physics. The physical scientist usually becomes a philosopher only after he has committed the fallacy of reification.

Nor is the philosopher concerned with questions about whether this or that exists, except in the domain of natural theology. With the exception of natural theology, philosophy has the same material object as natural science. No more than the scientist, need the philosopher ask whether the world of nature exists. But as a metaphysician considering the being of whatever is, the philosopher is inevitably led to inquire about the existence of beings *other than* the physical. Such beings are possible. Are they actual? At this point, the inquiry of the metaphysician is like that of the historian and, in general way, so is his procedure. As the historian passes inferentially from present sensible evidences to the determination of a past existence,—an existence which is, of course, homogeneous in ontological type with the present evidences,—so the natural theologian passes inferentially from the entire order of physical existence to the existence of a transcendent being. Both inferences are *a posteriori*, both involve the principle of causality. The essential differences are: (1) that basic metaphysical truths are needed to pass from one ontological order to another, and (2) our knowledge of the nature of that which is proved to exist is, in the theological case, only negative and analogical. Precisely because it is negative and analogical, it can be said to be derived from the realm of experience.

9. The differentiation of the three spheres of philosophical knowledge, —physics (the philosophy of nature), mathematics and metaphysics,— is first clearly made by Aristotle. Thus, in the *Physics*, he inquires how the mathematician differs from the physicist. "Obviously physical bodies contain surfaces and volumes, lines and points, and these are the subject-matter of mathematics. . . . Now the mathematician, though he treats of these things, nevertheless does not treat of them as the limits of a physical body; nor does he consider the attributes indicated as attributes of such bodies. That is why he separates them; for in thought they are separable from motion, and it makes no difference, nor does any falsity result, if they are separated" (II, 2, 193^b22–35). The physicist is concerned with things whose forms, though analytically separable from matter, do not exist separately. It is the business of the primary type of philosophy, metaphysics, to consider "the mode of existence and essence of the separable" (II, 2, 194^b15). And in the *Metaphysics* we find: "Physics deals with things which are inseparable from matter but not immovable, and some parts of mathematics deal with things which are immovable but probably not separable, but embodied in matter; while the first science deals with things which are both separable and immovable. . . . There must, then, be three theoretical philosophies, mathematics, physics and what we may call theology, since it is obvious that if the divine is present anywhere, it is present in things of this sort" (VI, 1, 1026^a 13–21). Cf. *Metaphysics*, XI 3, 4.

The Aristotelian distinction of the three divisions of philosophy is thus made in terms of the mode of being of their proper objects: the object of physics is material and changing; the object of mathematics consists of abstractions from the physical object, forms which are analytically separable from matter in motion, but do not exist apart from matter; the objects of metaphysics are forms which are actually separated from matter and self-subsistent. This method of making the distinctions defines the subject-matter of metaphysics too narrowly, identifying it with knowledge of transcendent objects, making it natural theology. Similarly, it overemphasizes the formal object of mathematics and fails to indicate that the material object of mathematics is the same as that of physics. The capital text for confusing the two parts of metaphysics,—ontology and natural theology,—has long been the famous passage which says that "the first philosophy considers being *qua* being, both what it is and the attributes which belong to it *qua* being" (*Metaphysics*, VI, 1, 1026^{a}33). To avoid such confusion, two interpretations must be made of this text: first, that metaphysics considers the being of anything which is, the attributes of any being according to its mode of being (ontology); and second, that metaphysics considers *that which is* simply and absolutely, both that such pure being is and what its attributes are (natural theology). The material object of ontology can be the same as that of mathematics and the philosophy of nature; it is only in so far as metaphysics is natural theology that its material object is not physical existence.

It is true to say that metaphysics is knowledge of being. But this must be understood, first, in the sense of the formal object of metaphysical knowledge, namely, anything *considered* as being; and only second, in the sense of the material object of that part of metaphysics which is natural theology, namely, being as such *existing* simply. The central term of metaphysics is being, and this carries with it all the transcendentals which are convertible with being. But transcendental terms are essentially analogical in their universal predicability. The subject-matter of metaphysics is, therefore, everything which is, according as it is. (The existential questions about transcendent beings are a very special part of metaphysics.) The marks of a metaphysical proposition can be simply enumerated: it is about (1) being, or (2) any term which is convertible with being, such as the transcendentals, or (3) any division of being, such as act and potentiality, or (4) any term which is convertible with these divisions, such as form and matter. It is in this sense that it can be said that metaphysics is about anything *qua* being and the attributes which belong to it *qua* being. The opusculum *De Ente et Essentia* of St. Thomas Aquinas is a much better example of a metaphysical treatise than is the *Metaphysics* of Aristotle. Cf. J. Maritain, *Sept Leçons sur L'Être*, Paris, 1932–33; and N. Balthasar, *L'Abstraction Métaphysique et l'Analogie des Êtres dans l'Être*, Louvain, 1935.

Philosophy is knowledge of existing things, and not of ideas. Mathematics, in so far as it is philosophical, is not knowledge of abstractions as such, but of physical things considered formally at a certain level of abstraction. Metaphysics is also knowledge of physical things, —though not exclusively,—considered at an even higher level of abstraction. It is this maximum grade of abstraction which enables metaphysics to include within its scope beings which transcend the physical order.

The distinction of the three departments of philosophy is better made by Aquinas than by Aristotle, because it is made explicitly in terms of the grades of abstraction. The Thomistic analysis includes all that is sound in the Aristotelian account, and avoids its difficulties and ambiguities. The theory of abstraction enables us to understand how physics (the philosophy of nature), mathematics and metaphysics,–except for natural theology,–have the same object materially, i.e., physical existences, but different objects formally. Vd. St. Thomas Aquinas, *In Librum Boetii De Trinitate*, Q. 5, Q. 6, A. 1. (This elaborate and subtle analysis is summarized in a single passage in the *Summa Theologica*: I, Q. 85, A. 1, ad. 1, 2.) Nor is this inconsistent with an ontological distinction between the objects of physics and metaphysics, in so far as the latter is natural theology. As St. Thomas says, "the proportionate object of the human intellect, which is united to a body, is a quiddity or nature existing in corporeal matter; and through such natures of visible things it rises to a kind of knowledge of things invisible" (*Summa Theologica*, I, Q. 84, A. 7). Physical things are the *proper* (proportionate and appropriate) object of human knowledge, but only being,–infinite being,–is its *adequate* object.

The three grades of abstraction can be understood as degrees of remotion from matter. The first grade, like total or extensive abstraction, departs from matter only in so far as matter is the principle of individual or numerical diversity. Thus, the physical thing is seized in its universality, but as fully subject to the material conditions of change. This formal object constitutes the domain shared by the natural sciences and the philosophy of nature. The second grade departs further from matter, disregarding the matter of physical things in so far as it is the principle of change and motion, but regarding it in so far as it is the principle of dimensionality and quantity in things. This formal object constitutes the domain of mathematics. The third grade departs furthest from matter, disregarding every accident of the thing which is due to matter except the radical accident of contingency in being itself; positively it regards matter only as having being through form and it is, therefore, able to regard form as being apart from matter. This formal object constitutes the domain of metaphysics, both ontology and natural theology. Cf. Maritain, *Les Degrés du Savoir*, Paris, 1932: pp. 72–74.

This analysis raises three problems. (1) The relation between the philosophy of nature and the natural sciences. They would appear to have the same formal object. In a sense this is true. They are both concerned with the physical thing as subject to motion and change. But the philosophy of nature has an ontological interest, whereas the sciences of nature consider only the phenomenal surface. If the formal object, constituted by the first grade of abstraction, be called *ens mobile*, the difference can be stated as follows: the philosopher is concerned with the intelligible *being* of the changing thing; the scientist with its sensible *motions* and *changes*. Limited to the data of common experience, limited by the restrictions of ontological analysis to essential traits, the method of philosophy is incapable of achieving demonstrable knowledge of nature in its phenomenal variety and contingency. This is the task of science, which, by experiment and measurement, is able to determine observable properties from observable properties. The philosophy of nature seeks only to demonstrate the *ratio* of the being of changing things; or, in other words, the ontological principles which underlie the phenomena of change. The sciences of nature seek to discover the interconnexion of the phenomena of change, the correlation of the accidental variables which, in their covariancy, present to us the uniform face of a changing world. To the extent that the specific natures of physical substances escape man's power of definition, the philosopher must be content with generic distinctions among the types of bodies and their operations. But the scientist, not concerned with definitions that grasp essential natures, is able to make multifarious accidental classifications that introduce relative order into the maze of phenomenal variety. The philosophy of nature is one, but the sciences of nature are many. Their multiplicity arises from the different cuts which can be made in the phenomenal order, separating this sort of thing from that, this type of change from that. Generically, all the natural sciences have the same material object; but they differ, as particular divisions of natural science in general, by having different material objects, different segments of the phenomenal world of changing things. Cf. Maritain, *op. cit.*, pp. 76–79; also *La Philosophie de la Nature*, Paris, 1935.

(2) The philosophy of nature must not be confused with metaphysics, although it is continuous with metaphysics in its ontological interest. Both, in a sense, are concerned with being. But the philosophy of nature considers the being of the changing thing as changing, whereas metaphysics considers the being of the changing thing only as being. The philosophy of nature may, thus, be thought of as an application of metaphysics. The ontological principles it employs are derived from metaphysics, but they are used by the philosopher of nature to understand change, and the thing which changes in so far as it changes. In other words, the philosophy of nature has some independent principles. It is not merely applied metaphysics. Cf. J. T. Casey, *The Primacy of Metaphysics*, Washington, 1936: pp. 93–94.

A philosophy of nature is impossible unless it is founded upon metaphysics. Lacking metaphysical principles, it would be, what it is so frequently in modern times, nothing more than a conjectural embroidery on the fringe of natural science. It would not be philosophy in short, but the guess-work of persons who are dissatisfied with the superficiality of science. The other error in modern times is worse: the identification of metaphysics with the philosophy of nature. It is implicit in the speculations of Descartes and Spinoza. It is made explicit for the modern tradition in the bad scholasticism of Christian Wolff, who divided metaphysics into ontology (general metaphysics), on the one hand, and cosmology, psychology and natural theology (special metaphysics) on the other. (Vd. I. Gredt, *Elementa Philosophiae*, Fribourg, 1932: II, p. 2.) Kant learned these distinctions out of Baumgarten's *Metaphysica*, the text-book which he made the basis of his lectures. His failure to understand the difference between metaphysical problems, on the one hand, and the problems of cosmology (the philosophy of nature) and psychology, on the other, is largely responsible for all the nonsense that is written about metaphysics since the 18th century, as well as for the excessively dogmatic *naturphilosophie*, Hegelian absolutism and its *sequelae*. Vd. A. D. Lindsay, *Kant*, London, 1934: Ch. II, VI.

(3) Mathematics is not in the same line with metaphysics and the philosophy of nature. It has no ontological interest. This does not mean that the formal object of mathematics has no place in the order of actual existences, but rather that the mathematician is not concerned with that order, as are the metaphysician and the philosopher of nature. When the mathematician discusses existence, when he postulates or demonstrates existence, he means only to assume the *possibility* of his object or to show, by construction, that it is possible, i.e., not self-contradictory within the rules laid down by his postulates. The possible, in this sense, may include both what can be real or actual and what is *merely* ideal or fictive, a construction of the intellectual imagination, an *ens rationis*. As Maritain points out, since the order of real things includes both the actual and the possible and the order of ideal beings includes both the possible and the fictive, there are inherent in mathematics, as knowledge of ideal beings, two opposed tendencies. On the one hand, in so far as it is concerned with the possible as a division of the real, it is knowledge relevant to the physical order and is properly associated with the natural sciences and the philosophy of nature. On the other hand, in so far as it is primarily concerned with its own constructions and with the possible only as a division of the ideal, it is something apart, something tangential to the whole hierarchy of human knowledge, since the natural sciences, like the philosophy of nature, are concerned with the real as the actual. (The natural sciences are in line with metaphysics and the philosophy of nature only in so far as they are concerned with the actual rather than the possible, but they are in line with mathematics in so far as they are concerned with the surface of substantial being, with the relation and order of accidents. This explains how mathematics can be aligned with science against philosophy, despite the fact that, being non-investigative, mathematics *as knowledge* is philosophical in type. Cf. P. Descoqs, *loc. cit.* in Note 6, on p. 136 *supra*.)

The problem of the classification of mathematics is a difficult one. There can be no question that in method and as a type of knowledge, it is philosophy rather than investigative science. Yet only to the extent that it is construed as knowledge of the real does it belong properly with philosophy. As so construed, I have used it to exemplify the difference between philosophical and scientific knowledge; otherwise, the exemplification would have been false. But it need not be so construed. In the modern world it is for the most part regarded either as knowledge of ideal constructions or as a purely conventional logistic. Yet this prevailing interpretation of the nature of mathematics does not prevent it from being of immense fertility in physical applications or from providing regulative principles to all those natural sciences which try to be metrical. The inner duplicity of mathematics is thus exhibited. Mathematics is like an incarnate angel suffering from schizophrenia. It seems to have affinities for two worlds, the strain between which it can endure only through a fundamental ambiguity. Yet the paradox of its nature is that almost in proportion as it more and more madly explores the ideal realm of its construction, does it become more and more useful in physical applications to the real. Cf. Maritain, *op. cit.*, pp. 78–83.

It is doubtful whether there is any cure for the madness of mathematics. But it can at least be kept from infecting the rest of philosophy and science. The history of both philosophy and science, from Descartes and Leibnitz on, records the spread of the mania for a universal mathesis. The most recent example of the derangement of both metaphysics and the philosophy of nature under the influence of mathematics is in the writings of A. N. Whitehead. (Whitehead's "scientific cosmology" is strictly not a philosophy of nature, which must employ independently established metaphysical principles. Rather it is an ontological projection of natural science, a reification of relational or mathematical logic. Vd. Notes 20b and 47 *infra.*) The dominance of mathematical physics over the other empirical, but non-mathematical, sciences is another example. What protection is there to ensure the rectification of the intellect in the line of the actual? In the sphere of philosophy, it is metaphysics, superior to mathematics in its grade of abstraction and therefore regulative of it as well as of all other bodies of knowledge. The philosophy of mathematics which is today largely the principles of logistic must become a metaphysical consideration of the objects of mathematical thought. In the sphere of the sciences, it is the philosophy of nature which, sharing the ontological light of metaphysics, must exert a counter attraction upon the empirical disciplines. But mathematics, because it is of a higher grade of abstraction than the philosophy of nature, is regulative of the natural sciences in its own right, whereas the philosophy of nature can be regulative only by virtue of the metaphysical principles it incorporates. It is an unequal struggle which, in the modern world, is becoming more and more a victory for mathematics in the sphere of science. The amazing technological utility of mathematical physics is an important factor in this trend. But this must not occur in the sphere of philosophy, where mathematics is of little or no utility and metaphysics is paramount.

One further point must be made. In an earlier discussion, the independence of philosophy and science as bodies of knowledge was argued. (Vd. Note 6b *supra.*) Such independence is, of course, reciprocal. It means that scientific knowledge is autonomous in its own sphere as philosophical knowledge is in its. Two qualifications must now be added. (1) Knowledge of a higher grade of abstraction can be regulative of knowledge of an inferior grade. In this sense, metaphysics and mathematics are regulative of natural science. This does not mean that metaphysics or mathematics can determine the conclusions of scientific research,–so far science is autonomous,–but rather that the interpretation and formulation of these conclusions may employ principles which science must take from philosophy because they exceed its powers. (2) Knowledge of an inferior grade can exert a material influence upon knowledge of a superior grade by supplying it with new exemplifications of its principles or by requiring it to extend its principles to new fields. In this way, the progress of the natural sciences may have an effect upon mathematics and the philosophy of nature and, indirectly, even upon metaphysics. But this does not abrogate the formal independence of philosophy, any more than mathematical physics ceases to be an empirical science because it employs mathematical formulae. Vd. Note 10a *infra*.

10. As we have already seen (Note 6b *supra*) the different grades of abstraction indicate why there can be no conflict between metaphysical and mathematical philosophy, on the one hand, and natural science, on the other. They are concerned with formally distinct objects. Yet the fact that there exists a mathematical physics,–in which mathematics is regulative with respect to physical formulations, and physical research is provocative of further mathematical analysis,–may lead some to suppose that philosophical and scientific knowledge are not reciprocally independent in such a way that conflict between them is impossible. This must be shown, and it can be most readily shown to a contemporary audience by taking the case of mathematics. Everyone knows that a mathematical question cannot be properly answered by any sort of empirical research. We may not be able to answer it at all, but if we can, we can do so without the benefit of investigation of an observational sort. It follows that if empirical methods are totally ineffective in the answering of mathematical questions, knowledge which is obtained by these methods cannot be inconsistent with such answers as are achieved by the appropriate method of mathematics. The principle, in short, is that if a cognitive procedure is incompetent to answer a question, it is equally incompetent to propose anything as a refutation to answers obtained by a method which is adapted to that type of question. If there can be no empirical mathematics, there can be no empirical or investigative refutations of mathematical propositions.

The same rule applies to metaphysics. The metaphysical object is even more incapable of empirical investigation than the mathematical, being of an even higher grade of abstraction. (Strictly, investigation, which always involves physical operations, is possible only within the sphere of knowledge constituted by abstractions of the lowest grade.) There can, therefore, be no empirical or experimental metaphysics, and equally no empirical or investigative refutations of metaphysical propositions.

The case of the philosophy of nature is, of course, the only difficult one, because what is, in general, the same formal object determine its sphere of knowing and that of all the natural sciences. But here, as we have seen, there is a subordinate formal distinction with regard to the aspect of the object being studied. The *being* of the changing thing is incapable of investigation; only the *phenomena of change* itself are open to empirical research. Investigation is, therefore, gratuitous in the philosophy of nature, but indispensable for the advancement of the natural sciences. Here the emphasis should be placed upon the necessity of research in the particular fields of natural science. The problems of optics, hydrodynamics, organic chemistry and genetics cannot be solved philosophically, any more than the problems of the philosophy of nature can be solved investigatively.

It should be said here that psychology constitutes the peculiar case which it was the aim of these lectures to examine. Psychology seems to be classifiable along with optics and hydrodynamics as a special field of physics: its object is a particular physical thing, man, subject to particular types of changes, such as learning and deciding. But psychology also seems to be capable of development in the light of common experience, and to violate the rule that in the particular fields of physics, investigation is indispensable. As we have seen, both indications are correct. Psychology is unique in that it is both a special natural science and a branch of philosophy, the only one which deals with a particularized physical object. It does not have this special status because of any distinctive formal constitution of its object of knowledge. Rather its uniqueness is due to the reflexivity which obtains in man's knowledge of himself.

10a. For an adequate discussion of the special problem of the philosophy of nature in relation to the changing content of natural science, vd. J. Maritain, *La Philosophie de la Nature*, Paris, 1935; *Les Degrés du Savoir*, Paris, 1932: pp. 83–144; and W. O'Meara, *Science and a Philosophy of Nature*, Proceedings of the American Catholic Philosophical Association, 1936: pp. 123–128.

The general solution of this problem can be indicated briefly here. As Maritain points out, "scientific data are like illustrations which it is normal for the philosopher to use to embody his ideas." This is particularly true for the philosopher of nature. Here the advance of scientific knowledge renews and enriches the matter which the philosopher can use for exemplification. Thus, for example, modern cytology and embryology have a descriptive precision which requires the philosopher to refine his formulation of substantial change, i.e. the process of generation. This dependence of philosophy upon natural science is material throughout. "The changes it brings in its train affect especially that imagery whose importance is after all so great with regard to the vocabulary and the halo of associations which envelop the didactic terms themselves. To imagine, however, that the philosophical doctrines must be transformed as the result of scientific changes would be as absurd as to imagine that our soul is transformed according to the diversity of the foods we assimilate" (*Les Degrés du Savoir*: pp. 100–102). In short, scientific facts can at best bring new matter to the consideration of the philosopher. They are never the original data upon which his inductions depend, but merely the occasion for new exemplifications and, perhaps, refinements in formulation of principles already known. "It is an illusion to believe that in appealing to scientific facts without considering them in a superior light, one can decide a philosophical debate, that of hylomorphism for example. For themselves they say nothing about it. Don't torture them to get false confessions! Never solicit them! Of course, let us question them; and that supposes that we are already provided with some information. They must be brought into court, as numerous as possible, and one must refer to the learned scientist for everything which concerns their civil status, their experimental significance and the way in which they have been established. But it is only by bringing them in touch with philosophical knowledge already acquired elsewhere, and with philosophical principles, that one can draw from them an intelligible content that can be handled by philosophy, that one can discern and judge what is their ontological value" (Maritain, *op. cit.*, pp. 115–116).

This can be explained by the analogous relation of mathematics and experimental physics. Experimental data are never the logical ground of mathematical discoveries; but new physical data may nevertheless provoke or occasion mathematical research, with the consequence that mathematical formulations are provided which subsume the data. It must be noted here that the empirical data do not test, verify or refute in any way, the demonstrable truths of mathematical analysis; nor are they the matter which generates those truths inductively. The data only discriminate between mathematical formulae which are or are not applicable to the physical world. If two formulae are applicable so far as the data are concerned, it is for the mathematician to choose between them by criteria of elegance and simplicity. The principles of the philosophy of nature are *similarly* related to the inductively established facts of natural science. The latter may provoke more precise formulations or even require an extended interpretation of old principles. To this extent the progress of scientific knowledge may cause development in the philosophy of nature. But whereas scientific progress is a transition to new and better knowledge, definitely enlarging or replacing the old, the philosophical development is not progressive in this way; rather it is a richer understanding of principles already known. It is intensive, not extensive. And it must be reiterated,—so widespread and entrenched is the popular illusion to the contrary,—that the propositions of the philosophy of nature are not founded upon scientific facts, nor can they, therefore, be "supported" or "refuted" by scientific knowledge. The relation of material dependence is one of exemplification.

What is here said of the relation between natural science and the philosophy of nature can be more sharply said of that between natural science and metaphysics. The philosophy of nature is, in a sense, an intermediary between metaphysical truths and scientific facts. The latter can be seen to embody the principles of metaphysics only after their ontological significance has been interpreted in the light of natural philosophy. One example will suffice to make this clear. The biologist gives us a mass of precise descriptive knowledge about the observable characteristics of embryonic development. These facts will not tell the natural philosopher what substantial change is. But they will enable him, perhaps, to delineate within this complicated phenomenal pattern the distinctions of substantial and accidental change. The facts will thus become illuminated with ontological significance. Then, and only then, will the metaphysician be able to determine the mode of being of a foetus. This is strictly not an advance in metaphysical knowledge; we are not learning what a substance is, but whether the foetus is a substance. Through such application of metaphysics we obtain a better understanding of an embryo than science can give us, though,—be it ten times repeated,—not a more useful one for the practice of obstetrics.

These points can be simply summarized. (1) The influence of the sciences upon philosophy is entirely material; it is psychological rather than logical. (2) The influence of philosophy upon the sciences is twofold: (a) it is positive or informative, in the way in which mathematics supplies empirical physics with formulae and principles; (b) it is negative or regulative, in the way in which metaphysics restricts science to the solution of phenomenal problems. (3) The philosophy of nature is regulative by virtue of its metaphysical principles; it is informative only after its substantial concepts and ontological principles have been transformed by relational logic and made applicable to the phenomenal order. Vd. Note 47 *infra*.

11. In the *Timaeus* Plato constructs the science of nature as an application of mathematics. In the *Republic*, he proposes music and astronomy, along with arithmetic and geometry, as pure mathematical studies, to be divorced as far as possible from observations (528 E–531 C). This again indicates the duplicity of mathematics, which continues to our day in the tradition of mathematical physics. Aristotle recognized this duplicity and distinguished both mathematics and physics from that mixed or intermediate kind of science which combines them, treating of problems that are formally physical in terms of principles which are formally mathematical. Thus, he writes of

"the more physical branches of mathematics, such as optics, harmonics and astronomy. These are in a way the converse of geometry. While geometry investigates physical lines but not *qua* physical, optics investigates mathematical lines, but *qua* physical and not *qua* mathematical" (*Physics*, II, 2, 194^a6–11). The mediaeval tradition of the Quadrivium recognized this distinction by separating the pure mathematics of arithmetic and geometry from their respective applications in music and astronomy. The latter involved the arts of measurement. St. Thomas clearly distinguished applied mathematics from physics. The former he treated as a science *intermediate* between mathematics and physics. Vd. *In Librum Boetii De Trinitate*, Q. 5, A. 3, ad. 5, 6, 7.

And at the beginning of modern physical research, the distinction is preserved both by Newton and Galileo. The title of Newton's greatest work tells the story: *The Mathematical Principles of Natural Philosophy*. Galileo, in the *Two New Sciences* enumerates perspective, astronomy, mechanics and music as sciences in which "mathematical demonstrations are applied to natural phenomena." In contrast, the tradition of physiology from Galen to Claude Bernard and J. B. Haldane is that of a purely physical science, the principles of which have the same formality as the problems they are employed to solve. Galen's work on *The Natural Faculties* plainly reveals that the principles he is applying to the analysis of the facts of vegetative functioning are derived from Aristotle's *Physics*, i.e., a philosophy of nature. For an illuminating discussion of the paradoxes which arise from the failure to distinguish mathematical from physical solutions of physical problems,—paradoxes of the sort that attended the popular, and even the technical, misunderstandings of the theory of relativity,—see Maritain, *Theonas,* New York, 1933: pp. 61–102.

12. Galileo's procedure was applicative rather than inductive in the strict sense of the word. By mathematical reasoning he first arrived at a formulation of the rate of acceleration of bodies falling freely to the earth, and then proceeded to test his equation by the measurement of a carefully constructed experimental case. The numbers which he obtained from the observation of the times and distances indicated by a ball rolling down an inclined plane were sufficiently accurate approximations to the ideal numbers required by his formula to assure him that his equation applied to the natural motion, the changing quantity of which he sought to define. It is perfectly clear that he did not first construct the experiment, make the measurements, and then from the resulting data sheet of observed times and distances *induce* the proposition that the acceleration was as the square of the times. The apparatus available to him made such a procedure impossible. Let us suppose, however, that he had such instruments as photoelectric cells and chronometers. Considering the problem of acceleration, he might then have constructed the following experiment. At various distances from the top of a metal tube, he could have placed

photo-electric cells which would be activated by the passage of an opaque body to affect the registrations of a chronometer. Dropping a ball through this tube, and reading the clock, he would then immediately obtain numbers which stated the covariation of times and distances. From these numbers the formula for the rate of acceleration could then be readily induced.

This indicates that the formal relation between the observed data and the general proposition is the same whether the procedure is applicative or inductive. The difference is psychological. In the inductive procedure, the universal is discovered in the particular. Experiments aid induction by creating a particular case which approximates ideal conditions, separating the irrelevant and accidental conditions from the relevant and essential. In the applicative procedure, the universal, already known, is located in the particular, and is thus tested or verified. Experiments are as useful for application as for induction, because the location of the universal in the particular requires the creation of an approximation to the ideal.

13. A scientific proposition is here called analytic when it is capable of an aetiological interpretation. But the causal interpretation is always something added to the content of the proposition which, strictly, is descriptive and not explanatory. The natural sciences, mathematical or otherwise, as bodies of theoretic knowledge, do not treat of causes any more than they do of substances. The physionomic statements of biology and the functional formulae of mathematical physics can, however, yield causal interpretations. In fact, in so far as they have any practical or operational significance, they must be so interpreted. Vd. Notes 16a and 47 *infra.*

A genuine causal analysis usually involves asymmetry in the temporal order and, what is more important, always an ontological asymmetry. The being of the cause does not depend on the being of its effect, as the latter does upon the former. The efficient cause is prior to the material and formal cause in the determination of a change. Functional statements, formulae of covariation, are essentially symmetrical. Any variable can be treated as independent or dependent. The equations of mathematical physics are functions and, in terms of mathematical principles, it is therefore arbitrary which variable is designated as the cause (independent) and which as the effect (dependent). The analytic statements of mathematical physics are thus seen to be descriptive rather than aetiological. From the time of Galileo, mathematical physicists have naturally disclaimed an interest in causes. Vd. Eddington, *The Nature of the Physical World*, New York, 1928: Ch. III, XIV. But mathematical physics is physics to the extent that it is experimental and observational. The investigative procedures necessary for the application of mathematics to nature involve the performance of physical operations upon physical things. In the construction of an experiment, in the performance of any complicated observation, the physicist operates by giving his descriptive formulae a causal interpretation. He does this or that in order to obtain this or that effect. The language which reports an experimental performance plainly reveals that the physicist knows the difference between the independent and the dependent variables. Yet this knowledge is practical or operational, rather than theoretic.

The same can be said for the formulations which are achieved by the non-mathematical natural sciences. These statements are, like the equations of mathematical physics, essentially descriptive, but they can also be viewed as analytic. Thus, the elements of a secular trend are asymmetrically ordered in time; this order can and, for practical purposes, must be causally interpreted. For the operations of research or for the practice of medicine, the descriptive knowledge which constitutes such sciences as physiology and pathology must be made to yield an aetiology.

The principles of aetiology are, of course, to be found in the philosophy of nature. The natural scientist as a technician, the engineer and the practitioner who apply scientific knowledge, are employing philosophical concepts when they make a causal interpretation of their descriptive knowledge for operational purposes. We must regard the detailed aetiologies which thus grow on the operational side of science as essentially practical, because they are not part of its theoretic content.

14. Vd. Note 6 *supra*.

15. Vd. Note 7 *supra*.

16. The position of Kant in the history of modern philosophy is strikingly defined by the errors of the 17th century which preceded him, and the errors of the 19th century which followed him. The whole story can be told in terms of before and after Kant. Kant used the words skepticism and dogmatism to name equally wrong extremes which diverge from the proper mean of discipline, critically self-imposed by sound philosophical procedure. Critical discipline in philosophy means two things: (1) the determination of the sphere of questions which can be answered without research or investigation; this in Kantian terms is the distinction between the pure and the empirical, the *a priori* and the *a posteriori;* (2) the delimitation of this sphere of inquiry, bounded as it is on one side by dogmatic theology, which requires faith as an auxiliary, and on the other by science, which requires investigation as an aid. The sphere of inquiry, thus determined and restricted, is the domain of philosophy. Those who deny it entirely, by error of defect, are skeptics. Those who transgress it in either direction, by error of excess, are dogmatists. Vd. *The Critique of Pure Reason*, Preface to the Second Edition (1787); *Prolegomena to Any Future Metaphysic*, Section 13, Remark III, and

Appendix C, critique of the fourth paralogism of transcendental psychology.

In the 17th century, or at least before Kant, philosophers had committed both errors. On the one hand, Descartes, Leibnitz and Spinoza were dogmatists. They tried by philosophical methods to answer questions which should have been reserved either for theology or experimental science. The badness of their philosophies, particularly their metaphysics, resulted from these confusions and transgressions. (To the extent that questions in natural theology concerning God, creation, the soul, are parts of larger questions which require sacred theology, founded on Revelation, for their adequate solution, Kant was right in regarding a purely rational approach to the whole question in each case as doomed to the frustrations of an illusory dialectic, a dialectic which did not properly recognize its own limits in philosophical mysteries. Descartes, Leibnitz and Spinoza deserved Kant's critique for violating the distinction between faith and reason, but unfortunately Kant himself misapprehended that distinction, denying to reason what is properly within its province,—metaphysics, both ontology and natural theology.) On the other hand, Hume was a skeptic. He tried to deny that there were any genuinely answerable questions about the realm of existence, other than those which required empirical research to answer. He refuted himself in doing so, because he employed the method of philosophy to answer a philosophical question, even though he answered it wrongly. Kant's critical regimen was an attempt to cure philosophy of these ills and to establish it within its own proper domain as vigorously as the sciences seemed to be flourishing in theirs.

The 19th century is the record of his failure. After Kant,—and in a sense because of him,—philosophers committed the same errors. On the one hand, the romantic and absolute idealists of the Fichtean or Hegelian sort were worse dogmatists than the metaphysicians of the 17th century, worse both because of the extent of their dogmatic excess and because they combined metaphysical dogmatism with the kind of epistemological skepticism that originated in Berkeley and Hume. On the other, in revolt against them, as Hume in a sense was in revolt against the "abstract" and "abstruse" philosophy of his 17th century predecessors, positivists and pragmatists of all sorts revived the error of skepticism,—philosophers denying that philosophy has an independent domain of inquiry and knowledge.

The state of philosophy after Kant is, in a sense, worse than its condition before Kant. The very errors of dogmatism and skepticism which Kant sought to correct not only recurred after him with greater violence, but, through commixture, became almost obscurantist in their impurity. The fault is Kant's. Had he repudiated Hume's premises instead of trying to avoid his conclusions, had he understood the tradition of European philosophy prior to the 17th century so as to have been able simply to correct the disorder of faith, reason and observation in Leibnitz, Descartes and Spinoza, he could have accomplished his critical reforms without the transcendental nonsense of the *Critique of Pure Reason*. Of course, he would have done nothing original; he would merely have regained the sound tradition of European philosophy prior to the Renaissance. That, of course, is too much to expect of almost any modern man. Discarding the burden of tradition, the heavy authority of human wisdom, and emphasizing the individual accomplishment that is marked by novelty and originality,–these are the correlative expressions of the protestantism and egoism which characterize modern thought. Kant is, indeed, the tragic hero of the modern story. He is a good man, rightly motivated and honest in execution, but with fatal defects of ignorance and pride. The catastrophe of the 19th century is the more painful as a tragic denouement because Kant came so near to being sound.

16a. The appraisal one makes of Hume and Kant must differ according as one views their work in relation to the natural sciences, on the one hand, or in relation to philosophy, on the other. In the first connection, they must be credited with having solved what can be thought of as the most critical problem of modern times. Our epoch is certainly distinguished from all others by the existence, amplification and application of empirical science. The novelty of science, its difference both in method and utility from philosophy, was recognized early in the 17th century. This new thing challenged the traditional theory of knowledge. It required a radical extension of that part of philosophy which has come to be called epistemology. In other words, just as the nature of philosophy is itself a philosophical problem, so is the nature of science. And in so far as Hume and Kant solved the latter problem, they made an epochal contribution to philosophy. Hume's radical insights were the basis for Kant's constructive formulations. Hume saw that empirical knowledge did not penetrate to the substance of things; he saw that it could not be a theoretic apprehension of causes, although the customary sequences which such knowledge described could, for practical purposes, be given a causal interpretation. He was the originator of the positivistic conception of science as restricted to observable relations among phenomena. Kant developed this positivistic conception constructively by discussing the forms and categories of empirical science, such as space, time, quantity, quality and relation; by reducing substance and causality to relational concepts; by understanding the role of mathematics and experimentation in the investigation of phenomenal reality. (Vd. *Metaphysical First Principles of Natural Science*. Kant did not realize, of course, that his own "pure physic" and transcendentally deduced categories were marks of an ill-conceived philosophy of nature.) The phenomenalistic positivism of the 19th century, as found in Comte, Mach and Mill, adds little if anything to the conception of science created by Hume and Kant. It does correct the *a priorism* of Kant by returning to Hume's view of the contingency of science. The logical positivism of the 20th century adds only the heuristic principles of relational and mathematical logic. The positivistic tradition, beginning with Hume and Kant, has done a great intellectual service in defining the traits and the limitations of scientific knowledge. It has not only solved a philosophical problem, but it has given the scientists, who gradually became self-conscious, an understanding of themselves. Vd. Eddington, *The Nature of the Physical World*, New York, 1928; Bridgman, *The Logic of Modern Physics*, New York, 1927; and similar works.

It is unfortunate, indeed, that the enlightening contribution of positivism was mixed with the darkness of denials. These also began with Hume and Kant. They solved one part of the problem (i.e., the nature of science); but their epistemological principles were not sufficiently refined or sound to solve the other part as well (i.e., the nature of philosophy). Although Hume proclaimed the principle of causality as the basis of his analysis of probability (vd. *An Enquiry Concerning Human Understanding*, Sections VI, IX); although Hume both discussed the enduring order of nature and advocated practical procedure in terms of causes and substances; and although he recognized in mathematics a body of non-empirical knowledge, treating it, of course, as "knowledge of ideas," Hume was unable to see the possibility of metaphysical knowledge. Of whatever does not contain "any abstract reasoning concerning quantity or number" or "any experimental reasoning concerning matter of fact and existence," Hume could say: "Commit it then to the flames: for it can contain nothing but sophistry and illusion" (*Op cit.*, Section XII, Part 3). Similarly, Kant was not able to see that his own critical philosophy, in so far as it was knowledge, was not empirical science and that, in consequence, non-scientific knowledge and knowledge of something other than the phenomenal order were possible. The fatal epistemological error in Kant's case, as in Hume's, arises from an inadequate psychology. Hume was a sensationalist. His failure to distinguish ideas from sense-images made it impossible for him to understand philosophical knowledge; in fact, it almost made it impossible for him to understand science. His positive contribution with regard to science was qualified by a raw empiricism and skepticism which Kant had to remedy. Unfortunately, the transcendental medicine was almost as bad as the disease. Kant's own psychological error was also on the nature of ideas. He failed to understand ideas as the products of intellectual abstraction, and hence did not see that the intuitive faculty of sense provided materials for abstractive and non-intuitive knowledge of an intelligible or noumenal order. As a consequence, Kant denied that there could be any knowledge of noumenal reality or of purely intelligible objects. As a further consequence, and one intrinsically damaging to Kant's conception of natural science, his psychological error distorted the nature of mathematics as intuitive knowledge of imaginative constructions. A fuller discussion of these psychological errors occurs elsewhere (Notes 21 and 22 *infra*). They are mentioned here only to remark that, on the one hand, the limitations of positivism as a theory of knowledge are due to bad psychology and, on the other, that much of the badness of psychology since the 18th century is due to a positivistic conception of knowledge. Alibert says in his Preface to *La Psychologie Thomiste et les Théories Modernes*, Paris, 1903: "Sans se proposer une étude spéciale du positivisme et du kantisme, l'auteur s'attache à combattre le principe de ces systèmes, celui du premier en particulier, dans les pages consacrées à la conscience intellective et à l'origine des idées de cause et de substance."

In its critical and negative aspects, contemporary logical positivism adds nothing new to the denials made by Hume and Kant, unless it be the hollow pretense that the dismissal of metaphysics as nonsense is supported by logical or grammatical considerations. Modern logistic in all its varieties,—whether relational logic or Cambridge symbolic logic or Viennese grammatics,—cannot consistently be regarded as *formal* and at the same time be used as a *criteriology*, a theory of knowledge. Neither formal logic nor universal grammar provide a basis for demonstrating (1) the impossibility of self-evident propositions, (2) the impossibility of philosophical knowledge, i.e., ontological propositions, (3) the reducibility of all propositions to atomic or elementary statements of sense-observation. The logical positivist's theory of knowledge is not *logical*; logic as logic is necessarily indifferent to the issue between positivism and realism; rather it is based on the same erroneous and inadequate psychology that generated the position of Hume and Kant. If the grammar and logistic of contemporary positivists were divorced from this bad psychology, which they seldom make explicit, the commotion which the Viennese have agitated in the shallow currents of contemporary thought would soon subside. Vd. Note 17 *infra*.

We can undo the errors of Hume, Kant and the whole positivistic tradition without in any way nullifying the intelligible rendering they made of scientific knowledge. On the contrary, if by correcting their errors in psychology, we can add a sound conception of philosophical knowledge, that by contrast will reflect new light upon the nature of science. This can be briefly done. Let us define philosophy, first, by affirming of it everything Hume denied of empirical science: it is knowledge of substance and causes; it goes behind the phenomena to a substantial reality; it has certitude where science is only probable; it is abstract rather than experimental reasoning. Then, in Kantian terms, let us say that philosophy is knowledge of the noumenal, but not transcendent, order (metaphysics as ontology, and the philosophy of nature), as well as knowledge of purely intelligible, and hence transcendent, objects (metaphysics as natural theology). With the denials of positivism thus removed, a sound and adequate epistemology enables us to understand the nature of philosophy, as the ancient tradition understood it, as well as the nature of science, according to the modern insight which most contemporary thinkers and scientists share. And how is this *rapprochement* of the two traditions to be accomplished? How is modern positivism to be retained for its vision of science and cured of its blindness to philosophy? Simply by an analysis of cognition which shows the cooperation of sense and intellect and which understands understanding itself as a faculty of abstraction rather than of intuition or of innate ideas. Such a theory of knowledge will correct the psychologism of Hume and Kant by recognizing the priority of metaphysics in philosophy.

There is one further comment on all this. One must not forget the radical difference between the modern and mediaeval epochs. The middle ages never doubted the intellect's ability to know reality and were interested in error only as pathological. In modern times, when as a matter of fact research has immensely increased man's knowledge, philosophers start by treating knowledge as a bewildering mystery, supposing that it is truth rather than error which must be explained.

17. The phenomenological question is, Whether man understands? and this is answered whenever we affirm that we do understand and mean thereby something distinctly different from what we mean when we affirm that we sense or imagine. The analytical question, What is understanding? is necessarily subsequent. The fact that we do understand cannot be altered by subsequent considerations concerning the nature of understanding, its relation to the senses and the brain, etc. *That understanding is* cannot be refuted by any analysis of *what understanding is*. It can be refuted only by a negative answer to the phenomenological question. It is impossible to give that negative answer and continue to talk intelligently. To those for whom this is not apparent, it can be shown by a logical analysis of the propositions which constitute the fabric of human discourse.

Propositions can be divided, first, according as their intention is singular or universal. The intention of a proposition is determined by the mode of signification of its subject term. On the grammatical side, the intention of a proposition is usually indicated by whether the words constituting the subject term are proper or common names. Within the singular intention, there is a further division into individual and particular intentions, according as the subject term has the minimum connotation of *this* or has the more fully determinate connotation of *this such and such*. Within the universal intention, there is the traditional distinction of first and second intention, according as the subject term has denotative reference to possible or actual members of a class or according as the subject term is shorn of all denotation except the designation of an *ens rationis*. The problem of the intention of the predicate term occurs only in propositions having universal intention. If the subject is in the first intention, the predicate must be so also. But if the subject is in the second intention reflexively, the predicate may either be in the second intention reflexively or predicatively. The propositions of mathematics are of the first sort; the propositions of logic, of the second.

The fact that human discourse cannot be interpreted without distinguishing between the singular and the universal intention is all that is needed to establish the distinction between sensitive and intellectual apprehensions.

Far from denying these distinctions, logical positivism has been unable to avoid them in its attempt to classify different orders of statement and to discriminate language about things from language about language. Unfortunately, contemporary analysts have not been able to achieve the clarity and subtlety of mediaeval logic in treating distinctions of this sort, partly because of the ill-concealed nominalism which is the core of all attacks on philosophy since the days of Hume. Nominalism is, of course, a psychological doctrine, a denial of intellect, a reduction of all knowledge to sense-knowledge. Nominalism has not only muddled the grammar and logic of contemporary positivists, but it has made it as difficult for them as for Hume to give an account of science which would be consistent with their denial of metaphysics.

18. The imagination is traditionally called the passive intellect because it is the faculty productive of experiences. An experience, as we have seen, is a sort of universal; the *quasi*-universality of the products of imagination has been recognized, in the modern tradition, under the head of generic or abstract images. Vd. Note 5 *supra*. Strictly, of course, images are not *abstract*. The word "abstract" can be said of them only with the signification that they have the potentiality for abstraction; they are the proximate matter upon which the intellect operates in the first act of abstraction. The difference between the perceptual image and the so-called generic image is that the former has an individual intention whereas the latter has a particular intention. The marks of determinate individuation can be lost without the loss of the marks of singularity. The generic image, therefore, provides the transition to the universal intention of the idea which can be abstracted from it. It is a mean between the extremes of sensitive and intellectual apprehension.

19. "When the act of imagination is hindered by a lesion of the corporeal organ, for instance, in a case of frenzy; or when the act of memory is hindered, as in the case of lethargy, we see that a man is hindered from actually understanding things of which he had previous knowledge." This indicates that "for the intellect to understand actually, not only when it acquires fresh knowledge, but also when it applies knowledge already acquired, there is need for the act of the imagination and of the other powers." In addition to the evidence from pathology and fatigue, this can be learned by anyone from his own experience, for "when he tries to understand something, he

forms certain phantasms to serve him by way of examples, in which as it were he examines what he is desirous of understanding. For this reason it is that when we wish to help someone understand something, we lay examples before him, from which he forms phantasms for the purpose of understanding" (St. Thomas Aquinas, *Summa Theologica*, I, Q.84, A.7). In the following article, St. Thomas proceeds to argue that the operations of the intellect are hindered by the suspension, through disease, fatigue or sleep, of the sensitive powers. In light sleep the senses are not entirely inactive, and the imagination may operate as in dreaming. "Sometimes while asleep a man may judge that what he sees is a dream, discerning, as it were between things and their images. Nevertheless, the common sense remains partly suspended; and therefore, although it discriminates some images from reality, yet is it always deceived in some particular. Therefore, while man is asleep, according as sense and imagination are free, so is the judgment of his intellect unfettered, though not entirely. Consequently, if a man syllogizes while asleep, when he wakes up he invariably recognizes a flaw in some respect" (*Ibid.*, Q.84, A.7, ad.2).

According to this analysis, the act of understanding is causally dependent upon acts of the bodily organs of sense and imagination, but it is not itself the act of a bodily organ. This analysis accounts for all the experimental and clinical evidences which modern researches have been able to add to the essentially correct knowledge which St. Thomas possessed through common experience. As the eye and the ear are the bodily organs of particular sensitive operations, vision and audition, so the cerebral cortex of the brain is the bodily organ of what St. Thomas would have treated as the various operations of the interior sense and which we, with some loss of detail, call memory and imagination. The cerebral cortex contains the primary reception areas for the various senses. Although all neurological evidence is against the specific localization in brain areas of any of the higher functions, such as learning or discrimination or judgment, the same sort of evidence supports the localization of the sensory reception areas. Thus, injury to the calcarine fissure of the occipital lobe can cause blindness though the eye is healthy and there are no lesions in the optic nerve. The neurological evidence, both experimental and clinical, supports the Thomistic analysis. Specific lesions can destroy the power of a particular sense or, if the lesion be central, destroy a particular field of imagination and memory, such as the visual or the auditory. But such destruction does not destroy intellection, or what the neurologist calls the "higher mental functions". They may be hindered or impaired by the loss of sensitive or imaginative powers, but they cannot be destroyed without the total annihilation of all sensitive functions. The powers of the understanding continue to operate as long as sense-organs and brain are sufficiently intact to provide it with any matter to operate upon. The neurological evidence shows precisely what St. Thomas held: that understanding is causally dependent on sense and imagination, but is not directly the function of a corporeal organ, such as the cerebral cortex. The nervous functions are the material, but not the efficient or formal, cause of intellection.

Another sort of evidence is relevant and favorable to the Thomistic analysis. Muscular fatigue can be increased to a point at which the muscle being studied is no longer able to operate. But all the experimental studies of so-called "mental fatigue" have been unable to discover any similar phenomenon of total collapse. The weariness of the individual doing incessant mental work over long periods of time is discovered to be muscular. This physical weariness affects mental activity, as that is measured by the time taken and the errors made in performing such operations as arithmetical calculations. In other words, if we speak of a man's mind becoming weary, such predication of weariness is *per accidens*. The weariness of the body, impairing the operations of sense and imagination, hinders understanding "inasmuch as the intellect requires the operation of the sensitive powers in the production of phantasms" (*Ibid.*, Q.75, A.3, ad.2).

In conclusion, it must be pointed out that the sort of evidence which is gathered by modern physiological and neurological research does not establish the proposition that understanding is not the act of a bodily organ. (Vd. the authorities cited in Note 36 *infra.*) That proposition is established by philosophical demonstration, independently of all such evidence. The present discussion merely makes explicit the compatibility of the scientific facts with the philosophical proposition, by showing that these facts are relevant to the way in which the understanding depends on sense and imagination.

20. The word "cosmology" is sometimes used to name that part of metaphysics which is knowledge of the mode of being appropriate to physical things. It is sometimes used, even more narrowly, to name the metaphysical propositions which are involved in the philosophy of nature, and sometimes it is used as a synonym for the philosophy of nature. It is a regrettable name and carries with it the distortions of the Wolffian tradition which have infected modern philosophy, scholastic and otherwise. Vd. Note 9 *supra*. "Cosmology" should be restricted to mean the philosophy of nature. It is not a branch of metaphysics, but it necessarily presupposes metaphysical principles. I used the word in Lecture II to indicate that metaphysical principles were being discussed *only* in so far as they were involved in the philosophy of nature. I could not in the scope of that lecture discuss the deeper ontological significance of those principles or their significance for natural theology. Where in that Lecture I talk superficially of four metaphysical doctrines I mean four philosophies of nature, four "cosmologies", which are divergent because arising from different metaphysical positions. Thus, the traditional name "hylomorphism" is more appropriately applied to a philosophy of nature

than to a metaphysic. Hylomorphism names a metaphysical doctrine only in so far as an analysis of the physical order in terms of matter and form rests upon ontological insights, that being is divisible into potentiality and actuality, into essence and accident, etc.

Some clarification would be achieved if the word "cosmology" could be used, in contradistinction to "philosophy of nature," to designate two peculiarly modern aberrations: (1) the illicit extrapolation and projection of scientific knowledge into an imaginative world-view, and (2) the attempt to solve the problem of the unity of the phenomenal world. The philosophy of nature treats of the interconnexion of individual substances only in terms of causality. Any attempt to pass beyond the pluralism of primary substances causally connected must lead either (a) properly to the unity which pervades things because they are gathered and ordered in Divine Providence, and this is strictly a theological unity,—or (b) improperly to the kind of monism which denies plural substances and uses a part-whole analysis to solve the problem of the one and the many. The "block-universe" which results from the latter alternative, with its absolute determinism, makes it impossible to account for real contingency in nature, which is intelligible only in terms of Aristotelian pluralism and which is compatible with Providence. (Aristotelian pluralism is a pluralism of individual substances. It must not be confused with neo-Platonic pluralism which is a pluralism of forms hierarchically received in one pervasive matter, which has some being apart from form. Vd. Note 21 *infra*.) The point to be reiterated here is that modern "cosmologies," from Leibnitz and Spinoza to Hegel and Whitehead,—having their ancient prototype in Plotinos,—are neo-Platonic confusions, influenced by the relationalism of science, on the one hand, and by unacknowledged borrowings from theology, on the other. Vd. Notes 20b and 25 *infra*.

20a. "When Descartes established the scientific dichotomy between mind and body, he provided both the *raison d'être* of modern psychology and the mystery which it has never completely dissolved. Descartes cut the world in two, into mind and matter, just at the time when science was about to begin the course of development which has made it the dominating influence in modern civilization. We all know how successful the physical sciences have been and we can also see that biology has prospered in abandoning a vitalism and identifying itself with the physical side of the Cartesian dichotomy. If Descartes was right, if there are these two worlds, then the success of science in attacking the one forms a challenge for the creation of a science of the other. This view is common in psychology. When psychologists speak of the classification of the sciences they are usually sure of only two sciences—psychology and physics. Yet, if psychology is coordinate with physics and if the scientific method is applicable to both, then it seems strange that psychology has come such a little way when physics has ramified into many fields and has come so far" (E. G. Boring, *The Physical Dimensions of Consciousness*, New York, 1933: p. 3; by permission of D. Appleton-Century Co.).

And Freud says: "Strictly speaking, indeed, there are only two sciences—psychology, pure and applied, and natural science" (*New Introductory Lectures on Psychoanalysis*, New York, 1933: p. 245).

20b. Absolute idealism is a subtle form of dualism. This is revealed by the historical transformations which produce Hegel out of Leibnitz and Spinoza, through Kant. The point of origin is, of course, Descartes. Making Platonic errors in psychology and misusing Aristotelian terms in metaphysics,—i.e. using them as a neo-Platonist does, —Descartes gave birth to the monstrosity of mind and matter as the changing independent substances which constitute the being of the phenomenal world. Both Spinoza and Leibnitz tried to change the unintelligible face this gave the world, but neither did more than accomplish a cosmetic disguise. The mask of monism which they imposed was not the genuine substantial unity of matter and form. Add now the complicating factor of the English tradition in psychology with its multifarious errors and you get Kant, whose bewilderment takes the form of the most elaborate philosophical analysis made in the modern world. The utterly incomprehensible rift between the noumenal and the phenomenal orders takes the place of the Cartesian bifurcation. Though the language and much of the meaning is different, the essential paradoxes of the two dualisms are the same. In both cases, the world is irremediably split asunder, and the transitivity that is indispensable for coherence is either abolished or rendered inexplicable. Hegel, in attempting to avoid the *insolubilia* in Kant, does much the same that Spinoza and Leibnitz did with Descartes, and in consequence he resembles them. The monism of the Absolute is applied to heal the wound caused by the diremption between the noumenal and the phenomenal orders. Within this One there is still the dualism of Appearance and Reality,—the plurality of inadequate, even self-contradictory, beings which constitute the phenomenal world, somehow embraced in the transcendent fullness and intelligibility of the noumenal real.

If it be said that hylomorphism is also dualistic, it need only be answered that it is a dualism which renders the unity of things at once intelligible and does not require the immanence of a transcendent One, which is the last contradiction in the Hegelian series,—so great that it blurs all the others into the background. A philosopher should be able to appear wise without making the man of common sense appear to be a fool. This is the obvious merit of Aristotle and St. Thomas; and the equally obvious failure of Descartes, Leibnitz, Spinoza, Kant and Hegel. Of these, Kant's failure is the most striking because he so well recognized the errors of materialism and idealism. But he never discerned their modern source in the dualism of Descartes. If Kant had understood the union of matter and form in *being* as well as in *experience*, if he had grasped the connection of the noumenal and the phenomenal as the procession of *being* and *operation*, he might not have been followed by Hegel and Marx as he was preceded by Spinoza and Leibnitz. Cf. Note 16 *supra*.

In a sense there are only two positions, monism and dualism. The only monism which is not a dualism in disguise is absolute materialism and it is untenable on many counts. The only dualism which does not require a super-imposed one for either the unity or the intelligibility of things is hylomorphism. The face of nature that it perceives is clear and whole. The *plurality* of individual substances constitutes the *one totality* of things by their causal connections. Any deeper understanding than this of the oneness of the universe is theological and not metaphysical: the immanence of God, not substantially, but by Power and Providence. Whitehead's criticism of Aristotelian cosmology is based on his failure to understand that "the disjunction of primary substances" is qualified by their causal connection and that Plato's doctrine of the Receptacle and Leibnitz's monadology achieved a better vision of the unity of the world only at the expense of confusing metaphysics and theology. Beyond causality there is no philosophical problem of the interconnection or procession of things. Vd. *Adventures of Ideas*, New York, 1933: Ch. VIII on Cosmologies and Ch. IX on Science and Philosophy. Whitehead's *Process and Reality* is at best a current version of Plato and Leibnitz. Vd. Note 25 *infra*.

21. I have often been tempted to use the name "dialectical materialism" for the traditional metaphysics of Aristotle and St. Thomas Aquinas; for if the Marxists fully understood their own doctrine, they would be hylomorphists or formal materialists. Marx and Engels said they rejected the simple-minded, mechanistic materialism of their day, the 19th century forms of a doctrine which had its historical antecedents in the ancient Greek atomists, and in the philosophy of Hobbes. This materialism was unable to give a satisfactory account of change, physical or historical, and reduced itself to skepticism or subjectivism whenever it tried to explain the processes of cognition. The phenomena of change require the notion of contraries which inhere in matter disjunctively and lead to a conception of matter as having the potentiality for the opposite contrary whenever a given form determines it actually. The contraries are forms; they are determinations of matter. The perpetual process of change is understood when it is grasped that no single form determines matter absolutely, i.e., exhausts its appetite or potentiality for contrary forms. Efficient causality in change is the energetic reduction of the potentiality of matter for a given determination to that determinateness actually. The Hegelian dialectic appealed to Marx because of its obvious apparatus of contraries and oppositions. Marx used it mainly

in the sphere of human history; it supplemented the inadequacy of simple materialism as an account of historical change. Marx rejected the idealistic premises of Hegel, quite properly, but failed to explain why the principles of change he learned from the Hegelian dialectic did not apply to the processes of the material and infra-human world. He lacked the philosophical sophistication and technique to see that the dialectical materialism he was looking for, the materialism which could give a consistent and adequate account of all natural and historical processes, as well as of the knowledge of them, was the materialism of Aristotle and St. Thomas Aquinas. As the result of this failure, Marxian materialism today is in an unstable equilibrium between the position which it definitely rejected,–simple, absolute materialism,–and the position which its premises indicate it is trying to achieve. (In this connection, it should be noted that Marx's doctoral dissertation involved a critique of Democritus. Vd. F. Mehring, *Karl Marx*, New York, 1935: pp. 53–59. Unlike Marx, Engels wrote Hegelianism more thoroughly into his materialism and insisted, with manifold inconsistencies, upon a dialectical process in nature. Vd. his essay on *Ludwig Feuerbach and the Outcome of Classical German Philosophy* (1888). Professor Hook has recently exposed all the contradictions in Engels on this point. Vd. *Dialectic and Nature* in the Marxist Quarterly, I, pp. 253–284 (April-June, 1937). In what follows I am treating Marxism as if it were free from the philosophical ineptitudes of Engels.)

That Marxian materialism must be the formal materialism of Aristotle and Aquinas can be simply shown. The Marxian recognizes the difference between physical and historical change, i.e., the motions studied by the physicist and biologist and the unique course of development to be found in human history. In fact, it was precisely this recognition which led him to supplement "natural science materialism" by "historical materialism" and to borrow from Hegel the principles of dialectic to describe the pattern of history. It is true that historical movement is *partly* dialectical. But that it is only partly so and that the processes of infra-human nature are not dialectical, in a univocal sense of the word, the Marxian has not been able to explain because he developed his position as a too-simple negation of Hegel's idealism, itself the negation of materialism. The solution of these difficulties is to be found in the Aristotelian distinction between material and rational potencies, the potentiality of prime matter and the potentiality of the intellect. Matter is able to receive contraries only *disjunctively*. It is this fact which explains the characteristics of physical change, in which matter is the substratum. Material motions are not asymmetrically progressive but cyclical, from one contrary to another and back again; thus, the phenomena of generation and corruption, of growth and decline, even of local motion and alteration, are understood in the philosophy of nature, the basic principles of which are matter and the contraries. But the intellect, or reason, is able to receive contraries *conjunctively*, as species embraced in a genus. The opposition of species is not the simple negation of A by not-A; it is the relation of contraries, both of which are positive terms, negating each other only partially within the positive ground of the genus. The way in which the intellect receives contraries and resolves their opposition by ascending to a concept which unifies them, indicates the essentially dialectical character of its procedure. In short, as the potentiality of matter gives physical motion its distinctive character, so the power of mind is the source of dialectical motion; matter is the substratum of contraries disjunctively received, mind is the substratum of contraries synthesized.

In the physical world, only man has an intellect. Therefore, dialectical motion will occur only in human history, and there only to the extent that the intellect is operative as a cause. The asymmetrical line of progress, which is characteristic of dialectical change, is most apparent in intellectual history, what is called the history of ideas, and much less so in social, economic and political development. But man is not a pure intellect. He is an animal and many material factors are among the causes of his activity. To the extent that matter is causally effective in human history, it is not simply or purely dialectical. This is true even of intellectual history. The history of philosophy is hardly an unbroken or undeviating progress. In its alternating advances and declines, it partakes of the character of material change; yet there is dimly discernible that dialectical movement forward which indicates that the intellect is operative in intellectual history. The line of progress is even more obscured in social and economic history, probably because the efficacy of material factors is greater there. Yet to the extent that there are genuine advances, the intellect is at work, and one's optimism about future progress must depend upon how much power one attributes to the intellect in its struggle against material forces.

Hegel, denying matter and making an Absolute Mind the basic ontological principle of change, fell into two errors: (1) he failed to see that only human history is a dialectical motion; and (2) he failed to see that no change is purely dialectical because material factors are always present in some degree and, hence, he was an unqualified optimist about progress. The Marxian has tried to avoid all of these Hegelian errors: he has distinguished natural change and human history; he has admitted regressions as well as advances. He is not a naive optimist precisely because he is a materialist. Yet he cannot be simply a materialist because, in negating Hegel, he does not wish to return to the mechanical materialism which Hegel's insight about dialectical motion negated. Dialectically to negate the negation, he must become a formal materialist, a materialist who distinguishes between the potentiality of matter and the power of mind. He will then realize that his philosophy of history is nothing but a reading of the facts of historical change, in so far as these are known, in the light of psychology, an analysis of man as a rational animal, in whom rationality is limited by animality. Strictly, there is no philosophy of history, i.e., no separate branch of philosophy with principles of its own. What the Marxian propounds as a philosophy of history is merely an interpretation of known historical change in terms of the principles of the philosophy of nature and of man, i.e., philosophical psychology. (He may, of course, include prophecy in his exposition, as an extrapolation of the curve which past history obscurely reveals.) Finally, Marx's recognition of a genuine contingency in historical change requires him to reject the block-universe of any absolute monism and to take the pluralist view of many individual substances causally connected. Vd. Note 20 *supra.*

In short, no materialism can account for physical change without adding to matter the formal principles of the contraries (*sound* natural-science materialism); nor can materialism account for dialectical change without adding to matter and the contraries the principle of mind (historical materialism). Formal materialism comprises all these principles. It is the only philosophy which includes them all and is able to give an intelligible account of their relation, of the substantial union of form and matter and of intellect as the substantial form of man. If Marxian doctrine wishes to avoid the errors of atomism, on the one hand, and the errors of Hegel, on the other, it must eventually learn that, as a philosophy, it is formal materialism. Only formal materialism can understand the world studied by the natural sciences and the order of history. Only formal materialism is dialectical materialism.

The history of philosophy contains many instances of failure to achieve the perfection of dialectical materialism. There is, first of all, the Platonic error which assigns to matter apart from all forms some actual existence,—the being of the receptacle in the *Timaeus.* This leads inevitably to the error of the plurality of substantial forms which dominates all the neo-Platonic thinking of the Middle Ages, even when it is ostensibly an effort to reconstruct the Aristotelian metaphysics and philosophy of nature. The tradition of hylomorphism is, for the most part, corrupted by neo-Platonism. The perfection of this doctrine has seldom been achieved. The philosophy of St. Thomas is its consummate expression, in many respects an improvement upon the Aristotelian sources.

Corrupt hylomorphism leads to a second and worse error, the Cartesian error of explicit dualism which assigns separate substantial existence to both matter and form. This contains the seeds of a third error, the worst of all. The problems of cognition are insoluble in terms of Cartesian premises, and beginning with Locke's criticism of innate ideas, we pass in a series of psychological mistakes to the subjectivism of Berkeley and the skepticism of Hume. In the course of this episode in intellectual history, the substantial existence of matter is denied. Kant's failure to establish a sound metaphysics,—

although matter and form are the leading principles of his analysis of experience,—thus finally leads to the absolute idealism, or spiritualism, of Hegel. Facing the issue between spiritualism and materialism, Marx attempted to employ the dialectical principles of the former and to retain the honest realism of the latter. The cycle would have been completed had Marx been able to weld the two into a sound philosophy of dialectical materialism.

Neo-Platonism, Cartesian dualism and Hegelian idealism are all corruptions of, or derivations from, the doctrine of formal materialism. Of the cosmological alternatives, only atomistic materialism is an independent doctrine; in fact, it is the philosophy which Aristotle most honors as being nearest to the facts, when he considers the attempts of his predecessors to analyze the processes of change. Vd. *De Generatione et Corruptione*, I, 2. Aristotle accepted materialism in part, and corrected its inadequacies by enriching it with the Platonic theory of ideas, transforming them both by his conception of substance as a union of form and matter, and rendering the analytically separable principles of form and matter intelligible in terms of actuality and potentiality, which constitute the primary division of being. It is interesting to note that both Platonism and atomism make the error of giving matter an actuality apart from form, and that both lack the concept of substance, all forms being equally the accidental determinations of matter. The concept of substance is crucial, carrying as it does the distinctions of essence and accident, of existence and operation, as well as the distinction of actuality and potentiality. It avoids the atomist's mistake of making quantities the prime, if not the sole, determinations of matter, but unless it is rightly understood, the ever-present error of pluralism begins the process of corruption which allows formal materialism to degenerate into dualism and idealism. Cf. Note 20b *supra*. (It should be added here that the concept of substance which is indispensable to a sound metaphysics and philosophy of nature is negligible to, in fact, should be disregarded by, the natural sciences. This point expresses the basic difference between philosophy and science as types of knowledge: the former penetrating to the ontological center, the latter staying on the empirical surface. It is significant that the concept of substance is placed by Kant in the category of relation. Natural science cannot employ it in any other way. As E. Cassirer shows, science progressively *reduces* substance to function, i.e., being to operation, the noumenal to the phenomenal.)

Spinoza is almost *sui generis* in this account of the transformations of metaphysical doctrine. He is certainly not a materialist, not an idealist, nor simply a Cartesian dualist. He comes nearest to being an Aristotelian formal materialist. Substance is constituted by the composition of inseparable formal and material principles (the attributes of thought and extension); neither of these principles has being in itself; only substance is. There is furthermore the distinction between essence and accidents (the infinite attributes and the finite modes). So far the analytical terminology appears to be Aristotelian. But the absence of the distinction between potentiality and actuality, the absolute unity of substance and the denial of individual substances which are *per se* and *in se* but not *a se*, the perplexing definition of the attributes which regards each separately as expressing the whole essence of substance, combined with the infinite plurality of attributes,–these are indications that Spinoza's *Ethics* is a confusion of many strands in the philosophical tradition. Primarily, it is a confusion of the neo-Platonism of mediaeval Jewish and Arabic thought with the dualism of Descartes. It must be remembered that the neo-Platonists of the 12th and 13th centuries talked the language of Aristotle even when they defiled his principles. This accounts for much of Spinoza, who, like Leibnitz, made the mistake of trying to solve in philosophy the theological problem of the procession of creatures within the embracing totality of an immanent One. Vd. R. P. McKeon, *The Philosophy of Spinoza*, New York, 1928: Ch. I on the background of Spinoza's thought. As Professor McKeon says, "Spinoza could not know that the cartesian distinction of body and mind was to wipe out the aristotelian distinction of matter and form; if he could have thought of it in those terms he might have hoped that his treatment of extension and thought be confused with neither, or at least that it be recognized to be nearer to Aristotle than to Descartes" (*op. cit.*, p. 51). The other element which complicates the characterization of Spinoza's philosophy is the absolute monism that has its ancient expression in the doctrine of Parmenides,–or the All-One of Plotinos,–and its modern form in the absolutisms of Hegel and Bradley. The truth which Parmenides grasped is a truth in natural theology,–the absolute oneness of absolute being; the error which Parmenides made, and which Aristotle corrected, was the error of giving this principle a cosmological interpretation. The result is, of course, pantheism, with its failure to acknowledge the real existence of modes of imperfect being and modes of imperfect unity. That Spinoza could contrive a novel doctrine by the mixture of these errors, can be explained by the fact that he lived at a time when philosophy and theology were disordered with respect to each other. Vd. Note 16 *supra*. Cf. A. E. Taylor, *Some Incoherencies in Spinozism*, in Mind, N. S. 182, pp. 137–158. Professor Taylor exposes the way in which Spinoza's argument covertly admits the plurality of individual substances while at the same time Spinoza dismisses such pluralism as a "vulgar notion."

22. As we have already seen, absolute idealism in so far as it is *absolute*, arises from the Kantian distinction between the unconditioned and the conditioned, which Hegel converts into the absolute one of Reality and the relative many of Appearance. Vd. Note 20b *supra*. But in so far as it is *idealistic*, there is no difference between the so-

called objective idealism of Hegel and the subjective idealism of Berkeley. Both result from the same error in the analysis of cognition. The opposition here is not between idealism and materialism but between idealism and realism. This can be shown simply as follows.

The basic principle of realism in the theory of knowlege is that sensations and ideas are not *that which* we know primarily, but *that by which* we know *what* we know of *that which* we know. They constitute both the instrumentalities of knowledge and its content, but not its objects. (Ideas are objects only secondarily in reflexive knowledge. We can understand that we understand, or in other words we can understand the primary object of knowledge, the thing, as something understood, the idea.) As the instrumentalities of knowledge, ideas refer the mind intentionally to that which it knows,—the order of existing things. To identify the *id quo* and the *id quod* of knowledge is to identify the objects of knowledge with its content. This is the root of all subjective idealisms. Locke is the chief source of this error in modern times, for in the Introduction to his *Essay Concerning Human Understanding* he defines an idea as "whatsoever is the *object* of the understanding when a man thinks" (I, 1, ¶ 8). (Italics mine.) Locke's common sense realism saved him from the consequences of this statement, though not from the inconsistencies he had to suffer in order to avoid the consequences. But Berkeley and Hume, with perverse logic, preferred to reduce themselves to the absurdities of subjectivism and solipsism. (For a full discussion of the realistic principle which distinguishes the *id quo* and the *id quod* of knowledge, vd. Maritain, *Les Degrés du Savoir*, Paris, 1932: Ch. III, Le Realisme Critique; also *Réflexions sur L'Intelligence*, Paris, 1931. Cf. G. E. Moore, The Refutation of Idealism and related papers in *Philosophical Studies*, New York, 1922. For a magnificent statement of the crucial importance of realism in contemporary thought, vd. Professor Gilson's address at the Harvard Tercentenary in September, 1936; also *Le Réalisme Methodique*, Paris, n. d.)

The same error is the root of all objective idealisms. The difference arises from the metaphysical status of the ideas which are the objects of knowledge. If we combine the premises, (1) that the objects of knowledge must be existences and (2) that ideas are the objects of knowledge, we reach the conclusion that ideas must exist *per se*, prior to and independent of the mind which knows them. In its primitive form this is Platonic idealism, called extreme realism in the Middle Ages because it answered the question about the status of universals by assigning them real subsistence. In modern times, objective idealism assimilates the Parmenidean doctrine of the one, to produce the pantheism of the One Absolute Idea. This is Hegelianism in all its varieties. (If one describes Hegelianism as a neo-Platonic combination of Parmenides and Heraclitus,—the immanent One which is perpetually in Process, constituted by or at least involving the Ideas,—one can discern how close are the affinities between Hegel and Spinoza, on the one hand, and between Bradley and Whitehead, on the other. Plotinos is in them all.)

Further, the same error is the source of phenomenalism among Hume's followers, and it is unmistakably present in the psychological doctrine of positivism. There is some justice in the Marxian charge that positivism and pragmatism, accepting the phenomenalism of Mach or Mill, are idealism in disguise.

The critical point can be expressed in another way in terms of the distinction between *secundum se* and *quoad nos.* The thing *as known* is *quoad nos.* But knowledge is a proportion between intellect and thing, and the thing which measures the adequacy of the intellect in knowing is the thing *secundum se.* If the instrumentality of the idea as the medium of knowledge is ignored, no difference is possible between the thing as it is, *secundum se*, and the thing as it is known, *quoad nos:* and it is impossible to distinguish truth and falsity. If, on the other hand, the meaning of *quoad nos* is not qualified by the intentional reference of knowledge to its object, there is again no distinction between the thing as it is and as it is known, and we are imprisoned in the world of our ideas. Radical objectivism and complete subjectivism seem to be opposite errors but they are the same essentially and arise from the same failure to see that ideas as the instrumentality of knowledge relate its subject and object by intentional reference and separate them according to the mode of being of the thing, *secundum se* and *quoad nos.*

This is related to the problem of the way in which men have ideas. In the history of thought, there have been only three solutions: (1) ideas are intellectually intuited, as sensible things are sensed; (2) ideas are innate principles of the understanding itself; and (3) ideas are in the intellect only as a result of abstraction from sense-experience. The first and second of these positions are combined in the Platonic tradition which, through St. Augustine, influenced Descartes and Malebranche and, through Malebranche, Berkeley and Hume. (Cf. E. Gilson, *The Spirit of Modern Philosophy*, New York, 1937: pp. 15 ff.; 86 ff.) It is through the illumination of the innate ideas, the seminal reasons, by the light of ideal objects, that intellectual intuition takes place. Through light we see light. The distinction of Kant is that he denied the first position and embraced the second; in fact, he opposed the first so vigorously that he also denied the reflexive power of the understanding to know its own ideas in second intention. In the Platonic tradition ideas exist *per se* because they are the objects as well as the content of knowledge. According to Kant, purely intelligible objects, if there are any, transcend our knowledge because the ideas, the pure concepts of the understanding, serve only as the forms of judgment, the matter of which must be provided by sensuous intuition. In contrast, the third position, taken by Aristotle and St. Thomas, denies that ideas exist *per se;* agrees with Kant in the sense that such intelligible objects as separate souls, the angels and God, are not capable of being known intellectually by abstraction but only negatively and analogically by construction; but makes the intellectual knowledge of sensible things,—the apprehension of their intelligible being,—as genuine as the sensitive knowledge of their accidents and operations. Ideas are not the forms but the content of judgments. Apart from and prior to judgment, they are the simple apprehensions of the quiddities of sensible things, an apprehension which requires both an intuitive phase, on the part of sense, and an abstractive phase, on the part of intellect. The doctrine of abstraction is, thus, crucial in psychology, as the doctrine of substance is in metaphysics and the philosophy of nature. Misunderstanding or error in regard to the one is always and everywhere correlative with misunderstanding or error in regard to the other. These are the twin fallacies of Platonism in European thought productive of all the basic speculative departures from the truth, except atomistic materialism which is correlative with sensationalism in psychology and the denial of ideas. Though metaphysics is logically prior to psychology, it seems clear, in modern times at least, that the psychological error is the original and generative one.

That the Platonic error of making ideas the objects of intuitive knowledge is the challenging mistake in the psychology of cognition can be judged from the effort St. Thomas made to correct it and, more than that, to guard against the many ways in which it intrudes itself. Vd. *Summa Theologica,* I, Q. 84, AA. 1, 2, 3, 5, 6. The Platonic error about the nature of the soul as a substance, rather than as the formal principle in the composite substance of man, follows from the erroneous supposition that the intellect knows ideas directly by intuition rather than the nature of things through them, by abstraction from the materials made available by sense and imagination. The unity of man is thus destroyed and the extremity of Cartesian dualism is the inevitable consequence.

It is interesting to note that a sound cosmology is materialistic and that a sound theory of knowledge is realistic. There is not only a harmony between these two parts of philosophical doctrine, not only a felicitous union of them in a sound psychological analysis of the nature of the soul, but, what is most striking, there is the agreement of a sound philosophy in all its parts with common sense, with public experience, with the plain facts known to every man. (Even Whitehead who treats the doctrine of substance as the villain in European thought cannot, as a matter of common sense, avoid it in his concept of "a Society." Vd. *Adventures of Ideas,* New York, 1933; pp. 260–267.) Idealism and dualism in all their forms are forced to justify their departure from common sense by renouncing it as superficial and illusory or by despising it as unlearned and gross. But subtlety alone, or subtlety and novelty, are marks merely of intellectual ingenuity and not of soundness. The philosophy of Aristotle and St. Thomas is both subtle and sound.

22a. What is said in the text of Lecture II at this point is restricted to "schools" of scientific psychology. I am disregarding those writers who, directly or indirectly, discuss psychological questions in the Aristotelian and Thomistic tradition. They fall into three groups: (1) They are philosophers, such as Brentano or even Husserl, whose expositions are entirely philosophical psychology but not entirely Thomistic. (2) They are neo-Scholastics, such as Dom T. V. Moore or Father R. E. Brennan in this country, who have attempted to put together the principles of Thomistic psychology and the findings of modern research, in physiology as well as psychology. Vd. *Dynamic Psychology*, Philadelphia, 1924; and *General Psychology*, New York, 1937; also *Experimental Psychology* by Father H. Gruender (Milwaukee, 1932). (3) Such books are to be distinguished from expositions of the Aristotelian-Thomistic analysis of soul, regarded entirely as a part of philosophy, such as I. Gredt, *Elementa Philosophiae*, Fribourg, 1932: I, pp. 328–488; or C. Alibert, *La Psychologie Thomiste et les Théories Modernes*, Paris, 1903.

The chief problem raised by all these books, though in different ways, is whether the two bodies of knowledge, same in subject-matter but distinct in method and type of knowing, should be left in separation or joined in a well-ordered doctrine which is psychology, both philosophical and scientific. Since most scientific psychologists would deny that there is any valid knowledge other than that acquired by research, the problem is not for them. It is rather for the philosophers who, unlike the scientists, recognize that psychological investigation does contribute knowledge which is relevant to their principles and analyses. The solution which seeks to establish the unity of psychology by ordering the results of empirical research and philosophical analysis, seems to me the better one. But the problem is not solved until the right principle of order is used. It is at this point that current expositions seem to me regrettably defective, especially the undue importance which neo-Scholastic writers attach to physiological details and the vagaries of experimental data. Vd. Note 32a *infra*.

23. The hierarchy of substances is the hierarchy of the perfections of matter and this in turn can be expressed in terms of a hierarchy of properties or operations. The principle of order is as follows: a given perfection A is higher than B, if the presence of A entails the presence of B, but not conversely. Thus, life is a higher perfection of matter than existence, because whatever is alive exists but not everything which exists lives. Similarly, in the realm of living things, sensitive powers are higher than vegetative, because not everything that grows is sensitive, but nothing is able to sense which does not also grow. And understanding is highest in the order of vital operations, because it necessarily entails vegetative and sensitive powers, but is not entailed by them. Substantial forms are named according to their highest power or property. Those forms which confer life upon matter are

distinguished from those which merely confer existence, by being called souls. A body alive is matter besouled, as a body existing is matter informed. In the realm of living things, vegetative, sensitive and intellective souls are distinguished according to the vital operations with which the matter thus besouled is endowed. The hierarchy of the natural sciences is determined accordingly: the study of material existences, the physical sciences; the study of living things, the biological sciences. In so far as all living things are besouled, psychology is a biological science. In so far as man shares many of the powers and operations of other living things, he can be studied biologically. But in so far as man, through having an intellective soul, exceeds the animal kingdom, psychology as the study of the specific nature of man becomes a science apart from the rest of biology. That psychology is not merely a biological science turns ultimately upon the proposition that the operations of understanding are not the acts of a bodily organ. It follows from this proposition that man is hierarchically graded with respect to all other living things as they in turn are graded with respect to inanimate bodies. The order of the sciences is, therefore: the physical group, the biological group, and human psychology.

24. Human psychology is like animal psychology to the extent that men and animals share many vital operations, i.e. sensation and imagination, locomotion, the passions, not to mention all the vegetative functions. If the distinctive intellectual power of man is ignored, there is no essential difference between human and animal psychology. Vd. Note 23 *supra*. The programme of behavioristic psychology involved an attempt to reduce human to animal psychology. It failed, not because human behavior is so much more complex than animal motions, but because it is radically different. A science of animal behavior is possible because the motions of animals are either instinctively determined or the products of reflex habituation. But human behavior is voluntary and human habits are voluntarily formed. The resulting contingency in the phenomena of human behavior makes them much less susceptible to scientific formulation. Cf. *Art and Prudence*, New York, 1937: Ch. 9.

25. The "philosophy of science,"—in so far as it concerns the ordering of the sciences,—is a rendering of the philosophy of nature, in so far as it considers the hierarchy of physical things. The order of the sciences of nature must depend upon the order of their objects. What we have distinguished as the Aristotelian and the Cartesian philosophies of science are strictly correlative to Aristotelian and Cartesian cosmologies. And these, in turn, depend upon different metaphysics. If we are bound by simple consistency, we are not free to take one position in the philosophy of science and another, which is not its correlative, in the philosophy of nature or metaphysics.

Nor is one free to choose a metaphysical position according to the view of science or of man's nature which, *for other reasons*, one prefers to take. Quite the contrary! If one proceeds according to reason, the resolution of the issues in metaphysics must come first. This subsequently determines (1) the account one gives of the order and relation of the natural sciences, and (2) the position of psychology. If either of these two determinations is given temporal priority, it must be done in ignorance of metaphysical presuppositions. Such is usually the case among scientists who talk about the outlook of their science or of the sciences, unaware that they are betraying metaphysical judgments which would shock them if made explicit. Psychologists especially are given to philosophizing unwittingly, as witness the introductory chapter of any treatise or text-book of scientific psychology.

Even worse is the construction of what pretends to be a philosophy of nature out of the reigning concepts and laws of natural science. Whitehead's *Process and Reality* is such a "scientific cosmology," an attempt at a "speculative synthesis" which will be for our epoch what Plato's *Timaeus* and the Cartesian cosmology were in their day. (Vd. *op. cit.*, New York, 1929: Preface and Ch. I.) What Whitehead takes to be the central problem of cosmology is not a philosophical problem at all, namely, the problem of the inter-connection of the totality of things. There is little to support Whitehead's interpretation of the Receptacle in the *Timaeus* as Plato's principle for solving this problem. There is even less evidence to show that the Greeks ever considered the problem which Whitehead formulates. It is a typical modern problem, beginning with Descartes and occupying Leibnitz and Spinoza. It originates in the 17th century, partly because these philosophers failed to distinguish the problems of the philosophy of nature from those of metaphysics and theology, and partly because they converted natural science into a cosmology. The theologian is able to consider the totality of things in their interconnection and in process only in so far as their nexus and order is Providential. But Providence is not a principle in philosophy. It is only as a theologian, aided by revealed truth, that St. Augustine can develop a doctrine about history or that St. Thomas can discuss the procession of creatures. The neo-Platonic tradition confused theology and philosophy. This is true even of Plotinos who was not aided by Holy Scripture. There are traces of Plotinos in Descartes and Spinoza and Whitehead. These modern thinkers, all neo-Platonists, are pre-occupied with a problem which is not Greek but Christian and which, in the Christian tradition, belongs to theology and not philosophy. Their "cosmologies" are not philosophies of nature, but attempts to answer this problem by "ontologizing" science. Again, the influence of the *Timaeus* is apparent. Plato did not conceive the philosophy of nature as related to metaphysics and as having principles of its own. He told what he called a "likely story" about the realm of becoming, basing it upon the science of his day, particularly mathematics. That is what Descartes did, and what Whitehead is re-doing.

I use the phrase "scientific cosmology" to name a projection of the relational analyses of science *behind* the phenomena to which they properly apply. Such projection is a reification of mathematical relations, of the relational logic of science, but it is not a philosophy of nature, first, because the method of philosophy is not to interpret the findings of science, and second, because the conceptual limitations of science make that knowledge incapable of providing any genuine philosophical insight. One example will suffice. The concept of substance has no place in science which, as Cassirer points out, studies functions, or correlations of accidents. (Vd. E. Cassirer, *Substance and Function*, Chicago, 1923.) Whitehead, illicitly projecting natural science into a cosmology, makes the denial of substance pivotal, and naturally turns to the Platonic and Cartesian traditions to support his exclusion of what must be the central term in the philosophy of nature, which seeks to answer ontological questions properly and does not look to the sciences for help they cannot give. As I have already indicated (Note 22 *supra*), Whitehead does not succeed in avoiding the concept of substance. His enduring societies, personal or otherwise, are Aristotelian primary substances. But his analysis of their nature makes, on the one hand, the typical Platonic error of a plurality of forms in that societies are composed of societies, though ultimately they are reduced to the togetherness of actual occasions of the ingression of the ideas, and shows, on the other hand, that a society is a relational rendering of substance, which is appropriate to the sciences of phenomena but not to ontology. Vd. Note 47 *infra*.

26. Cf. Aristotle, *De Anima*, III, 3–8; St. Thomas Aquinas, *Summa Contra Gentiles*, II, 59–78, and *Summa Theologica*, I, Q.75, AA.2, 5; Q. 76, A. 1; Q. 84, AA. 1, 2, 3, 4, 6; Q. 85, AA. 1, 2.

The argument can be reduced to the following propositions. (1) Knowledge involves some *communication* of the knower and the known. (2) A thing is known in so far as its form is somehow in the knower. (3) Whatever is received is in the recipient according to the mode of being of the recipient. (4) Forms in matter are individual because that is the material mode of reception. (5) Sensitive knowledge is the apprehension of things in their individuality because sensation is the act of a bodily organ and sensible forms are therefore received materially. (6) Man understands as well as senses, i.e., man knows intellectually. (7) Intellectual knowledge is the apprehension of things in their universality. (8) Therefore, the intellect must receive universal forms. (9) But no form is universal according as it is received in matter. (10) Therefore, intellectual reception must be immaterial, which is to say that understanding is not the act of a bodily organ. This last proposition is the capital premise for the conclusion that the soul, having this immaterial mode of operation, must also to that extent have an immaterial mode of being, and hence it is not only the substantial form of the body but is capable of separate self-subsistence upon the corruption of the composite. (Cf. Whitehead's reasoning which comes to the conclusion that "in some important sense the existence of the soul may be freed from its complete dependence upon the bodily organization." *Adventures of Ideas*, New York, 1933: p. 267.)

27. Vd. my analysis of artistic production in a paper on *Creation and Imitation: An Analysis of Poiesis*, published in the Proceedings of the American Catholic Philosophical Association, 1935: pp. 153–174. The intellect is the principle, not only of philosophy and science, but of art and morality; of art, because intentional making requires that the artist order his material according to a form which he possesses in abstraction from any matter; of morality, because the moral act must be a voluntary one, and the will is appetite as intellectually determined to an object. With respect to all means, all partial goods which are the subject of choice, the will is free because the intellect, operating in the practical order, determines the appetite imperfectly. Human freedom is proportionate to this indeterminacy.

28. The Marxian conception of man as a manufacturing, or machinofacturing, animal is another indication that Marxism must become a truly dialectical, or formal, materialism. Marxian materialism in its present development cannot give a satisfactory account of the way in which men multiply material things according to specifications. In this respect it is as inadequate as the simple, mechanical materialism which it so resolutely rejected. If the Marxian seems equally resolute not to follow out the intellectual consequences of that rejection, one is led to suspect that he *dislikes* the consequences rather than that he is unable to discover them. He must then be charged with superstition and ignorance; the first because one does not make rational judgments according to one's likes, and the second because if the Marxian fully understood *all* the consequences of his implicit premises, both speculative and practical, he would see that he had no reason to dislike them.

It should be added, in commentary on the text at this point, that the material out of which man makes useful productions is not prime matter but the formed matter of substances; and that the artificial forms which he imposes upon these materials are not substantial forms, but accidental determinations of composition and order. These qualifications for the sake of metaphysical precision do not, of course, diminish the force or alter the direction of the argument.

28a. What is perhaps the most striking fact distinguishing man as radically different in kind from all other animals, is the fact of human history, the fact of cultural development. As Allers says, "the fact of human progress alone would show the impossibility" of the opposite view. "The inheritance of tradition and progress in technique are things not to be found in animals: a hundred thousand years ago the termites built their admirable houses just as they do today; but what a difference between the dwellings of primitive man and the sky-scrapers of modern New York!" (*The New Psychologies*, New York, 1933: pp. 33–4).

There is a nice paradox in this for the Marxists. Man is an historical animal because man is a rational animal. This does not deny the Marxian point that material causes operate in human history,—that what men make and do depends upon the material and animal conditions of their life,—but it does deny that material causation is sufficient to explain the phenomena. The material and animal conditions of human life are essentially the same as those for any other animal; but what men are able to produce under such conditions is different because the factor of reason or free intelligence has been added. Marxism distinguishes itself from simple materialism,—what it calls "natural science materialism,"—by adding thereto a materialistic account of history. But that account must either insist that material factors are the only essential causes and everything else is epiphenomenal, or it must acknowledge that in human history reason is an *independent* cause. In the first alternative, dialectical materialism, even though it is historical, is no better than natural-science materialism, because it is using the same principles, disguised in Hegelian language; it simply cannot explain the facts of man's progressive mastery over materials. In the second alternative, dialectical materialism, recognizing the role of reason in imposing forms upon matter, is hylomorphism. The Marxian can take the second position without altering his view of the shifting struggle of the classes, without yielding in his justifiable moral condemnations of capitalism. In fact, he is strengthened in the latter if he become a Thomist. (Vd. Note 21 *supra.*)

29. Brutes and men are alike in the possession of the powers of the *interior sense*, such as comparison and discrimination, memory, imagination, and estimation. The interior sense consists of powers which follow from the operations of the proper or special senses. As sensations are the functions of particular sense-organs and primary projection areas of the brain, so the operations enumerated under the head of the interior sense are functions of the total involvement of the brain, going beyond the activity of the primary areas of sensory reception. Another name for these powers in man is the *passive intellect*, because the performance of such operations as comparison and discrimination, imagination and cogitation is a kind of thinking. Men do a sort of thinking with images alone, the kind of thinking that occurs in reverie and day-dreaming. Such thinking does not require an intellect. To the extent that animals have brain power, they are able to do thinking of this sort. The one difference here between men and animals is that men possess an "intellectual imagination" able to com-

pound images freely. Animals, lacking intellect, lack this power. They can estimate but not cogitate. Vd. *Summa Theologica*, I, Q. 78, A. 4; Q. 81, A. 3, ad. 3. Cf. H. A. Wolfson, *The Internal Senses in Latin, Arabic, and Hebrew Philosophic Texts* in the Harvard Theological Review, April, 1935.

It is this similitude in human and animal powers which enables animal psychologists to construct experiments for the investigation of animal intelligence in problem solving. When, on the supposition that human intelligence differs from animal intelligence only in degree, experiments which use analogous problems, only more complicated, are constructed to test human powers, it is not surprising that the supposition is verified. This *petitio principii* is as much involved in the experimental work of the *gestalt* psychologists as in that of the behaviorists, although the former being more subtle conceals it better. When an experimental psychologist is able to make an animal solve a *scientific* or an *artistic* problem, he will have proved that animals have intellects as well as men. It is not necessary to take men into a laboratory to discover that they are intellectual.

30. The text does not answer Dr. Alexander's third question, concerning the biological utility of understanding. The utility of sense in the economy of animal life is, of course, its implementation of vegetative functioning by aiding the animal to satisfy his basic needs. Sensitive knowledge not only determines desires but helps to gratify them. It is difficult to say whether animals have any purely speculative mode of sensitive operation, i.e., a use of the senses purely for the sake of knowing. But we do know that men employ their cognitive faculties for both speculative and practical ends. On the practical side, intellectual knowledge determines desires and helps to satisfy them in the same way that the senses do. So far there can be no question about the biological utility of the intellect. But "biological utility" usually has the narrow meaning of "survival value" or "adaptation to environment" or the "satisfaction of animal wants." The intellect, therefore, has more than biological utility because it directs men in a mode of life which involves other goods than these. It directs human desire to intelligible goods which exceed all animal wants and which have nothing to do with survival value or adaptation to environment in the struggle for existence. Beauty and truth and justice are things for which men work, even die, because their intellects enable them to understand, and hence desire, goods that no animal seems to apprehend. Biological utility is so far transcended by the gift of intellect that men are given to intellectual operation for its own sake. Since the ultimate perfection of any thing lies in the performance of its proper operation, the intellectual life is the happiness to which all human virtues and external goods must be ordered. The latter are the goods of "biological utility." They are for the sake of the intellect rather than the intellect for the sake of them. One cannot praise

the intellect by talking of its biological utility; that is fitting praise for the senses. The intellect should be honored for its biological inutility because it is that power whereby men are able to live and love differently from animals. If, through a misuse of the intellect, men become unhealthy, ill-adapted and even unhappy, that must be charged to the animality which complicates man's attempt to lead a human life.

31. Aristotle, in the *Metaphysics*, compares the species of things to integral numbers, which differ in species by the addition or subtraction of unity. And, as St. Thomas adds, in the *De Anima* "he compares the various souls to the species of figures, one of which contains another, as the pentagon contains and exceeds a tetragon" (*Summa Theologica*, I, Q. 76, A. 3). The type of continuity which obtains among natural forms is like that of the series of whole numbers. It is not the continuity of a dense series, between any two members of which there is an infinite number of intermediates. To speak of it as a continuity at all is only for the sake of emphasizing that each member of the series contains its hierarchical inferiors and is contained by its hierarchical superiors. To the extent that each member exceeds, or is exceeded by, another in terms of an indivisible unit, discontinuity predominates. This unit is the specific difference. To deny this unit difference is to deny species, since species cannot be different kinds if they differ only in degree. The radical error in *The Origin of Species* is the attempt to define species as the extremes of a series of graded intermediates, differing quantitatively. Species are said to *originate* through the extinction of the intermediate varieties. It is this error which the discovery of mutations corrects and which changes the interpretation of all of Darwin's data. Whether mutations produce accidental or essential differences is not here the question. If they are only accidental, mutations do not constitute an origin of species; but the varieties of species which result are discontinuous. In any case, therefore, the true maxim about nature's work in the order of generation is the contradictory of *natura non facit per saltum.*

31a. "The intellect knows itself not by its essence, but by its act. This happens in two ways: In the first place, singularly, as when Socrates or Plato perceives that he has an intellectual soul because he perceives that he understands. In the second place, universally, as when we consider the nature of the human mind from knowledge of the intellectual act. . . . There is, however, a difference between these two kinds of knowledge, and it consists in this, that the mere presence of the mind suffices for the first, the mind itself being the principle of action whereby it perceives itself, and hence it is said to know itself by its own presence. But as regards the second kind of knowledge, the mere presence of the mind does not suffice, and there is further required a careful and subtle inquiry. Hence many are ignorant of the soul's nature and many have erred about it" (*Summa Theologica*, I, Q. 87, A. 1). Here St. Thomas distinguishes between the facts of experience, as they are known to all men, and the analysis of them which the philosopher makes by "a careful and subtle inquiry." Psychology as a body of philosophical knowledge arises with the analysis of such apparent facts as that men understand, that men have habits, etc. The reflexive action of the intellect is the source of these facts, but the understanding of them,—the analysis of the habits, powers and ultimately the nature of man from a knowledge of his operations,—is not different in method from the philosophical penetration into the nature of other things, whose phenomenal manifestations are not known reflexively. Cf. Note 17 *supra.*

32. Any investigative study of rational processes can do no more than determine the accidents of rationality in operation. In the first place, a scientific investigation cannot proceed upon the assumption that men are not rational without self-contradiction. The fact of reason is a brute fact of experience. It underlies the existence of science itself. It does not wait for science to establish its existence. Rationality is no more discovered by psychological investigation than gravitation is discovered by physical investigation. The physicist determines certain quantitative accidents of gravitation, the rate of acceleration of bodies falling toward the earth, the relation of the mass and the distance to gravitational force, etc. Scientific psychology starts from the commonly known fact that men are rational and proceeds to investigate the circumstances and qualifying accidents of rational performances.

That this is so is clear, in the second place, from the data which the investigative psychologist has collected. The data of the experimental laboratory, of psychometric research, and of clinical studies, do not define the essence of reason. They cannot. What is discovered can be summarized as follows. (1) Behavioristic experiments have shown that under many circumstances human beings solve problems by "trial and error" rather than "rational thought." Such data have been misinterpreted to mean that human beings are not rational, or that animals are. But, as we have seen, all that the experiments show is that trial and error problems are solved by trial and error, in the case of men as in the case of animals. Vd. Note 29 *supra.* (2) Psychometric research has determined the quantitative accidents of intelligence. It has shown the way in which the different operations of man's rational ability are related to each other in terms of quantitative correlations. It has measured the relation of rational power to other abilities. It did not discover the fact of individual differences, but it has made this fact quantitatively significant and precise by manifold measurements. (3) Clinical studies, by psychiatrists and psychoanalysts, have documented what is commonly known about the relation of reason to the passions. They have not studied rationality but rather the conditions under which rational men do not operate rationally because they are also animals. They have determined, in short, the accidents of irrationality in men. They did not discover that fact. (4) Experimental and clinical studies by physiologists and neurologists have determined, but not discovered, the dependence of rational performances, and also the pathology of reason, upon various bodily conditions, such as fatigue, brain lesions, etc. In some instances, they have been able to measure this dependence by fairly precise quantitative techniques.

The scientific evidence does not tell us what reason is or what rational operations are. It does not establish the existence of reason or the equally obvious facts about its pathology, the abeyance of reason and irrationality. The data cannot be interpreted to mean that men are not rational or that human and animal intelligence differ only in degree. Their only significance is the determination of the extrinsic conditions and the qualifying accidents of reason as an ability and in operation.

Philosophical psychology rests upon the same obvious facts of common knowledge, which scientific investigations have, at best, supplemented by the sorts of determinations enumerated above. But, starting from these facts, it proceeds in a different direction because its interest is in definitions and causes rather than in the correlation or measurement of phenomena. It seeks to understand these facts; it seeks to determine the essence of rationality, not its accidents. The philosophical analysis defines the intellectual power, distinguishes its subordinate abilities, determines the different fields of its operation, divides the several acts by which the power is fulfilled, and formulates the relation of reason to those other powers of man which, though not intrinsically rational, participate in rationality either as its instruments or by its ordination. For all of this analysis, even when it becomes exceedingly subtle, only the facts of common experience are needed. The scientific evidence adds nothing that is *essential.* At best, it contributes exemplifications of what is independently known.

The foregoing discussion has singled out the study of reason, in its speculative dimension, as a cognitive power. But what has been said applies to all *human* behavior, because human behavior is specifically different from animal behavior in so far as it is rational or participates in reason. The phrase "human behavior" has become ambiguous, largely through the errors of that scientific "school" which claims this to be its subject-matter. If it means the whole field of human conduct, the development of human character and the social intercourse of men, and if the scientist aims to discover the causes of human behavior in this sense, the scientific effort is doomed to failure. Human behavior is voluntary and contingent in a way that the rest of natural motions are not. Reason is a first cause in human behavior, and the essential operations of this cause are not susceptible to scientific investigation. Vd. Note 24 *supra.* It should be added here that investigative psychologists, for the most part, have not yet learned the lesson positivism has taught physicists, namely, that science is incapable of being theoretic knowledge of causes. Vd. Note 16a *supra* and Note 47 *infra.*

But "human behavior" can be given a more restricted meaning. It can mean the operations of specifically human powers. The subject-matter of psychology is human behavior in this sense: the powers and acts of men,—what the psychometrist calls the abilities and performances. Common experience provides the basic facts concerning the existence of these powers and acts. Philosophical psychology analyzes their essential nature. Scientific psychology investigates their external conditions and their accidental traits. In short, philosophical and scientific knowledge differ in psychology according to the general difference in their type. Vd. Notes 6b and 9 *supra.*

32a. The uniqueness of psychology makes it difficult to define. It is the only body of philosophical knowledge which deals with a single species of physical thing. It is therefore the only body of philosophical knowledge which has a subject-matter capable of being investigated scientifically. It is not a part of the philosophy of nature because there are no other parts strictly coordinate with it. It is rather a special application of the principles of natural philosophy; yet it is not merely that because it has primary inductions of its own from the data of reflexive experience. Whereas the philosophy of nature considers the mode of being of any changing thing,—the types of such contingent beings, the kinds and conditions of change,—philosophical psychology studies particular phenomena of change,—the operations of human nature, the formation of habits, etc. To this extent it is like scientific knowledge, though it differs both in method and in aim: it is not investigative and it seeks definitions; its principles are in the order of substance and causality.

Another way of indicating these difficulties is to classify the questions which relate to man: (1) Questions concerning the self-subsistence of the human soul, and its mode of being, belong to metaphysics and, within metaphysics, to natural theology. (2) Questions concerning the mode of being of man as composite of form and matter, of soul and body, and, in view of the subsistence of the human soul, questions concerning man's unity belong to metaphysics in the province of ontology. (3) Questions concerning man as living, as subject to generation and corruption, and to accidental motions, belong to the philosophy of nature. (4) Questions concerning the specific nature of man, his powers, habits and operations, belong to psychology. (4a) In so far as these questions are concerning the essence of man, the essence of his powers and their essential relationships, the answers must be achieved by philosophical analysis from the data of reflexive experience. The answers constitute philosophical psychology. (4b) In so far as these questions are concerning the accidental conditions of human operation and accidental determinations of man's powers, the answers must be achieved by investigative research, by special observations and measurements. The answers constitute scientific psychology.

Strictly then, psychology begins with the fourth type of question. The answers to the second and third types are necessarily presupposed and may, therefore, be properly included in the exposition of philosophical psychology, but the distinctions in type should be preserved for the sake of clarity. It makes a difference whether the locus of an argument is in metaphysics, in natural philosophy, or in psychology proper. Questions of the first type cannot be answered except *a posteriori;* in the order of knowing they presuppose psychological analysis itself (Type 4a). There is good reason to restrict the discussion of these questions to treatises on natural theology. If we turn now to what are strictly psychological questions, we can see at once the relation of Types 4a and 4b. The principles of philosophical psychology are presupposed by any sort of scientific psychology: essential distinctions are the ground for accidental determinations. As the natural sciences in general can be informed and regulated by the superior conceptual order of mathematics or the philosophy of nature, so the science of psychology is informed and regulated by the special philosophical analysis of its own subject-matter. All of the basic questions in psychology are purely philosophical. Denial or ignorance of philosophy is the cause not only of the inadequacies of scientific psychology but also of the vain controversies of the "schools." On the other hand, just as the sciences provide exemplifications of superior principles, so the empirical findings in psychology exemplify the relevant philosophical principles. This does not mean that exemplification is the sole contribution of scientific research. It also adds a wealth of detailed knowledge about all sorts of accidents, which philosophy cannot reach to. It would lose its proper posture if it tried, as history unfortunately reveals. This briefly indicates the ordering principles for the exposition of all knowledge relevant to man. Vd. Notes 36c, 39c and 46 *infra.*

Two comments remain to be added. (1) If the word "psychology" were restricted to name the consideration of the soul itself, either as the formal principle of living things or as self-subsistent, and if "anthropology" were used to name the study of man specifically, his nature, powers and operations, then the body of knowledge which is a special branch of philosophy as well as a special natural science would be called anthropology, and psychological questions would belong to the philosophy of nature and to natural theology. (2) Man is of all natural things the one with which man is most intimately acquainted, the only one whose specific nature he is able to comprehend fully. In the light of this fact, it may be thought paradoxical that scientific efforts in psychology are among the most recent and least successful. Why should not a science of psychology be better *qua* science than any other? The paradox is removed when it is realized that the greater knowability of man for man produces as its natural result in the hierarchy of human knowledge, not the *best* science, but rather the *only* body of philosophical knowledge relevant to a species of physical thing. Those who will not recognize this fact must remain perplexed about the poorness of psychology as a science although men are so well acquainted with themselves. Those who acknowledge the existence of philosophical psychology can learn from it why the obstacles to the investigation of human nature are so great, so great that psychology will never achieve the precision and plenitude of physics.

33. The ancient and mediaeval tradition not only relegated developmental problems,—the growth of character, the types of human life,—to the field of ethics, but also located the discussion of certain other psychological topics in practical treatises on ethics, rhetoric and poetics. Professor McKeon promises soon to publish a paper on the history of the treatment of the passions, showing how this topic passed from a locus in rhetoric to poetics, then to ethics, and finally in modern times to physiology and pathology. Ancient and mediaeval treatises on psychology dealt in detail with sense and intellect in their speculative dimension. In so far as sense and intellect are involved in the operations of appetite, the acts of the passions and the will, they are in the practical dimension, directed toward the end of action rather than the end of knowledge. It, therefore, seemed appropriate to place the discussion of these topics in practical treatises. Aristotle pointed out that the moralist must be a student of psychology, as the physician is a student of physiology. Vd. *Nichomachean Ethics*, I, 13, 1102ª 16–25. But the subject-matter of physiology is essentially the same, whether it is studied academically or for practical purposes in a medical school. So, too, the psychological analyses that Aristotle develops in the *Ethics* and the *Rhetoric*,—the nature of will and the conditions of voluntary action, the types of pleasure and love, the operations of practical reason, in the *Ethics;* the passions, their nature, the conditions of their arousal, and their course, in the *Rhetoric*,—are strictly psychological regardless of their practical contexts.

St. Thomas makes a similar disposition of topics. In the Treatise on Man, after he has enumerated and analyzed all the powers of man, he proceeds to the detailed analysis of the operations of one of these powers, the intellect, reserving for other treatises the consideration of the acts of the other powers. "The acts of the appetitive part of the soul come under the consideration of the science of morals; wherefore we shall treat of them in the second part of this work, to which the consideration of moral matters belongs" (*Summa Theologica*, I, Preamble to Q. 84).

Such allocations of psychological topics to various parts of a systematic philosophy must not obscure the unity of the subject-matter of psychology, which comprises all the powers and acts of man, the appetitive as well as the cognitive. The parts of Aristotelian psychology can be gathered together from the *De Anima*, the *Ethics* and the *Rhetoric*, as in the case of Aquinas, they can be collected from the Treatise on Man and from the Treatises on Human Acts, the Passions, and Habit in the *Summa Theologica.* The collection will readily form the systematic whole of philosophical psychology. That Aristotle and St. Thomas made the disposition they did of its parts is ultimately a matter of relevance and convenience in exposition,—the dependence of practical philosophy upon psychological principles, and the avoidance of repetition. To suppose otherwise would lead one to say that Spinoza had no doctrines in metaphysics, physics and psychology because all of these are contained in a book called *Ethics.* (Cf. Alexander Bain's division of his psychological doctrine into two treatises: *The Senses and the Intellect* and *The Emotions and the Will.*)

33a. When a natural scientist seeks to "explain" the phenomena which he is describing, he usually turns to another science which describes a lower order of phenomena. Thus, the psychologist turns to neurology and physiology for explanations, the biologist to the chemist, the chemist to the physicist. What is meant by "lower" here is simply that the system of phenomena which one science studies *includes* systems of phenomena studied by other sciences. The latter sciences, dealing with the included systems, are lower. But this reference of higher to lower sciences for the sake of explanation is not a reduction of the sciences because the proper task of each is the description of a special segment of phenomenal reality. The phenomena of life may be explained mechanically,—at least, in so far as explanation is "scientific,"—but they are not mechanical phenomena. Vd. Note 13 *supra* and Note 47 *infra.*

34. The word "perfection" must be understood in its metaphysical sense primarily. The ethical meaning is derivative. Forms perfect matter in so far as they actualize its potentialities. The fulfillment of anything's potentialities is its completion or perfection. The substantial form is, in this sense, the first perfection or act of a thing's being. It is the term of generation. But in so far as the thing which is substantially actual has powers of operation, there are second perfections or acts, i.e., the operations of these powers. The ethical meaning of perfection follows from the metaphysical insight that goodness and being are correlative, and that anything is good in proportion as it achieves actuality. The highest perfection of a thing is its fullest actuality. To judge a thing we must, therefore, know its specific powers of operation. Vd. Aristotle, *Nichomachean Ethics*, I, 7.

For a discussion of the hierarchy of perfections in nature, vd. St.

Thomas Aquinas, *Summa Theologica*, I, Q. 76, AA. 3, 4. The evolutionist similarly grades the lower and higher forms of life. Evolution exhibits a hierarchy of perfections in nature. Cf. Note 31 *supra*.

35. "There is no other substantial form in man besides the intellective soul; and the soul, as it *virtually* contains the sensitive and nutritive souls, so does it *virtually* contain all inferior forms, and it alone does whatever the imperfect forms do in other things. The same is to be said of the sensitive soul in brute animals, and of the nutritive soul in plants, and universally of all more perfect forms with regard to the imperfect" (*Summa Theologica*, I, Q. 76, A. 4). I have underlined the word "virtually" because its full analytical significance is essential to understanding how St. Thomas avoided the error of the plurality of substantial forms. An inferior form, virtually contained by a superior form, is not actually present as a form but only operatively present in the order of powers which the superior form involves. As habit is a mean between an operative power and its act, so a virtual form is a mean between the potentiality of substantial being and its act. A single substance has a hierarchy of powers, but not a hierarchy of forms. "Of one thing there is but one substantial being. But the substantial form gives substantial being. Therefore of one thing there is but one substantial form. But the soul is the substantial form of man. Therefore it is impossible for there to be in man another substantial form besides the intellective soul" (*Ibid.*).

A single example may make this clear. On a sheet of blank paper, a triangle is present *potentially*. It can become physically actual there through the addition of three connected straight lines. On a sheet of paper on which a square is drawn, a triangle is present *virtually*. It can become actual there first by the drawing of the diagonal and then by the removal of two sides. Whatever has the form of a square is thus said to contain the form of a triangle virtually; and although the properties of a square are not identical with the properties of a triangle, they include the latter properties. The triangular properties are, of course, not the same in the square, in which the triangle is present only virtually, and in an actual triangle. In the same way, the human soul includes an animal soul virtually, and all the properties, i.e., powers, of animal life are present in human nature, though differently because they are subordinated to a higher power. (Thus, a man and an animal, but not a vegetable, can suffer emotionally caused indigestion, and only a man can suffer thus by worrying about ideas.)

This point can be seen *analogically* in the processes of development and decay. When an infant or a cretin idiot becomes a man, a potentiality is actualized. When a man suffers *dementia praecox* and decays to a persistent catatonic stupor, a virtuality is actualized. The distinction is strictly exemplified in the processes of generation and corruption.

36. Vd. Notes 19 and 32 *supra*. Cf. C. J. Herrick, *The Brains of Rats and Men*, Chicago, 1926; K. S. Lashley, *Brain Mechanisms and Intelligence*, Chicago, 1929; G. E. Coghill, *Anatomy and the Problems of Behavior*, Cambridge, 1929; W. G. Summers, *The Psychology of Sensation* in The Proceedings of The American Catholic Philosophical Association, 1934: pp. 104–113.

36a. In his Introduction, Dr. Alexander says that human infants show only animal characteristics, and that the difference between men and animals "comes gradually about during the individual's development from an ovum to an adult" (pg. xiv *supra*). While it is true that an infant is not fully a man, it must be understood that the infant is actually a potential adult. Even though the infant at birth behaves as an animal and only that way, the infant is not even then actually an animal because it can become a man as an animal cannot. The educability of an infant, like the curability of a cretin idiot, signifies the possession of powers not shared by animals. It is this difference in powers which marks the essential difference between animals and men. Generation and development must not be confused. The infant is born a human being, and not an animal; it develops into an adult. The development is with respect to powers and not specific nature; the adult differs from the infant not in power simply, but in habits and operations, i.e., the developments of power. Vd. Note 35

36b. Those who tell the history of psychology usually recognize this division but as usually misunderstand its significance because they are positivists. Supposing as they do that the only valid and adequate knowledge in this field must be scientific,—the result of experiment or research,—they treat what precedes the middle of the 19th century as the era of "pre-scientific psychology," which means, of course, that they treat it as a period in which philosophers "speculated rationally,"—a polite way of saying "guessed,"—about problems later to be investigated when scientific method reached psychology. They may even use the phrases "philosophical psychology" and "scientific psychology," but they do not attribute to the former any status as established knowledge; it consists merely of "systems," or "hypotheses" which do not become knowledge until they are tested by scientific research. Thus it is clear that the historians of psychology, explicitly or implicitly, take a positivist view of the nature of philosophy. What is worse, they proceed for the most part as if modern philosophy were intelligible other than as an attenuation of the ancient and mediaeval tradition, confounded by the repetition of old errors. That they have little respect for philosophical psychology is pardonable considering that they start with Descartes and Locke. Thus, in a hundred pages dealing with "the preparation for experimental psychology within philosophical psychology," Professor Boring devotes three to Aristotle and none to any mediaeval writer. He admits that Aristotelian traces can be found in all modern psychology; in fact, "many modern fundamental concepts of psychology can be found in Aristotle, and the historian can show for some of them a continuous descent. For this history, however, the reader must go to other sources. It is enough, as we begin with Descartes, for us to realize that he is by no means the first systematic psychologist" (*A History of Experimental Psychology*, New York, 1929: p. 158). Vd. the seven pages devoted by G. Murphy to the "intellectual background of seventeenth-century psychology" in his *Historical Introduction to Modern Psychology* (New York, 1929); and the chapter on "prescientific psychology" in E. Heidbreder's *Seven Psychologies* (New York, 1933). Although Professor Brett gives a whole volume to ancient and patristic theories, and another volume to the mediaeval and early modern period, in his three-volume *History of Psychology* (New York, 1921), he, like the others, writes as if the transition from ancient to modern philosophy, and from philosophy to science in psychology, were unqualified progresses. Until the anti-philosophical virus of positivism is completely overcome, an adequate history of psychology will not be written. Until psychologists rid themselves of this version of the history of their subject, "schools of psychology" will persist in interminable controversy about ungenuine issues, and scientific work will be misled by the failure to recognize that the basic questions in psychology are philosophical and cannot be answered by research. This is the root of error in psychoanalysis. Freud is a positivist. Vd. *New Introductory Lectures on Psychoanalysis*, New York, 1933: Ch. 7 on A Philosophy of Life.

Furthermore, most historians of psychology who write from the scientific point of view, confuse philosophical psychology with what Wolff and Kant called "rational psychology." Vd. Note 39c *infra* and cf. C. Alibert, *La Psychologie Thomiste et les Théories Modernes*, Paris, 1903.

36c. In writing a treatise on the soul rather than a treatise on man, Aristotle betrays the influence of Plato and the pre-Socratics. His method of reaching his own doctrine through a consideration of his predecessors has unfortunate consequences in this case. The *De Anima* lacks unity of subject-matter. It not only combines philosophical and scientific questions, but is concerned with problems that must be distinguished according to their various formalities. Thus, its questions concerning soul in general and the grades of soul constitute a problem in the philosophy of nature, the problem of living things in the order of composite substances. This can be seen in another way. To the *Physics*, which contains the most general considerations of the philosophy of nature, the *De Caelo* adds a treatment of local motion, the *De Generatione et Corruptione* a treatment of substantial change and alteration, and the *De Anima* a treatment of the motions which are vital operations. The interest of the *De Anima* extends to a consideration of vegetative, locomotive and sensitive powers *per se*, as acts of bodily organs. The questions raised here are physiological and belong properly to investigative biological science. So the consideration of plants as wholes, as composites, is botanical science, and the consideration of animals as composites is zoology and, perhaps, animal psychology,—both in the biological domain and scientific in type. That part of the *De Anima* which is not a section of the philosophy of nature, on the one hand, or dispersed among the biological sciences, on the other, is the treatment of human nature. To the extent that the analysis of human powers and acts arises from man's reflexive knowledge of himself, the *De Anima* is philosophical psychology. But as such it is not knowledge of the soul *per se*, but of man who, as a composite substance, has these vital powers by virtue of having as a principle of his life a soul of human grade. Vd. Note 32a *supra.*

37. The three Platonic errors in psychology are: (1) the substantial separation of soul and body, (2) the assignment of sensitivity to the soul as a power of operation apart from bodily organs, (3) the operation of the intellect in the direct intuition of ideas, apart from sensitive knowledge. Aristotle and St. Thomas corrected these errors by painstaking analysis, but Descartes returned to two of them (1 and 3) and bequeathed the "problem of the soul," in an insoluble form, to modern psychology. For a citation of the Thomistic texts in which the refutation of Platonism is accomplished, vd. Note 22 *supra. Summa Contra Gentiles*, II, Ch. 56–79 should be added. For a critique of Descartes, vd. Maritain, *Three Reformers*, New York, 1932: pp. 53–89; *Le Songe de Descartes*, Paris, 1932; *Réflexions Sur L'Intelligence*, Paris, 1931: Ch. II.

38. Vd. Note 33 *supra.* Distinction must be made between two kinds of psychological knowledge which occur in the practical treatises of Aristotle. (1) Propositions about the nature of man and about human powers and operations. (2) Propositions about types of human character, the conditions which influence human development, the variables of human behavior, the contingent circumstances of action, etc. Knowledge of the first sort is strictly speculative philosophy. Such propositions have the universality and certainty that mark speculative knowledge. Knowledge of the second sort is necessarily uncertain and inexact. Such knowledge is not "scientific," to use Aristotle's words, but "practical." We desire it chiefly because it is useful in directing conduct, and not for its own sake. Psychological knowledge of the first sort provides ethics with some of its leading principles. But these principles cannot be applied without knowledge of the second sort. That part of contemporary psychology and social science which is concerned with human behavior in the large, is of the latter kind,—practically useful knowledge about the general facts of life.

38a. The magnificence with which St. Thomas perfects the Aristotelian tradition is more evident in psychology than anywhere else, except natural theology. For one thing, where Aristotle treats human nature as a part of the study of soul in general, St. Thomas makes man the central object of psychological analysis and subordinates the discussion of soul thereto. Strictly, soul as substantial form cannot be in itself either a material or formal object of knowledge. Man can be such an object, and psychology is not adequately defined in subject-matter until it treats of man rather than the soul. (We are, of course, here considering only human psychology or what would be better named anthropology. The consideration of soul as self-subsistent belongs to natural theology.) Furthermore, where Aristotle refutes Platonism and materialism, St. Thomas purifies Aristotle himself of the tendencies to these very same errors which his neo-Platonic commentators could easily read into his texts. The Thomistic rendering of Aristotle is not only an answer to Averroes, Avicenna and Ibn Gebirol, but to Duns Scotus and Roger Bacon, to Descartes and Leibnitz as well, because as an exposition of the errors of Platonism, it is so much clearer than the account which Aristotle gave.

With respect to such crucial matters as the relation of the active and the possible intellect, it may even be conceded that Averroes was nearer to a right reading of the Aristotelian text than St. Thomas. But in the issue against Averroism, Aquinas was right philosophically, and those who praise the Averroistic reading are really admitting that Aristotle himself was more of a Platonist than St. Thomas was willing to construe.

39. Vd. Note 37 *supra.* Though he followed Descartes and was much influenced by him, Spinoza was a better psychologist. Yet he could not solve the problem of the unity of man by making mind the idea of the body. This led to the identification of mind as knower with the ideas it knows. The account of understanding and knowledge given in Book II of the *Ethics* suffers from the denial of universals *in abstracto*. Book III is an excellent analysis of the passions. The separation of theoretical psychology (Books II and III) from its practical application to the problems of conduct and happiness (Books IV and V) provides a model of systematic order which unfortunately is seldom imitated by other modern writers.

39a. We have already discussed many errors of Kant's philosophical psychology, his misconception of the intellect as a faculty of judgment rather than abstraction, his distinction of understanding and reason as scientific and dialectical,—in which he curiously distorts the Platonic division of the knowledge segment of the divided line (vd. *Republic*, VI, 509 D–511 E),—his failure to understand the faculties as the powers of man rather than as the mysterious operations of the transcendental ego in constituting experience. But at least he did proceed in terms of faculties, at least he did see that the separation of powers was not inconsistent with their unified operation,—even though he spoke of this as a transcendental unity,—at least he did understand that scientific psychology was restricted to the phenomenal order,—even though he did not see how it could be constituted as an experimental and mathematical science. All of these insights were lost or nullified by Herbart who succeeded him at Königsberg. Herbart denied the genuine distinction between rational, or philosophical, and empirical psychology, conceiving psychology at once as an empirical, mathematical and metaphysical science. As Boring points out, it was on the mathematical side that Herbart influenced Fechner who, also influenced by Weber, surmounted Herbart's Kantian repudiation of experimentation in psychology. It is not Herbart's misconception of the method or status of psychology as a science which is most important, however; that was remedied by Fechner and Wundt. It is rather his misconception of its subject-matter. Herbart rejected the analysis of faculties, and with it he rejected man as the subject-matter of psychology. Instead he attempted to formulate the relations of active ideational elements,—an analysis of consciousness which was a sort of animated associationism. (Vd. Heidbreder, *Seven Psychologies*, p. 65 ff.) Thus, the British and German lines converge on Fechner and Wundt to frustrate the early efforts to found a scientific psychology by reason of an impossible definition of its subject-matter. If it were true, as Boring says, that Herbart's attack on faculty psychology rejected a "kind of analysis to which psychology has never returned" (*History of Experimental Psychology*, p. 242), there would be no psychological science today. Fortunately it is not true; both psychometrics and psychoanalysis, however much they are indebted to Herbart and Fechner, have returned to the study of the abilities, habits and performances of men; neither are concerned with the elements of consciousness as such. Thus, Spearman writes: "The attacks made long ago by the Herbartians appeared to be irresistible; no serious defense was even attempted. Yet the sole permanent effect of these attacks was only to banish the word 'faculty', leaving the doctrine represented by this word to escape scot free. As much may be said for the onslaught of Thorndike" (*The Abilities of Man*, New York, 1927: p. 39). Cf. C. Pratt, *Faculty Psychology*, Psychological Review, March, 1929: pp. 142–171.

It is often said that Herbart's discussion of the vitality of inhibited ideas,—inhibited as a result of conflict with other ideas, and active though they are below the limen of consciousness,—is not only a memory of Leibnitz's *petites perceptions*, but also an anticipation of the Freudian notion of the active, though repressed, unconscious. (Boring denies a direct influence here. Vd. *op. cit.*, p. 246. Allers, on the contrary, claims Freud to have been influenced by Herbart through Breuer. Vd. *The New Psychologies*, New York, 1933: p. 4.) But the nature of the active unconscious cannot be explained either in Leibnitzian or Herbartian terms, and it remains a mystery in Freud. The problem is solved only by the conception of habit as a mean between potentiality and act, and hence as an active tendency toward operation although not fully operative. Vd. Note 55 *infra.*

39b. Until the recent attacks, made from different angles by behaviorists and by psychoanalysts, text-books of psychology defined the subject-matter of their science as consciousness, or the phenomena of consciousness. In doing so, they betrayed the unfortunate influence of either the Cartesian or the British tradition. The content of consciousness or, what is the same thing, immediate experience, cannot be the object of any body of knowledge, scientific or philosophical. Immediate experience belongs to all knowledge as its brute datum. An adequate account of the "content of consciousness" can be given only by reporting the data and concepts of all the natural sciences, of philosophy, of poetry, of law and morality. But such an encyclopedia is not psychology. Beyond that, there is only the report of one's personal experiences and biography. The chief difficulty of most of modern psychology, in so far as it is influenced by Descartes and Hume, is that it has no subject-matter which it can properly call its own. Lacking subject-matter, it can hardly become a science, not to mention clear philosophical analysis. Santayana aptly described it as "literary psychology" and added that it is better written by poets than by empiricists or experimenters. (Scientific psychology rightly discarded Soul as subject-matter, but failed to select Man.)

It is extremely significant for the translation which Lecture IV attempts between Aristotle and Freud, to note that both the Freudian and the contemporary Thomist criticize the subject-matter of modern psychology in the same way. The Freudian rightly objects to the narrowness and superficiality of academic psychology. It is limited to the study of the ego and of consciousness,—the phenomena of immediate experience. In contrast, Freudian analysis is truly a "psychology of the deeper layers," a study of the whole man, of all the powers of the soul. So Alibert objects to the contraction of psychological subject-matter due to positivism and phenomenalism: "A la différence de la psychologie Thomiste, qui avait pour objet l'âme prise avec l'ensemble de ses puissances, conscientes ou inconscientes, la psychologie moderne n'en accepte qu'une partie: savoir, le moi, ses facultés et leurs phénomènes" (*La Psychologie Thomiste et les Théories Modernes*, Paris, 1903: p. 9.)

39c. The distinction between rational and empirical psychology, instituted by Wolff, adopted by Kant, and still flourishing among many neo-scholastic writers, has been the source of much confusion in the modern history of psychology because of ambiguity in the words "rational" and "empirical." They convey both a distinction in subject-matter and a distinction in method. Originally, the subject-matter distinction was primary. For Wolff and Kant, rational psychology was a branch of metaphysics, treating such questions as whether the soul is self-subsistent and what is its mode of being, in separation from the body, as a simple substance. As we have seen, such questions strictly belong to natural theology and in some part require the supplementation of sacred theology and revelation. Vd. Note 32a *supra*. Empirical psychology is the field of faculty analysis; it is concerned with man and not with the soul *per se*. (The object of rational psychology is a purely intelligible and simple being; the object of empirical psychology is a sensible being, a composite of form and matter; hence there is some justification for the use of the words "rational" and "empirical" to distinguish knowledge of these different objects. As so used, the words have no methodological connotation whatsoever.) As Alibert makes the distinction in subject-matter, rational psychology deals with ontological questions and questions of existence, and empirical psychology deals with dynamological and phenomenological questions. (Vd. *La Psychologie Thomiste et les Théories Modernes*, Paris 1903.)

Wolff's use of the words "rational" and "empirical" to name this distinction in type of question had extremely unhappy consequences because in post-Kantian thought the words acquired a specious methodological meaning,—"rational" naming the supposedly *a priori* or purely dialectical method of philosophy, "empirical" naming the *a posteriori* or investigative method of science. (I say *specious* because philosophical knowledge, though dialectical rather than investigative, is as much *a posteriori*, as much the result of inductions from experience, as science. There is no knowledge which is purely rational or purely empirical.) Kant's attack on rational psychology is based on the same grounds as his attack on every part of what he thought was metaphysics, namely, that ontological knowledge of noumenal and transcendental being is impossible. (It must be remembered here that Kant accepted Wolff's ill-advised classification of the parts of special metaphysics as psychology, cosmology and theology.) But Kant was not attacking rational (philosophical or, even in his sense, *a priori*) as opposed to empirical (scientific and *a posteriori*) knowledge. He distinguished between pure or rational physics and empirical natural science; he made the same methodological distinctions in psychology; in fact, Kant's own philosophy is in large part philosophical psychology, dealing with questions which belong to empirical psychology (in subject-matter) but, in his terms, rational in method. It is ironic, therefore, that Kant should be cited by historians of psychology as authority for the position that philosophical psychology (identified by them with rational psychology) is impossible.

These confusions can be clarified only if we are able to eliminate the treacherous words "rational" and "empirical." We can then properly order the related distinctions in subject-matter and in method. (To show how these eliminations can be made, I shall use the words in what follows to make substitutions for them.) 1. *Subject-matter*: (a) "psychological" questions concerning existence and mode of being of the soul: rational psychology; (b) "anthropological" questions concerning the nature of man, his powers, habits and acts: empirical psychology. 2. *Method*: (a) philosophical, by analysis of the phenomena of reflexive experience, involving *a posteriori* inferences from operations to powers and nature: rational; (b) scientific, by investigation of the phenomena of human behavior, reaching accidental determinations of powers and acts: empirical. Now, it should be noted, in the first place, that philosophical method is not rational in Kant's sense of *a priori;* like scientific method, it also depends upon the data of experience and in the same way, though the data are different. And, in the second place, it should be noted that whereas the subject-matter here called "anthropological" is capable of both philosophical analysis and scientific investigation, the subject-matter here called "psychological" is restricted to philosophy. Yet even these ontological questions are not answered *a priori,* but only by *a posteriori* inference from the facts concering human nature which are the basic facts of philosophical psychology. This *a posteriori* inference from knowledge of human nature to questions concerning the soul differs from the *a posteriori* inference from the facts of human operation to knowledge of the powers and essence of man in that the former requires special metaphysical premises. This is important because it indicates the impropriety of treating questions concerning man and questions concerning the soul as if they were parts of a single subject-matter. The relation between empirical and rational psychology,—when these words name a subject-matter distinction,—is that of premises to conclusions, but the conclusions require additional premises not provided by empirical psychology. The relation between empirical and rational psychology, —when these words name a methodological distinction,—is that of accidental to essential determinations of human nature and its mode of life. Here there is a real unity: empirical psychology as a subject-matter combines and orders two bodies of knowledge which have the same subject-matter, man, but differ in method, as philosophical and scientific. Rational psychology as a subject-matter is purely philosophical, a group of questions in metaphysics (more narrowly, in natural theology, since the primary question is one of existence of a transcendent, simple, purely intelligible being, i.e., the separated soul). These latter questions are solved in terms of the knowledge provided by empirical psychology, in so far as it is philosophical, and by strictly metaphysical principles (knowledge of substance and cause).

When the distinctions are thus understood and ordered, the errors of Kant become plain, and plainer still those who followed and misunderstood his errors. Kant not only made the positivistic error of denying the possibility of rational psychology as a branch of natural theology, but he failed to see that the field of empirical psychology included problems capable of clear philosophical solution and also problems capable of scientific determination by methods which, in so far as they are mathematical and experimental, do not differ from those employed by physicists. Only to the extent that rational psychology includes questions concerning the mode of being of the separated soul was Kant right in saying that rational psychology exceeded the bounds of reason and belonged to the province of faith (sacred theology). Such questions are not capable of being solved within the limits of philosophy. Any attempt to do so must lead to paralogisms and dialectical frustrations. But the question, Whether the soul has any self-subsistence, is as much a purely philosophical question (in natural theology), susceptible of clear affirmative answer, as the question, Whether God exists.

40. The contrast between Wundt and Brentano can be made in terms of their analytical principles, as well as in terms of their methods. In method Wundt was an experimentalist whereas Brentano was frankly a philosophical psychologist. But the issue between Wundt's principles and those of Brentano is philosophical. It is in no way affected by whatever experimental evidence was obtained in the laboratory at Leipzig. Titchener's discussion of this opposition proceeds without reference to "scientific data." Vd. his *Systematic Psychology: Prolegomena*, New York, 1929; cf. E. G. Boring, *A History of Experimental Psychology*, New York, 1929: Ch. 18 on act psychology in relation to experimental psychology.

41. It is to Alexander Bain rather than to William James that we owe the reintroduction of the concept of habit into psychological theory. Vd. G. Murphy, *Historical Introduction to Modern Psychology*, New York, 1929: p. 111. But neither of these writers fully realized its true significance, because neither placed it in the context of the distinction between power and act. Their partial and confused consideration of habit is one among many indications of how attenuated the vestiges of a sound tradition can become.

42. "All the movements in psychology that have led to self-conscious schools–Wundt's physiological psychology, introspectionism in America, functional psychology, *Gestalt* psychology, behaviorism, but not animal psychology nor the mental tests–have been philosophical movements, conducted, for the most part, by men who would eschew philosophy and rely solely upon the experimental method. The degree to which the text of this book has entered upon quasi-philosophical and systematic matters, while purporting to be an account of the history of experimental psychology, is a measure of the admixture of philosophy with experimentation within psychology. Ever since their foundation, the journals of psychology in all countries have been weighted down with 'theoretical' papers that are really expositions of psychologists, untrained to philosophy but writing on philosophical

matters. Incompetent work can be ignored, but a division of the mind within psychology is not healthy. Inevitably it must hinder work in the individual and thus the most rapid progress in the science. There is too much to psychology now for psychologists to master their own material and philosophy too" (E. G. Boring, *A History of Experimental Psychology*, New York, 1929: pp. 660–661; by permission of D. Appleton-Century Co.). Boring's complaint can be reversed for much of contemporary philosophy. These philosophers,–the pragmatists, positivists, etc.,–have given psychology up, or what is much worse, they have adopted the "theory" of one or another "school" of so-called scientific psychology. In fact, bad psychology is the villain throughout the history of modern philosophy. It works havoc enough in Descartes, Hobbes and Kant, but that is as nothing to the ruin which follows upon its being made, by Locke and Hume, the "first philosophy" in place of metaphysics.

43. Much of the experimental evidence which has been obtained by researchers who have espoused *gestalttheorie* is in the field of animal psychology. In this respect, the gestalters and the behaviorists are alike. They are alike, furthermore, in that they are both reactions against introspectionism of the structuralist sort, and in that both regard men and animals as differing only in degree. As the behaviorist uses the concepts of reflex and conditioned reflex to explain human and animal behavior without distinction, so the gestalt psychologist applies the concepts of configuration and insight to both human and animal perception and learning. They differ with respect to their main interests: the behaviorist concerns himself chiefly with sensori-motor coordinations and emotions; the gestalt psychologist primarily with visual perception and problem solving. Gestalt experiments are, for the most part, more ingenious, and the neurological hypothesis which *gestalttheorie* so largely depends upon is much more sophisticated than the earlier behavioristic neuro-mythology of the reflex arc. But Lashley's neurology, as a basis for behavioristic interpretations, has been recognized by Köhler to be essentially the same as the psychophysiology suggested by his *Die physischen Gestalten in Ruhe und im stationären Zustand* (1920). Cf. *Gestalt Psychology*, New York, 1929: Ch. IV.

Both behaviorism and gestalt psychology started out as great reform movements in experimental psychology but although both stimulated many departures in experimental work, especially of a physiological sort or concerned with animal behavior, neither has achieved the fruition it promised,–the establishment of a science of psychology. In this respect, of course, they are no worse than all the other movements generated by Wundt's laboratory. Cf. E. G. Boring, *A History of Experimental Psychology*, New York, 1929: Ch. 22 on *Gestalt* Psychology and Behaviorism.

44. The chapter headings of a recent text-book of psychology,—*Psychology, A Factual Textbook*, by Boring, Langfeld, Weld and others (New York, 1935),—reveals the structure of psychology to be nothing more than a collection of topics that have been experimentally investigated. They are as follows: the nature of psychology, the response mechanism, psychological measurement, vision, audition, taste and smell, somesthesia, intensity, the perception of spatial relations, temporal perception, the perception of movement, perceiving, learning, imagery, pleasantness and unpleasantness, emotion, action, thought and personality. The greater part of this material is physiological, and of that the greater part is sense-physiology. The same picture of psychological subject-matter can be obtained by examining *The Foundations of Experimental Psychology*, Worcester, 1929. Experimental psychology began in the physiological laboratory and seems to be returning to it, if it ever departed therefrom. Boring has attempted to make a virtue of this defect by turning psychology into a systematic interpretation of physiological data. Vd. *The Physical Dimensions of Consciousness*, New York, 1933. Cf. on this point, H. P. Weld, *Psychology as Science*, New York, 1928.

45. The inductive sterility of experimental research in psychology is plain to anyone who has examined vast amounts of data and found no significant generalizations yielded by them. What are the "laws" of learning, of reaction time, of memory, of perception, of attention, of association? These are all fields in which the pile of raw data is tremendous. At best the generalizations with which experimental reports conclude are matters of common sense knowledge, given an air of precision and elegance by a pseudo-technical language and a parade of metrical determinations. I do not mean to say that we have not learned a great many details about the functioning of sense-organs, muscular fatigue, drug-effects, the role of the glands in emotional disturbance, and so forth. But this is all physiology. The criteria by which we shall know that an experimental science of psychology exists are few and simple: (1) its generalizations must not be common sense knowledge, but genuinely novel inductions from experimental evidence; (2) its generalizations must be about specifically human operations and must be incapable of assimilation to physiology; (3) its generalizations must be compendant, i.e. they must hang together by sharing a few simple concepts, in the way in which the formulae of mechanics are rendered compendant by such concepts as time, space and mass. By this test experimental psychology is still in limbo, if it is in potentiality at all.

Dr. Crichton-Miller (*Psychoanalysis*, New York, 1933: p. 7) quotes William James as writing to James Sully in 1890 that "psychology is like physics before Galileo's time—not a single elementary law yet caught a glimpse of. A great chance for some future psychologue to make a name greater than Newton's; but who will then read the books of this generation? Not many, I trow." He adds, in comment, that forty years later William McDougall declared Freud to have done more for psychology than anyone since Aristotle. It is reasonable to suppose, he says, that James would have accepted Freud as the Newton he was looking for. (The comparability of Newton and Freud is also proposed by Dr. J. S. Van Teslaar, *An Outline of Psychoanalysis,* New York, 1924: p. 362.) Leaving comparisons aside, it is certainly true that the contribution of Freud to scientific psychology, as measured by criteria which William James seems to have shared, is genuine. Psychoanalysis is psychological science: it defines the scope of its subject-matter properly as man; its method is investigative; it is inductively fertile. Vd. Note 39b *supra.*

The only other genuine contribution is that made by psychometrics. It satisfies the same criteria. It can be viewed either as separate from what is ordinarily called experimental psychology or as including it, because all the metrical data gathered by psychological research can be used to apply mathematics to the quantitative accidents of human abilities and acts. In either view, psychometrics is an existing science of psychology. Two qualifications must be made, however: first, that psychometrics is applied mathematics and adds little conceptually to psychological analysis; second, that it presupposes the concepts of philosophical psychology,–which is concerned with the essence of human operation,–and is satisfied to make precise determinations of the quantitatively variable accidents. The formulae of psychometrics,–not only precise, but genuine contributions to knowledge,–are, like those of mathematical physics, functional statements. They do not, therefore, solve the aetiological problem. The psychometrician is not concerned with human behavior in the large or with its causes. He is in theory a faculty psychologist,–dread name for the doctrine of powers and acts, abilities and performances, –and in practice he is a mathematician who tries to make crude measurements approximate rational equations. The amazing thing is the degree to which he has succeeded in this effort. It is in the spirit of Fechner rather than of Wundt that psychological experimentation has proved fruitful,–the spirit of Fechner's method, but not of his Cartesian ideology. The latter has obscured the bloom. Perhaps, all of experimental psychology can be assimilated to psychometrics. This may be the meaning of Boring's effort in *The Physical Dimensions of Consciousness,* but it is vitiated by his inability to avoid or cure the chronic Cartesian affliction by substituting an ambiguous monism. To effect the consummation with clarity and without pretension the philosophical analysis which is faculty psychology must be explicitly recognized as providing the conceptual matrix for the mathematical formulations. I say "without pretension" because by such acknowledgment it will be conceded that psychometrics can add to the traditional account of the essence of human nature only the determination of accidental details. This, after all, is the business of empirical science in any field,—the description of phenomenal relationships. Vd. L. L. Thurstone, *Vectors of Mind*, Chicago, 1935: pp. 44–54 also C. Spearman, *The Abilities of Man*, New York, 1927: pp. 38–39. Spearman more than Thurstone recognizes that psychometrics employs the the concepts of faculty analysis, and is thus subordinated to philosophical psychology. Vd. Note 39a *supra.*

45a. The criterion of subject-matter is in some respects the best to use in searching for a science of psychology. We have already shown that a science, distinct from physiology, can be constituted only by taking human nature as its object. Philosophical psychology is similarly constituted. It approaches the essence of man in terms of an analysis of the proper powers flowing from that essence, and in the course of that analysis, it studies the relation of the powers in operation and habituation. Scientific knowledge, limited by method and in aim, to the phenomenal order, studies the accidental determinations or conditions of the powers in operation, and correlates observable relationships synchronically or diachronically. Scientific psychology may, of course, be either like mathematical physics or like the non-mathematical biological sciences.

All the errors and false starts of modern psychology can be stated in terms of misconceptions of subject-matter. Thus, philosophical psychology blocked itself as soon as it took for itself (1) the task of describing the states of the soul as a separate substance or (2) the task of describing, genetically or chemically, the contents of immediate experience or the elements of consciousness and their combination. In so far as investigators or experimenters accepted either of these definitions of their subject-matter, they too were doomed to fail in their effort to create a science of psychology. Out of the despair which was the inevitable consequence within the first half century of the experimental effort, were born the extreme reactions of behaviorism and animal psychology. But animal psychology, if it is a science, cannot be extended to man, despite the behaviorist's effort to do so. Behaviorism is thus either animal psychology or reducible to human physiology. The tremendous mass of experimental findings, common to all schools, can be assimilated to *one* psychology only by interpreting them somehow in the light of a unified subject-matter, the only possible subject-matter, man or human nature. The distinction of psychometrics and psychoanalysis is that they have taken this as their subject-matter. It should be added that human behavior is included in that subject-matter only if by "behavior" is meant the performances or acts of human abilities. Vd. 39b *supra.*

45b. The history of psychiatry should, of course, be told in relation to the history of psychology. Unfortunately, it is the least developed part of the history of medicine. The Noguchi Lectures of Dr. Gregory Zilboorg on *The Medical Man and the Witch During the Renaissance*

(Baltimore, 1935) are a substantial contribution to the subject,—intelligent scholarship to be extended, one hopes, to other periods, particularly the Greek and Hellenistic. Dr. Zilboorg points out that "psychology—that is, academic psychology—contributed little if anything to psychopathology. The process is here reversed in that medical psychology has always been the pioneer in the general field, stimulating the most important advances in the study of normal psychology" (p. 204). And thus writes Alibert: "La *psychopathologie* ou *psychologie morbide* a rendu et continue á rendre les plus grands services à la psychologie normale" (*La Psychologie Thomiste et les Théories Modernes*, Paris, 1903: p. 16). One must ask, therefore, whether the advance made by psychopathology in conceiving "mental disease" as a natural phenomenon does not impugn the adequacy of philosophical psychology.

So far as the organic psychoses are concerned, there is no problem. The pathology of the nervous system is of the same sort as other organic disorders. The mental aspect of these psychoses is to be understood in terms of the functional dependence of reason upon sense and imagination which are directly functions of bodily organs. St. Thomas recognized that the operation of reason is affected by an individual's organic condition, whether that be a matter of native temperament, fatigue or lesions. Vd. Note 19 *supra*. (This applies both to cognition and volition.) The functional psychoses,—dementia praecox, cyclothymia and paranoia,—are rapidly being assimilated to the organic group, and there is every reason to expect that medical research will discover their physical pathogenesis and conditions. It is inevitable that all mental disorders will eventually fall into two groups: organic diseases (the psychoses) and abnormalities of character (the neuroses). There is no middle ground. The so-called functional psychoses are at present anomalies due to ignorance. Cf. R. E. Brennan, *A Theory of Abnormal Cognitive Processes, According to the Principles of St. Thomas Aquinas*, Washington, 1925; and C. A. Dubray, *The Theory of Psychical Dispositions*, Washington, 1905: pp. 157 ff.

The analyses of the neuroses,—the determination of the types of character and the account of their development,—does not, of course, belong to philosophical psychology; in the ancient and mediaeval traditions, these problems belonged to ethics which depended for its theoretical principles upon psychology. Nor is there any question that we have made an advance in subjecting the neuroses to scientific study. Psychoanalysis is the great gift which practical medicine has made to psychology as a science. This advance does not alter any philosophical principles, however. It is clear that in the strict meaning of "disease" only the body can suffer lesions; the intellect as such cannot be diseased, though it can be affected by a diseased body. Abnormalities which are not strictly diseases are the results of habit formation, contrary to the *norms* of good conduct; in other words, vicious characters. Psychoanalysis has learned much by investigating the nature and development of moral character, but it has *discovered* nothing which is inconsistent with the principles of philosophical psychology, nor can it, either as knowledge or as therapy, ever be more than an aid to the moralist. Vd. Notes 61 and 62 *infra.*

That the modern history of psychiatry is a record of the struggle of scientific inquiry against the practices of the Church may be true, but it is not relevant to the point under discussion. That the Devil, being of angelic nature, can cause the movement of matter and thus be one,—but never the sole or sufficient,—cause of human activity is a theological doctrine. This doctrine is thoroughly compatible with all philosophical knowledge, but demonology is not in itself a part of philosophical psychology. Furthermore, it is as much beyond the power of scientific evidence to refute the existence of demons as to establish the existence of angels. Science, philosophy and theology view "mental disease" in terms of causes of different orders. Logically, there is no conflict between them; in fact, they are necessarily complementary. But this is not to say that actually and historically there were no conflicts between scientists and churchmen who exceeded the bounds of theological doctrine or who even converted what was merely theology into a dogma of faith. The Dominican Inquisitors who composed the *Malleus Maleficarum* were far from being good Thomists, and the ecclesiastical and temporal authorities who applied it in practice were equally far from being good Christians. It is not only psychiatry which has progressed since the days of Johann Weyer, but theology and the Church as well. Unfortunately, the kind of naive demonology which guided the Inquisitors in their efforts to extirpate witchcraft can still be found today among those psychoanalysts who have reified such analytical terms as complex and super-ego into demonic forces with which neurotics,—nay, all of us,—are supposed to be possessed. Historic roles are reversed. Today, the Thomist must exorcise the "demons" out of psychoanalytical theory. To do this the only instrument he needs is Ockham's razor. Vd. Notes 48 and 51 *infra.*

46. In the light of Note 45 *supra*, the text at this point requires a word of explanation. Unless the word "non-mathematical" is carefully noted, the statement that psychoanalysis is the *only* science of psychology is inconsistent with the acknowledgment that psychometrics is an inductively fertile field of experimental research, employing psychological concepts.

The honors must be divided between psychometrics and psychoanalysis, the one mathematical and experimental, the other non-quantitative and clinical. Both provide genuine contributions to our knowledge of man by means of investigative techniques. Neither is reducible to physiology. The three criteria which test the accomplishment of scientific knowledge in the field of psychology are satisfied, to some degree, by both. Psychometrics and psychoanalysis are related as the mathematical and the non-mathematical branches of physical science. Neither excludes the other or competes with the other in any way.

The interesting fact, which Lecture IV elucidates, is that the concepts of psychoanalysis, like those of psychometrics, are re-phrased versions of the traditional terminology of philosophical psychology,—the analysis of the powers of man and their operations. As psychometrics, employing these concepts, has added metrical determinations of the quantitatively variable accidents of human ability and action, and has embraced these determinations in functional statements of co-variation, so psychoanalysis has used the same concepts to formulate generalizations about human development and character differentiation, inductively extracted from a vast amount of clinical data. These generalizations are entirely qualitative: they are classificatory, or taxonomic, and physionomic, i.e. the formulation of secular alterations. Finally, psychoanalysis, no less than psychometrics, is not aetiological in the strict sense of that term. This is a limitation which arises from the very nature of scientific knowledge. Vd. Note 47 *infra*. But even in the sense in which scientific knowledge can be given a causal interpretation for the sake of practical applications, psychoanalysis,—in fact any scientific psychology,—fails. The failure is not due to any incompetence in scientific method or any lack of analytical skill in the interpretation of the evidence. The failure is the inevitable consequence of the fact that the subject-matter being investigated is human activity which, being voluntary, has reason for its essential cause. As psychometrics can do no more than study the quantitative accidents of this activity, so psychoanalysis must be content to study its biographical accidents. In either case, the knowledge, given an aetiological interpretation, throws light only on accidental causes. Success in an undertaking thus limited is appropriate glory for an empirical science.

For a discussion of the unity of psychology, achieved by the proper ordering of its philosophical and scientific domains, vd. Note 32a *supra*. In terms of this unity, peculiar to psychology, it will be seen that psychology is the only particular natural science which depends upon philosophy for its proper concepts and principles.

47. To understand the different problems of natural science, we must first distinguish between the mathematical and the non-mathematical types of science. The former aims to describe the phenomena in terms of functional formulations. That it eschews causes we have already seen. Vd. Note 13 *supra*. But mathematical physics is not only non-explanatory; it does not classify; it does not do morphological analysis; it does not describe changes in which time's arrow is real, i.e. secular trends. All the problems of a mathematical science are necessarily of the same sort because mathematics is undeviating in setting as the ideal the accomplishment of statements of the equational or

functional kind. As both Eddington and Jeans have pointed out, the aim is to express everything in differential equations. It is only in the non-mathematical natural sciences that different sorts of problems are genuinely discriminated. Since psychoanalysis is non-mathematical, these discriminations are a relevant concern.

The problems of the non-mathematical natural sciences cannot be understood except in terms of the concepts of the philosophy of nature. The possibility of classification is founded on the fact that whatever exists is specifically determined, i.e., is a substance possessing determinate characteristics, both essential and accidental. The possibility of morphological analysis is founded on the fact that substances as integral wholes are determinate organizations of parts. The possibility of temporal ordering arises from the fact that changes occur in regular sequences because individuals of a given species develop and change according to their determinate nature. But, as we have seen, natural science is not ontological knowledge. It does not apprehend substances; it does not employ real definitions. It must, therefore, transform concepts which are appropriate to the substantial order into concepts applicable to the phenomenal surface which science is able to investigate. The logic of science is not the Aristotelian logic of predication. That belongs properly to metaphysics and the philosophy of nature. Cassirer and Whitehead are right in so far as they insist upon the inapplicability of a predicational logic in scientific work. The logic of science is relational, and relational logic, in its non-quantitative form, is continuous with mathematical logic. The latter is, in a sense, a special case of relational logic. The non-mathematical natural sciences employ this general relational logic. Thus, substance is relationalized by the concepts of class, order and system. The phenomena can be classified, ordered, systematized by the principles of relational logic. Where the philosopher talks of substance, the scientist considers a persistent relational system, the structural form of which endures throughout substitutions of particular matter; where the philosopher is concerned with the attributes of substance, the scientist classifies relational systems; where the philosopher determines the integral parts of a substantial whole, the scientist distinguishes subordinate systems included in the relational structure of a larger system; where the philosopher discerns the uniform career of change which a substance undergoes because of its determinate nature, the scientist apprehends the relational transformations of system structure, distinguishing this serial pattern as a diachronic order of relations from the part-whole pattern as a synchronic order. (Whitehead's term "society" is the same in meaning as what is here called a "system." It is a relationalized version of substance. Vd. Note 25 *supra.*)

Two further points must be added. (1) Russell is right that scientific notions are conceptual constructions and not abstracted concepts. (Vd. *Our Knowledge of the External World*, Chicago, 1914.)

And (2) Bridgman is right that the empirical content of these notions is their reference to scientific operations and not ordinary perceptions or imaginations. The meaning of a scientific construction is determined by the operations it calls for. (Vd. *The Logic of Modern Physics*, New York, 1927.)

In short, the scientist deals only with the relations of phenomena; his conceptual schema, constructed entirely by a logic of relations, enables him to *impose or find* systems, classes and orders *on or in* nature. But which is it, impose *or* find? If he is a radical positivist, he will say "impose," almost in the manner of Kant. But since he will not attribute the imposition to a transcendental mind, science becomes for him conventional, using logical fictions which are practically expedient. If he is not an extreme positivist, or if he is a Platonist, he will say "find," holding that the relatedness of phenomena is a real interconnectedness, and that the discoveries of science are true or false according as they agree or not with what is independently the case. Such a scientist cannot avoid having a philosophy of nature. And he will either make the error of Whitehead, reifying the relational logic of science into a Heraclitean cosmology, in which the Ideas may be substituted for the Logos, or he will be guided by what is here the crucial principle, namely, that philosophy is knowledge of a different type, informed by a different logic. He will realize that the concept of substance is indispensable in the philosophy of nature as ontological knowledge and that a philosophy of nature, whose conceptual schema is constructed by Aristotelian logic, far from being incompatible with the aims and methodology of science, provides the only intelligible basis for the scientist's classifications and orderings of phenomena, if they are viewed as knowledge of an independent reality. The relations of phenomena are real connections, rooted in the determinate substantiality of the actual. Aristotelian science is bad for the same reason that "scientific cosmologies" are bad: both attempt to extend a logic, appropriate to one type of knowledge, to fields in which that logic is inapplicable. Similarly, Aristotelian philosophy is good for the same reason that modern science is good. As the former employs the logic of definition and predication for knowing the substance of things, so the latter employs the logic of relations for investigating phenomena. Contemporary issues which call upon us to choose between these logics, which ask us to adhere to science and forsake philosophy or which in the name of philosophy require a false apologetics for science, are obviously ungenuine. And just as obviously the modern synthesis is clear. It remains to be done. It will be done only when both scientists and philosophers learn the full wisdom of Maritain's principle: *distinguer pour unir*.

To return to the problems of the non-mathematical sciences: they are taxonomic (classification of relational systems), morphological (synchronic analysis: the part-whole ordering of inclusive and included systems), and physionomic (diachronic formulation: the secular ordering of systematic transformations). The taxonomic can be made to include the morphological as a special case. The latter is a classification of systems in terms of part-whole structure. Taxonomy, furthermore, is more than the mere identification of persistent systems; it involves the characterization of these systems in terms of relatively stable or unstable traits. (Scientific descriptions do not distinguish essence, property and accident, but the discrimination between universal laws and statistical generalizations is the relational analogue of the distinction among the predicables.) The transition from taxonomy, including morphology, to physionomy is a shift from a synchronic to a diachronic mode of ordering. Synchronic problems disregard change and time as its dimension. But this indicates that the separation of taxonomy and physionomy is only analytical. According as a system is of a certain type and structural form, so does it undergo systematic transformations; and conversely. (In the substantial order, one would say that according as a thing is, so does it change; its career of modification reveals its specific character.) Although the taxonomic and physionomic problems are correlative, they can be independently solved. As a matter of fact, however, they are seldom solved in complete independence of each other. Sciences which seem to be exclusively taxonomic and morphological, such as classificatory botany, zoology and anatomy, have a kind of partial autonomy, but they need to be completed by physionomic sciences, such as physiology and genetics. The latter sciences, of course, require the former. Lecture IV shows the correlation of the taxonomic and the physionomic phases of psychoanalytical research.

One problem remains. Can scientific knowledge be aetiological? Can science give an analysis of causes? The positivist rightly says No. The concept of cause is inextricably associated with the concept of substance. The notion of causality and the distinction of the four causes depends upon the concepts of actuality and potentiality and the distinctions of form and matter. Cause and substance belong together to the philosophy of nature. The same insight which excludes substance from natural science, must exclude causality. Since the days of Galileo, sciences of the mathematical type have restricted themselves to description. Explanation, in the sense of determining real causes, was clearly beyond their province. In the non-mathematical sciences, there is a relational substitute for causality, just as persistent system takes the place of substance. Uniform or at least usual sequences become the attenuated phenomenal substitute for causal relationship. The aetiological problem in science thus appears to be the same as the physionomic. Of course, the distinction of causes is lost, unless it be thought that vestiges of material and formal causality are retained in the part-whole analysis of morphology. Of all the causes, final cause seems most abhorrent to the scientist, although in the scientific reduction of causality to sequence the efficient is to the final cause as a beginning is to an end. In any event, it is clear that scientific knowledge of any field of phenomena is either mathematical and functional or non-mathematical and taxonomic, morphologic and physionomic. There is no aetiology in addition. If the scientist appears to talk or think causally, he does so by making the substitutions above indicated, but not by doing any further research or making new discoveries.

Yet the scientist cannot avoid talking or thinking in causal terms. The reason for this is that the scientist as an experimenter or investigator is also an artist or operator. Even though scientific knowledge is purely descriptive and does not *as such* contain knowledge of causes, the scientist must have such knowledge or he could not construct experiments in which he controlled certain conditions to produce certain effects. Because it is operational, all technology, including the art of research itself as well as the so-called applied sciences, presupposes an aetiology. But where does this aetiology come from if it is not strictly a part of scientific knowledge? The answer is that the man of common sense, the ordinary practical man, makes genuine causal determinations. He need not, like the philosopher, possess an analysis of the principle of causality and its relation to substance; he does not try to rise from a knowledge of proximate and instrumental causes to ultimate and principal causes; but he must, because he is a daily practitioner of one sort or another, know the causes of change in the things (substances) with which he deals. This knowledge of causes, being operative, is not an attenuated fiction. The kind of knowledge which the practical man of experience has of cause and substance is essentially the same as that which the philosophy of nature begins with and reflectively develops. And the scientist, as an operator in engineering or research, must use the same sort of knowledge. For all practical and productive purposes, the scientist can give his purely descriptive formulations a causal interpretation; he can convert his mathematical formulations into an aetiology by determining what is really the independent variable; he can translate his physionomy into a causal diagnosis or prediction by penetrating to relations of genuine efficiency beneath his secular trends. But it must be reiterated that the scientist does not make these conversions and translations as a *knower*, i.e., as a scientist, but only as a doer or maker. If the scientist could be merely a knower, he could avoid the concepts of substance and cause entirely. That he cannot avoid these concepts is due to the fact that scientific knowing involves real operations. Nevertheless, aetiology is no part of scientific knowledge, any more than ontology is. The scientist uses the concepts of substance and cause only when he must operate as any other practical man, and at that point his knowledge is of the same order. In exceptional cases, he may possess philosophical insight as well. The purity of theoretic natural science is that it is entirely descriptive in relational terms. The applied or practical sciences, such as engineering and medicine, are impure because they are aetiological and, therefore, require admixtures of common sense or philosophy. It is only because we sometimes permit their intimate relation to medicine to color them, that such sciences as physiology and pathology appear to be aetiological. In the strictly theoretic dimension, they are as purely descriptive as mathematical physics.

There is, of course, another sense in which the theoretic natural sciences are "explanatory," namely, by reference to phenomenal systems, described by other sciences and included as parts of the whole system which the science, making this reference, is investigating. Vd. Note 33a *supra*. This point does not alter the foregoing analysis. Cf. Dr. E. G. Salmon, *Physical Sciences and Causality*, Proceedings of the American Catholic Philosophical Association, 1936, pp. 117–123; also Dr. C. deC. DeKoninck, *Thomism and Scientific Indeterminism*, ibid, pp. 58–75.

48. Newton's famous dictum *Hypotheses non fingo* is repeated at the end of the *Opticks* (Book III, Q. 31) where, in discussing scientific method he says: "Hypotheses are not to be regarded in experimental philosophy." The word "hypothesis" has two traditional meanings which have for long made Newton's remark an almost unintelligible puzzle. (1) The sense in which Euclid speaks of an hypothesis, i.e. the knowledge which is available, through assumption or prior demonstration, for the solution of a given problem. (2) The sense in which the word has come to be used in investigative science. An hypothesis is a hypothetical proposition, in the form 'if P, then Q.' Such propositions constitute problems when they challenge us to establish the connection between P and Q. The theorems in Euclid are hypothetical propositions to be demonstrated. In this sense, every well formulated scientific problem is an hypothesis, a hypothetical proposition to be established or refuted by the evidence. The first meaning of hypothesis is involved also, since what the scientist already knows, —that which is given as the condition of the problem's solution,—is indispensable to the formulation of the problem and to the determination of what evidence will be relevant to its being solved. Scientists certainly employ hypotheses, in the first sense, and make hypotheses, in the second. Only in strictly exploratory research,—which is far from the ideal of scientific method,—does the scientist proceed without hypotheses. The ideal is quite opposite to this: research is good in proportion as all its hypotheses,—its conditions and its problems,—are explicitly defined.

What, then, did Newton mean by *Hypotheses non fingo?* There are two clues, one from etymology, the other from the context of Newton's writings. The word "hypothesis" has traditionally a logical significance. The closely related word "hypostasis" has traditionally an ontological significance. An hypostasis is a substance, that which underlies accidents and change as their subject. While no one who was well instructed in the philosophical tradition could confuse these two words, their closely related Greek roots make it possible for a modern scientist, even one of Newton's stature, to do so. That in fact he did so is evidenced by his attack on Descartes for making hypotheses in the sense of postulating what Newton called "occult substances" and "occult causes" to explain the phenomena of nature, e.g., the vortices. Newton was right in principle; he was insisting upon the positivism of science. Experimental philosophy, i.e., investigative science, is not concerned with the substance of things or their causes; it is concerned with accidents, mainly quantitative variables, with phenomenal change and its covariations or secular trends. Descartes did confuse the problems of philosophy and science in his physical writings. Unfortunately so did Newton. A man who really understood the sense in which a scientist does not, should not, make hypotheses would not have postulated the "aether" to "explain" the phenomena of light. Vd. *Opticks*, Book III, QQ. 18–24.

Philosophers do not *assume* or *postulate* substances or causes. The nature of substances and the analysis of causes is properly the field of philosophical knowledge. But when a scientist goes beyond his empirical evidence to make "hypostases" or to discover "occult" causes, he is guessing and, worse than that, he is violating the principles and scope of scientific investigation. The history of science is full of such violations, from Descartes and Newton to Darwin and Freud. Ockham's razor has been used by modern scientists to decimate metaphysics entirely, but it has too often not been used to cut off the growth of fictitious entities that have reified on the face of science.

49. Vd. Notes 13 and 47 *supra*.

50. While psychoanalysts cannot study the operations of reason essentionally, they can throw some light upon the external circumstances and accidental causes of rational behavior. The essential cause of any specifically human act is reason, but it is not the sole cause. To the extent that psychoanalytical observations have discovered the way in which environmental circumstances and biographical factors determine the conflict between reason and the passions, to the extent that the interpretation of the clinical data has isolated the predisposing conditions of irrationality, psychoanalysis has made a contribution to the aetiology of human activity. Just as the kind of "practical aetiology" which is involved in psychometrics can be useful in educational administration to allocate pupils and to apply the principles of pedagogy, so the kind of "practical aetiology" which is involved in psychoanalysis can be useful to the medical practitioner and the moralist. Vd. Note 47 *supra*. It is important to remember in both these cases that the scientific knowledge is inadequate because, even in the practical dimension, it deals only with accidental causes. The principles of pedagogy and of morality must include the kind of knowledge of man which only philosophical psychology can provide. The radical

flaw in contemporary educational practice can be traced to the kind of educational psychology which dominates our teachers' colleges and our schools of education. It is entirely scientific and, therefore, pathetically inadequate. The same can be said for much of contemporary morality, and particularly the sort that has been foisted on the world by behaviorism and psychoanalysis. Vd. Notes 24, 32 *supra*, and 61, 62 *infra*.

51. "In our opinion a presentation which seeks to estimate, not only the *topographical* and *dynamic*, but also the economic element, is the most complete that we can at present imagine, and deserves to be distinguished by the term *meta-psychological*" (Freud, *Beyond the Pleasure Principle*, London, 1922: p. 1). By the economic element Freud means the quantitatively variable factor of psychic tension that is related to the avoidance of pain and the production of pleasure. Cf. F. Alexander, *The Psychoanalysis of the Total Personality*, New York, 1930.

But the use of the word "metapsychology" is not fully explained by the statement that this part of psychoanalysis is concerned with the "total personality," that it is the most complete account that can be given. The metapsychological papers are more "theoretical," in what for a scientist is the bad sense of that word, than other monographs written by Freud and his students. It may be insisted that the metapsychology consists of the most general inductions from clinical data, but a careful logical examination of the documents will not support this doctrinaire effort to make all of psychoanalysis scientific. *Beyond the Pleasure Principle*, for example, reveals Freud as making hypotheses in the sense in which Newton said no scientist should make them. At the end Freud says: "We wish to make it clear that the uncertainty of our *speculation* is enhanced by the necessity of *borrowing* from biological science. Biology is truly a realm of limitless possibilities; we have the most surprising revelations to expect from it, and cannot conjecture what answers it will offer in some decades to the questions we have put to it. Perhaps they may be such as to overthrow the whole *artificial* structure of *hypotheses*. If that is so, someone may ask why does one undertake such work as the one set out in this article, and why should it be communicated to the world? Well, I cannot deny that some of the *analogies*, relations and connections therein traced appeared to me worthy of *consideration*" (*Op. cit.*, p. 78). Italics mine. This is not the way a scientist talks about the inductions he has obtained from the data of his investigations. It is rather the way Newton talks, as a guesser and "speculator," in the Queries appended to his *Opticks*. There Newton was being a "meta-physician" in the bad sense of that word which means "guessing beyond the evidence." Here Freud is being a "meta-psychologist." Furthermore, Freud's references to biology should be noted, because they indicate that he is guessing beyond the evidences of biological science, as well as exceeding the significance of his own clinical data.

The metapsychological writings contain two quite different kinds of material. On the one hand, there is the analysis of the structure of the soul (topography), of the functional interdependence of its parts (dynamics), and of the fundamental principles of psychic operation (economics). On the other hand, there is a variety of speculations about ultimate origins and causes which are fanciful conjectures, fruits of the myth-making power of evolutionary biology. That Freud himself recognized this difference,—though not in these terms,—is clear from his opening remarks in *The Ego and the Id* (London, 1928): "In my essay, *Beyond the Pleasure Principle*, published (in German) in 1920, I began the discussion of a train of thought, my personal attitude toward which, as I mentioned there, might be described as a sort of benevolent curiosity; in the following pages this train of thought is developed further. I have taken up those *ideas* and brought them into connection with various *facts observed* in psychoanalysis and have endeavored to draw *fresh conclusions* from the combination; in the present work, however, no further contributions are *levied from biology, and it consequently stands in a closer relation to* psychoanalysis than does *Beyond the Pleasure Principle.* The thoughts contained in it are *synthetic* rather than *speculative* in character, and their aim appears to be an ambitious one. I am aware, however, that they do not go beyond the baldest outlines and I am perfectly content to recognize their limitations in this respect" (*Op. cit.*, pp. 7–8). Italics mine, to indicate, first, that neither book is simply the product of investigative science, and second, that the difference between them is a difference between evolutionary speculations and a psychological analysis which may be sound even though it is not scientific.

The two parts of the metapsychology can be distinguished as Freud's philosophical psychology and his "speculative opinions." Neither is strictly *based* on scientific evidence in the sense in which a scientific induction is a generalization that is derived from the data. That Freud writes his philosophical psychology as if he were interpreting clinical data is intelligible in the light of his positivistic prejudices against philosophy, but his language cannot deceive us if we scrutinize the analysis and examine the data. Furthermore, a sound philosophical analysis of the structure and operations of the soul should be applicable to the clinical evidence as well as to the facts of common experience. That it is so applicable indicates nothing about its mode of derivation. It may even be that Freud obtained his philosophical insights from his clinical studies, as in the great tradition of psychology, those same insights were obtained by other men in the light of common experience. If Freud had had a greater knowledge of that tradition, he might have demonstrated the truth of his claim that "priority and originality are not among the aims which psychoanalysis sets itself" (*Beyond the Pleasure Principle:* p. 2). He would have found more in that tradition which anticipated his chief tenets than the myth which Plato puts into the mouth of Aristophanes in the *Symposium*. Vd. *op. cit.*, p. 74–75. If he had understood the way in which common experience is the source of philosophical analysis, he might not have had to apologize for his speculations by saying that he could not work out these ideas "except by combining facts with pure imagination many times in succession, and thereby departing far from observation" (*Ibid.*, p. 77). He would have been able to distinguish between the certainty of philosophical knowledge and those "speculative opinions" of which he felt obliged to say: "Self criticism does not render obligatory any special tolerance of divergent opinions. One may inexorably reject theories that are contradicted by the very first steps in the analysis of observation, and yet at the same time be aware that those one holds oneself have only a tentative validity" (*Ibid.*, p. 77).

That part of the metapsychology is sound which can be understood in the light of common experience and which, for the most part, can be translated into the analytical terms of the traditional anthropology of Aristotle and St. Thomas. That part which is sound is, therefore, not novel or original, for the most part, except in vocabulary. (The outstanding exception is the concept of repression. This is a genuine contribution to philosophical psychology. Vd. Note 55 *infra.*) The rest is either a perpetuation of the errors of Descartes which Freud learned from Fechner or, what is worse, "speculations" which are neither scientific nor philosophical knowledge. They are not even errors in philosophical analysis of the Cartesian sort. They are myths and fancies, guesses about "occult substances and causes", opinions which violate Ockham's principle that a scientist should not reify his imaginations or multiply hidden causes and convert them into a demonology. Vd. Note 48 *supra.* It is not surprising that the greatest novelty of the Freudian doctrine should be in the opinionative part of the metapsychology.

In writing of the metapsychology, I have considered those articles which the editors of Freud's *Collected Papers* have assembled under that head in Volume IV; also Papers XXI–XXIV of Volume II, and the separate monographs *Beyond the Pleasure Principle*, *The Ego and the Id*, *Group Psychology and the Analysis of the Ego*.

52. The parts of the body are organs. The parts of the soul are powers. As the whole soul is related to the body as the actuality of its organic potentiality for life, so the parts of the soul are the powers of the particular organs. They are not the acts of the potentialities of these particular organs, because these organs are not always active, as the body is alive actually as long as it is besouled. The parts of the body are sensible, physical things and are, therefore, capable of being known directly by observation. But powers cannot be observed. Nothing which is not fully actual can be observed. Our knowledge

of the powers of a body is the result of inference from the operations or changes which we can observe. Men are sufficiently acquainted through common experience with their own operations or changes to make an adequate division of the powers which constitute the parts of the soul. Anatomical division and classification, especially the histological, requires investigation. Psycho-topography does not. Furthermore, what many psychoanalysts like to suppose is not the case, namely, that Freudian topography is to the traditional analysis of the powers of man as histology is to gross anatomy. (It should be noted here that the way in which Freud "discovers" the unconscious is precisely the mode of inference which Aristotle and St. Thomas employ in passing from the operations to the powers. Freud, unfortunately, speaks of "assuming" rather than inferring, and reifies what he assumes. Vd. *New Introductory Lectures on Psychoanalysis*, New York, 1933: pp. 99–100. The modern attack upon the faculties proceeds in terms of Ockham's razor. But this, as we have seen, is due to a misconception of the faculties, as substantial agents rather than powers, active or passive. Locke's attack is much more applicable to Freudian writing which does appear to reify the parts of the psyche and to speak of them as if they were agents rather than psychic properties. The Freudian reifications can be corrected by the translation we have made of these parts into powers.)

Although both topography and what I have called the psychoanalyst's taxonomy are classificatory, they can be as readily distinguished as classificatory botany, which groups varieties of organisms, and anatomy, which classifies the parts of an organism of a given species. (Morphology is a kind of classification. Vd. Note 47 *supra.*)

53. The genetic problem, as the Freudian states it, consists of a set of questions which are intelligible only in terms of the myth of evolution. I say "myth" in order to refer to the elaborate conjectural history, which vastly exceeds the scientific evidence in the fields of genetics, palaeontology, comparative anatomy, geology and geography. This myth is the story of evolution which is told to school children and which they can almost visualize as if it were a moving picture. It is the concoction of such evolutionary "philosophers" as Herbert Spencer, Ernst Haeckel and Henri Bergson, as well as the invention of popularizers of science.

Questions about the origin of life or of various psychological structures are clearly historical, and neither scientific nor philosophical. If there is any philosophical question involved in all this discussion, it is a question about God, Creation and Providence which the well-disciplined philosopher knows is, for the most part, beyond the scope of natural theology. Only those modern thinkers, such as the Freudians and the Marxians, whose faith is the religion of evolution, can answer such questions dogmatically. They know all the answers in a way that no Christian theologian ever pretended to know them. Although Darwin confused the 19th century badly by the preposterous issue he agitated between evolution and "special creation", he at least recognized some limits to scientific knowledge and historical conjecture about ultimate origins.

In the case of individual development, the Freudian also uses the evolutionary myth. He analogizes ontogeny and phyologeny in the light of Haeckel's "biogenetic law". He supposes that the soul evolves from its primitive seed in the *id*, as the forms of life have come from some undifferentiated primary plasm. It is clear that this supposition outruns both scientific evidence and common experience. The genetic problem thus formulated can, therefore, be neither scientific nor philosophical. As Freud unwittingly indicated, it is a challenge to the myth-maker of an Aristophanic sort. Vd. *Beyond the Pleasure Principle*, New York, 1922: pp. 72–76.

Dr. Van Teslaar, discussing the significance of psychoanalysis, declares the contribution of Freud to be as revolutionary as Darwinism. Freud's addition of a "genetic, developmental, evolutionistic viewpoint" to psychology has resulted in "as radical a transformation of all branches of psychology as that which Darwin has inaugurated in the biological sciences." Dr. Van Teslaar acknowledges that much scientific criticism has been directed against Haeckel's biogenetic law, but insists that the facts support recapitulation. He adds: "Freud's discovery shows that in the course of its development the individual mind repeats racial history. The details of Freud's work amounts to a restatement of the recapitulation theory applied to the biologic history of mind. For the first time there has been disclosed to us the manner in which psychic recapitulation operates and its consequences" (*An Outline of Psychoanalysis*, New York, 1934: p. 375).

53a. The most compact statement of Freudian topography and dynamics is to be found in the lecture on The Anatomy of the Mental Personality in the *New Introductory Lectures on Psychoanalysis*, New York, 1933. Here Freud distinguishes and attempts to define the id, the ego and the super-ego, and shows that these divisions must not be confused with the distinctions of unconscious, pre-conscious, repressed unconscious. Cf. Healy, Bronner and Bowers, *The Structure and Meaning of Psychoanalysis*, New York, 1930: pp. 22–57; also pp. 192–267. For an equally compact statement of the traditional philosophical account of the powers of man and their cooperative inter-dependence, vd. St. Thomas Aquinas, *Summa Theologica*, I, QQ. 77–83. Anyone who can read the Freudian and Thomistic texts with ability to discern analytical equivalence beneath seemingly incommensurable vocabularies, can make in full the kind of translation which I briefly indicated in Lecture IV.

54. Vd. St. Thomas Aquinas, *Summa Theologica*, I, QQ. 80–82; I–II, Q. 17, AA. 7–9. "Some acts proceed from the natural appetite,

others from the animal, and others from the intellectual appetite" (I–II, Q. 17, A. 8). Cf. I–II, Q. 1, A. 2; Q. 6, A. 4. The natural appetite of animals consists of the tendencies of the various powers to the performance of their proper acts. This holds for sense and intellect as well as for the vegetative powers. There is, however, some justification for thinking of natural appetite especially in connection with these latter powers, because their operation is not determined directly by cognition or subject to will. If we regard natural appetite narrowly in the sphere of the vegetative as the inclination of these powers to their fulfilling operations, the concept thus restricted is equivalent to what in modern terms is the concept of biological needs, the basic urges or drives.

The remaining appetites, i.e., animal and human, are cognitively determined, by sense and intellect respectively. The difference between need and desire can be stated clearly in terms of the difference indicated between natural and cognitively determined appetites. A need is a biological want, arising from some condition of the vegetative organs. It is an indeterminate tendency to action, having no *particular* object as its goal. Thus, hunger, fatigue, sexuality are needs. A desire is a tendency toward a particular object, known through sense or intellect. The sensitive desires are, in large part, related to animal needs, as the desire for this morsel of food is related to hunger. Sensitive desires are acts of bodily organs; intellectual desires, the acts of will, are not. Sensitive desires cannot be reduced to needs. It is obvious that we often seek to possess an object of sensuality which we do not need. The problem of the nature of appetite,–whether it is a single power of the soul embracing the three forms here distinguished, whether the natural appetite is primary and the cognitively determined appetites are developments therefrom, whether there is any power of appetite, other than the natural, which is antecedent to sensitive and intellectual determinations,–consists of questions difficult to answer. But the facts of experience are clear and they require us to distinguish between indeterminate needs and definite desires. To ask why objects have a tendential mode of being for man, i.e., are objects of appetite when known, is as impossible a question as to ask why objects have an intentional mode of being, i.e., are objects of knowledge. Cf. Freud, *Instincts and Their Vicissitudes* (1915), and *The Unconscious* (1915) in *Collected Papers*, IV, London, 1925.

55. In view of the fact that "consciousness" was not a technical term in psychological doctrine until the late 18th century, it is not surprising that Aristotle and St. Thomas did not discuss "the unconscious". The Freudian can claim to have made an advance over the associationist and introspective psychologies which examined only the contents of consciousness, but he cannot extend this claim against the traditional philosophical analysis in which the basic terms are

power, habit and operation. On the contrary, if his conception of the unconscious is to be saved from reification as a level, province or structural part of the psyche, the Freudian must be freed from the prepossessions of 19th century psychology in which consciousness was entitized. It is not to anticipations in Leibnitz and Herbart, von Hartmann and Schopenhauer, that one must turn if one seeks a thoroughly analytical understanding of unconsciousness, but rather to the traditional doctrine of faculties. A Thomistic rendering of the unconscious will not only clarify the Freudian theory, but will show that the metapsychology is a poorly expressed version of this philosophical analysis. (It should be repeated here that a contemporary Thomist, such as Alibert, claims the superiority of Thomistic analysis over modern philosophical psychology to be precisely the fact that it includes the unconscious. Vd. Note 39b *supra.*)

In the first place, it is necessary always to replace the substantive words, "consciousness" and "unconsciousness" by adjectival or adverbial forms. Modes of potentiality and operation are being distinguished, not modes of being. In order to make the Thomistic translation, it is then necessary to consider how an Aristotelian would use the words "conscious" or "consciously" if he were to introduce them into a psychological exposition. The answer is simple and clear. That operation is conscious which is the act of a cognitive power, either sense or intellect; and that operation occurs consciously which, while not an act of cognition, participates in actual cognition; thus, either an act of sensitive appetite, a passion or emotion, or an act of will. (So a Freudian would say that ideational activity is conscious or that desires occur consciously in so far as they have ideational representation.) We can now ask to what "unconscious" and "unconsciously" apply. To answer this question, we must first distinguish between the primary use of the word "conscious", exclusively applicable to acts of cognition, and a derivative use to qualify objects cognized. Thus, the object which we know or desire, i.e. of which we are conscious, is said to be a conscious object or end. In the same way, there is a primary use of the word "unconscious" to distinguish all non-cognitive operations, such as the purely vegetative and locomotive; and a derivative use to qualify whatever cannot be directly cognized. Now, neither a power nor a habit is a direct object of sense or of intellectual apprehension. All powers and habits, including those of cognition itself, are therefore said to be unconscious in this derivative sense. Vd. *Summa Theologica*, I, Q. 87, AA. 1–3.

But, the Freudian will at once object, this is superficial, even though true. The psychological significance of the unconscious is that it is dynamic. A power of the soul, called "unconscious" because not an object of immediate cognition, is no different from an atom or an angel in this respect. The Freudian is right. We must proceed, therefore, to another conception of the unconscious, namely, as a mode of operation defined without reference to cognition. Here we must distinguish power, habit and activity according to their grades of actuality. A vital power is not a pure potentiality. It exists as the property of a living substance; it is a determinate accident. As possessing some actual being, a power also possesses a proportionate degree of operation. In so far as a thing is actual it can act. The essence of a power is an actual inclination to a particular mode of activity. If the power is a passive power it must be acted upon before it is fully actualized in activity, but short of such actualization, it is still an actual power and, as such, an energetic inclination, a dynamic disposition. If we use the phrase "perfect operation" for those acts which are determined by particular objects, then we can speak of the powers, actual tendencies not thus determined, as imperfectly operative. Powers are energetic factors in behavior because they are operative, though imperfectly. They are one part of what the Freudian means by the dynamic unconscious. To the extent that its behavior is directed by its powers, an organism behaves unconsciously.

Habits are another part of the dynamic unconscious. In the ordinary meaning of the word, a habit is acquired by the actual exercise of a power. Once acquired, the habit exists as a modification of the power. It is more determinate than the power because it has been formed by acts determined to particular objects, but less determinate than these acts because it regards only the species of these objects. In other words, a habit is not a perfect operation but only a tendency to such operation; yet as a tendency it is more determinate than mere power. Thus, habits have more operative actuality than powers; though their mode of operation is imperfect, they are less imperfect. We know that habits exist in all degrees of strength, ranging from something more than the imperfection of power to something less than the complete actuality of perfect operation. In all these degrees, habits are actual; according to their degrees of actuality, they have energy and are, therefore, weaker or stronger energetic factors in behavior. This applies to habits of cognition as well as to habits of desire. We can be said to think or desire unconsciously to the extent that our thinking or appetition is affected by our habits.

An instinct is like a habit in that it is only a tendency to action rather than perfectly operative; it is not mere power because it is always relatively determinate, i.e. an inclination to a specific mode of behavior. As an energetic factor, instinct does not differ from habit. Habits of great strength so closely resemble instincts as operative tendencies that they are called "second nature". This indicates the difference between instincts and habits. An instinct is native and not acquired. Instinct can be defined as a natural habit. This is a difference in mode of origin, not mode of operation, yet it is related to the latter. The alteration of instincts is different from the alteration of habits; the latter are less stable and more modifiable. (In the lower animals, instincts remain largely unmodified; in man they are usually, if not always, overlaid with habit formations. In man, instincts are nothing more than vegetative needs.) For our present purposes, it suffices to point out that instinctive tendencies are energetic factors in behavior and are a part of what the Freudian calls the dynamic unconscious.

Perfect operations, i.e. particular, perfectly determinate acts, remain. These can be properly spoken of as operations, in contrast to powers, habits, instincts, which are only more or less indeterminate tendencies to operation. But, as we have seen, all operations are not conscious. At this point, cognition becomes the essential distinction between those operations which are conscious or occur consciously and those which do not. Operation, whether conscious or unconscious, can be a factor in behavior in two ways: (1) being fully actual, an act can communicate its energy by reducing what is in potentiality to act and, in this way, one operation can be the efficient cause of another; (2) an act can determine a power, alter the strength of a habit, modify an instinct. The only strictly conscious factors in behavior are thus seen to be those acts which are conscious (cognitions) or which occur consciously (involve cognitions). All the remaining factors in behavior,—powers, habits, instincts and acts which are not cognitive,—are unconscious. These others could not be factors in behavior unless they had some actuality, the actuality of tendency if not the actuality of perfect operation. This actuality is the energy of the unconscious. And, furthermore, it is clear that no behavior is ever determined by conscious factors alone. The Freudian is right in comparing the proportions of conscious and unconscious energy to the visible and submerged portions of an iceberg. This quantitative fact must not, however, be misinterpreted. In the order of powers, reason is most perfect; in the order of factors, operation is more perfect than habit, i.e. has more actuality, as habit is more perfect than power. Conscious operation, and particularly rational operation or operation involving reason, is the prime factor in human behavior. Since habits are formed by operations, we can further distinguish habits which have been formed by rational operation from all other habits which are mere bodily dispositions. The former are more significant unconscious factors in human behavior than the latter.

So far we have done no more than to translate the imaginative language of Freud into the clear concepts of Thomistic psychology. (Freud, at one place, defines a process as unconscious "when we have to assume that it was active *at a certain time*, although *at that time* we knew nothing about it;" but then, a little later, he adds that the unconscious is a "mental province rather than a quality which mental things have." Vd. *New Introductory Lectures on Psychoanalysis*, New York, 1933: pp. 99–102.) But there is a further step in analysis which marks an original contribution made by Freud. Although it can be translated into Thomistic terms, the psychological insight conveyed by the concept of repression seems to be an addition to the traditional understanding of the relation of reason to the passions.

Freud says that "the essence of the process of repression lies, not in abrogating or annihilating the ideational presentation of an instinct, but in withholding it from becoming conscious" (*The Unconscious* in *Collected Papers*, London, 1925: IV, p. 98; vd. also the essay on *Repression*). Repression must be sharply differentiated from such inhibitive processes as renunciation or conscious abandonment of a tendency. I am indebted to Dr. Alexander for the statement of repression as a specific form of control mainly characteristic of the infantile personality, excluding certain tendencies not only from motility but from consciousness. It is due to the fact that the infantile or the weak ego cannot stand the temptation, and therefore the tendencies, in order to be checked, must be excluded not only from motor expression but also from consciousness. Repressed tendencies do not lose their dynamic efficiency, but express themselves through substitutive vents (symptoms), and they remain conserved in the unconscious in their original form. Being repressed they cannot undergo those modifications which are called sublimation (domestication of original non-adjusted tendencies). Freud stresses this last point, "that the repressed remains unaltered by the passage of time" (*New Introductory Lectures*, p. 105).

We must separate the fact of repression from the explanation of the origin and effects of repression. The fact of repression is best understood by distinguishing the repressed unconscious from both the pure unconscious and the pre-conscious. The pure or original unconscious consists of those unconscious factors in behavior which we have called powers and instincts; to these might be added all purely bodily dispositions and unconscious acts. The pre-conscious consists of those habits which are tendencies to conscious operation, habits either of cognition or desire. As factors in overt behavior or thought, they are unconscious, but they can also become conscious, e.g., the transition of an idea from memory to actual consideration. The repressed unconscious consists of the same sort of habits as the preconscious. Only tendencies to conscious operation can be repressed because repression is exclusion from consciousness of what, were it not for repression, would naturally occur as conscious operation. Repression does not destroy the habit which it bars from normal operation and development. The habit retains all its energetic efficiency as an unconscious factor in behavior and is not susceptible to alteration in the same way that normally operative habits are. Repressed ideas are those which we will not consider, but they remain in the memory, nevertheless, and have operative tendency. Herbart discussed repression in terms of the incompatibility of ideas. This is insufficient. The permanence of repression can be accounted for only as a habit of the will not to consider certain ideas. Acts of understanding, i.e., actual consideration, are within the power of the will. The will, like any other power, is subject to habituation. Repression must, therefore, be defined as a habit of the will not to consider a certain idea, and the idea which is the content of this habit belongs to the repressed unconscious in distinction from the pre-conscious memory.

The repression of desires, i.e., habits of the passions, is more complicated. It depends upon ideational repression because these habits are formed by conscious operation, involving the intellect. Emotional or appetitive habits exist as tendencies toward or away from objects which can be ideationally represented. Repression here consists in the exclusion of such representation. But the conative tendency, which may have a deep instinctive origin, remains with all the energy possessed by the habit according to its strength. As unconscious factors in behavior, such repressed habits can influence bodily dispositions and operations as well as conscious activities of thought or desire. In this respect they do not differ from other habits. But because they are repressed and are prevented from normal operation, their influence is indirect and by means of all sorts of substitutions. Symptomatic actions, dreams, wishful thinking are good examples of the influence of repressed factors. What is most important of all is that repressed habits are not subject to modification by conscious operation. Though the will was involved in the conscious formation of these habits, the will is barred by its own habit of repression from further direct control or modification.

The explanation of repression requires us to understand the nature of the will as intellectual appetite determined by the rational estimate of things as good and evil. "In popular language," Freud says, "the ego stands for reason and circumspection, while the id stands for the untamed passions" (*New Introductory Lectures*, p. 107). "The id knows no values, no good and evil, no morality" (*Op. cit.*, p. 105). It is the ego which is the agency of repression. But within the ego, reason and will must be distinguished. The will is moved by the reason in so far as the rational consideration of objects is the ground for approval or disapproval. Inadequate knowledge may, of course, result in wrong estimates of good and evil. But even if the estimates be right, the will may not be able to cope with the strength of the passions tending toward what should be avoided. The traditional analysis here goes no further than the distinction between the successful operation of the will in forming habits of desire in accordance with reason (the virtues) and the failure of the will with the consequence of undisciplined habits (the vices). It is at this point that the concept of repression extends the analysis. The pain of failure may cause the will to withdraw from its conflict with the passions. This withdrawal becomes repression when the will moves the reason not to consider the objects to which the passions tend. The repressed habits are not only undisciplined but, by the habit of the will itself, become free from subjection to reason. They are, therefore, worse than ordinary vices because they are vices which cannot be directly cured by ordinary rational or educative methods. They are protected from criticism by a vicious habit in the will itself. Repression can be defined as the vice of a will lacking fortitude in its relation to the passions. Repression is not the cause of moral vice; it is, on the one hand, the result of moral vice, and, on the other, the cause of its perpetuation. The cure of neurosis which, though Freudians do not admit it, is the beginning of moral reformation, must attack repression as the primary obstacle to the rectifying work of reason in the discipline of the passions. The will must be strengthened by a removal of the fears and resistances which underlie repression. The attack upon repression must be oblique because the habit of the repressive will prevents a direct appeal to reason. Such oblique attack is the essence of psychoanalytic therapy. Though the path is through the passions, through the gradual understanding of their objects and hence the reduction of repression, the goal is the restoration of reason, by means of a cooperating will, to its proper role of regulation in human life. The inaccessible portions of the id thus become open to the ego. Freud describes psychoanalysis as a work of reclamation. Its object is to strengthen the ego, to widen its field of vision, "so to extend its organization that it can take over new portions of the id. Where id was, there shall ego be" (*Op. cit.*, p. 112). How close this is to the goal of morality may be judged from Freud's further statement of the ideal that "the intellect–the scientific spirit, reason–should in time establish a dictatorship over the human mind. The very nature of reason is a guarantee that it would not fail to concede to human emotions and to all that is determined by them, the position to which they are entitled" (*Op. cit.*, p. 234). Not a dictatorship, but the *just* rule of reason is the condition of good human life. Cf. Notes 61 and 62 *infra*.

For a discussion of the relation of reason and the passions, vd. Note 57 *infra*. For an examination of the concept of the unconscious in the light of the traditional psychology, vd. G. Dwelshauvers, *Traité de Psychologie*, Paris, 1928. Cf. *L'Inconscient*, Paris, 1919. Also, C. M. Dubray, *The Theory of Psychical Dispositions*, Washington, 1905: pp. 157 ff.

56. It has been objected that this translation of the Aristotelian and Freudian vocabularies is superficial, and purely verbal. This objection is based on the ground that the special experience achieved by investigative science is much more complete and adequate in detail than the common experience upon which philosophical knowledge rests. Thus, it can be said that although both Democritus and Dalton used the word "atom", the concept of the former is "purely speculative" whereas the concept of the latter can be referred to many careful observations. It is true that pre-scientific speculations in regard to questions which are essentially scientific are incommensurable

with answers which result from investigation. Thus, popular notions about the causes of disease, based on ordinary experience, must give way before the science of pathology, because such questions by their very nature call for research. Democritus was not a scientist in our modern sense of that word. He was a philosopher. Dalton was a chemist. The word "atom" clearly does not mean the same thing for Democritus and Dalton. The questions Dalton answered cannot be answered by common experience or by philosophical analysis. But the questions Democritus did answer are not affected in any way by scientific evidence. Atomistic materialism,—a philosophical and not a scientific doctrine,—is the same in the 19th century as it was in the 5th century B.C. So far as Dalton was a materialist, as well as a chemist, he did not improve upon Democritus.

The situation in psychology is unique, because psychology is the only field of subject-matter that is at once scientific and philosophical. In so far as Freud is answering philosophical questions about man, all the clinical data at his command are logically irrelevant. In so far as Freud is answering scientific questions,—is solving the problems of taxonomy and physionomy,—the data are extremely relevant and should certainly be the source of better answers than those which can be given by common sense or by pre-scientific speculations in regard to such questions. The issue turns, therefore, on whether the points under review in this translation are philosophical or scientific. The question cannot be begged by denying the existence of a philosophical psychology, i.e. by asserting that *all* questions about man are exclusively scientific. I have attempted carefully to distinguish those problems in regard to which psychoanalysis can proceed scientifically, and those in regard to which it cannot. The problem of the structure of the soul is clearly not a scientific question. That is the problem on which Freud and Aristotle are being compared.

What is said above applies equally to the translation of Freud and Aristotle on the problem of the functional relationship of the various powers of the soul, i.e., the dynamic problem.

57. The following texts should be noted. "As the Philosopher says (*Politics*, I, 2) the reason, in which resides the will, moves by its command, the irascible and concupiscible powers, not, indeed, by a *despotic sovereignty*, as a slave is moved by his master, but by a *royal and politic sovereignty*, as free men are ruled by their governor and can nevertheless act counter to his commands. Hence both the irascible and concupiscible powers can move counter to the will, and accordingly nothing hinders the will from being moved by them at times" (*Summa Theologica*, I–II, Q. 9, A. 3, ad. 3). Cf. *Summa Theologica*, I–II, Q. 17, A. 17. "Whence it is that we experience that the irascible and concupiscible powers do resist reason, inasmuch as we sense or imagine something pleasant, which reason forbids, or unpleasant, which reason commands. But from the fact that the irascible

and concupiscible resist reason in something, we must not conclude that they do not ever obey" (*Summa Theologica*, I, Q. 81, A. 3, ad. 2). "The passion of the sensitive appetite moves the will, in so far as the will is moved by its object, inasmuch as, to wit, man through being disposed in such and such a way by a passion, judges something to be fitting and good, which he would not judge thus were it not for the passion. Now this influence of a passion on man occurs in two ways. First, so that his reason is wholly bound, so that he has not the use of reason: as happens in those who through a violent access of anger or concupiscence become furious or insane, just as they may from some other bodily disorder. . . . Sometimes, however, the reason is not entirely engrossed by the passion, so that the judgment of reason retains, to a certain extent, its freedom; and thus the movement of the will remains in a certain degree. Accordingly, in so far as the reason remains free, and not subject to the passion, the will's movement, which also remains, does not tend of necessity to that whereto the passion inclines. Consequently, either there is no movement of the will in that man, and passion alone holds sway; or if there be a movement of the will, it does not necessarily follow the passion" (*Summa Theologica*, I–II, Q. 10, A. 3).

In these and many other passages, St. Thomas formulates the relation of passion to reason and will. The only alternatives considered seem to be the dominance of the passions by reason, or the subordination of the will to the passions. Freud adds another course: repression, the willful withdrawal of reason from the conflict. Vd. Note 55 *supra*. The nearest approach to this psychological insight is made by Aristotle in his consideration of the incontinent man who is led by his emotions to do what he *knows* to be wrong. Incontinence becomes repression when the passions further lead one to ignore what one knows, if such knowledge would require reason to oppose passions over which the will does not seem able to exercise command. Vd. *Nichomachean Ethics*, VII. Aristotle points out that children are naturally licentious and incontinent, and that, in this sense, vicious adults, not governed by their reason, are like children who do not live according to the direction of their tutors. Or, as Freud would say, the neurotic adult behaves in an infantile fashion. He is neurotic because he has never outgrown being a child.

58. The question about the independence of reason and the passions, the ego and the id, must not be interpreted genetically. Whether the Freudian account of the evolution of the ego out of the id is right or wrong is not relevant. Nor does it matter whether the Freudian speaks of the ego as a function of the id. The point is one of freedom of operation. If the ego were not, in some degree, operatively free from the id, it could not control the id, as it does both by inhibition and domestication. The same is true of the id. If the id were not, to some degree, operatively free of the ego,–if, in Aristotle's terms,

reason ruled the passions despotically instead of royally,—there could be no conflict between ego and id, no independent determination of behavior by repressed tendencies, no problems of vice and neurosis. In short, the primary fact is the fact of conflict between two parts of the soul, the rational and the non-rational. This fact,—and no other is needed,—establishes the analytical point that the forces in conflict are operatively independent of each other to some degree. What is here being said does not apply only to reason and passion, ego and id; it applies equally to the conflict of two passions, such as love and fear. The fact of this conflict requires us to understand these two motions of the sensitive appetite as operatively independent of each other. I would go further and say that just as this makes it impossible to say that fear is *simply* a function of love or love of fear, in any intelligible meaning of the word "function", so it is impossible to say that the ego is *simply* a function of the id, or reason of the passions. This is the type of error which intrudes itself into Freudian dynamic analysis as a result of the evolutionary genetics to which psychoanalysis religiously subscribes. Vd. Notes 51 and 53 *supra*. Freud supposes that all psychic energy is originally vested in the id, and that the actuality of the ego is nothing but energy borrowed from the id. This error is corrected by an analysis which shows that each of the independent powers of the soul is unconscious energy. Vd. Note 55 *supra*.

59. The important point here is not how much scientific truth there is in the propositions contributed by the biological sciences to the "theory of evolution"; nor is it a question concerning the *facts* which constitute all that is scientific knowledge about the origin of species. Whatever is scientific knowledge cannot be gainsaid, either by common sense or by philosophy. But a right understanding of philosophy and science shows that the facts ascertained by science make no difference to the solution of questions properly answerable by philosophy. An "evolutionary philosophy" is therefore a violation of both science and philosophy. It is the kind of speculation which discredits them both, because it goes beyond the scientific facts, on the one hand, and makes philosophy appear to be a sort of guessing, on the other. That the facts of evolution caused such agitation in philosophical circles in the 19th century indicates how far from their proper domain philosophers must by then have wandered, how little they must have understood their own principles and the regimen of their method. That the facts of relativity theory did the same thing in the very recent past is further proof that philosophy has not yet recovered itself.

60. Vd. *Beyond the Pleasure Principle* and cf. Bergson's *Creative Evolution*. The ideological affinities are plain. I must confess that I originally misread Freud's work as being entirely analytical. I took

the death instinct to be the desire for freedom from the passions and the attainment of the peace of the contemplative life, which is a kind of death in life in itself. I had supposed that the basic ideology was derived from Schopenhauer, that the pleasure principle was the will to live, and the death instinct its negation. But I have since learned that the book contains a cosmic biological fantasy. Cf. G. Santayana's misreading in his review under the title *A Long Way Round to Nirvana* in The Dial, Nov., 1923: pp. 435–42.

Whatever be the right interpretation of the text, one point is clear. In so far as the metapsychology is genetic, it does not rest on psychological evidence exclusively. On the contrary it seems to depend more upon biology, and even then not upon the established scientific facts of the various biological sciences, but upon the conjectural history which I have called the myth of evolution. Freud is a great storyteller, as witness the imaginative sociology of *Group Psychology and the Analysis of the Ego*. Many of his stories have a merit common to all great fiction. They convey profound insights into human nature. But poetry and science are not the same; much less poetry and philosophy. A scientific psychology must appeal to nothing but psychological evidence and must not go beyond the strict confines of its investigatively ascertained data. It must plainly exhibit each of its propositions as the inductive product of these data. It must order these propositions in such a way that their compendancy and interconnections are clear. The writings of Freud, or for that matter of any other psychoanalyst, cannot pass this simple test. Psychoanalysts would do well, first, to separate their strictly psychological doctrine from all the adventitious materials and reified fantasies with which it is at present garnished; second, to expound this doctrine in a strictly logical manner rather than in the style and language of poets; and third, to separate sharply the truths they have achieved as scientists from the philosophical analysis that is obscurely discernible in the metapsychology. It would be better if they left philosophy to philosophers, or at least sought instruction from the tradition in which they are thinking, whether they know it or not.

61. The psychoanalyst's therapeutic aim can be described, negatively, as the elimination of repression. Repression stands in the way of the control of the passions by reason; or, in psychoanalytical language, it stands in the way of the total integration of the personality. As repression is relieved, there is a consequent re-invigoration of conscious control of the separated tendencies of the id. The ego and the id assume an harmonious functional relationship. Desires which are irrational, i.e., desires which violate the reality principle, are modified by reason through sublimation and domestication, so that they can be assimilated. The result, supposedly, is a unified and adjusted personality,—unified in itself through a rational ordering of the appe-

tites and passions, adjusted to the environment because reason moderates and modifies desire according to the dictates of reality.

I do not mean to deprecate the therapeutic technique of psychoanalysis by referring to it as an extraordinary trick. Rather I wish to praise its ingenuity, its artistry. Nor do I mean to suggest that the psychoanalyst underestimates the power of reason, which must be utilized to make men happy or healthy; or that he caters to the passions, coddles them, compromises with them. I readily accept the statement of psychoanalytical technique which Dr. Alexander has made for me. What appears to be catering to the passions is quite the opposite. The therapeutic effort is to lure the passions out from their recesses, to remove the barriers of repression, not in order to give the passions freedom, but for the sake of making them submissive to reason. To suppose otherwise is to misunderstand the central concept of repression. Repressed tendencies are not merely inhibited desires and impulses. They are tendencies which have become anarchic through a kind of secession from the rule of reason; or, as the psychoanalyst would prefer to put it, through the abdication of reason from dominion over them because they have too painfully challenged its commands. In any case, adjustment, harmony, health and happiness, depend upon the reduction of such anarchy to a minimum. Therapy, therefore, must enable reason to regain its full sovereignty. It does this through a process of emotional clarification, on the one hand, and through augmenting the power of reason by giving it a fuller knowledge of the intransigent passions, on the other. A psychoanalysis is at best a course of education concerning one's emotions. I have elsewhere described psychoanalytical therapy as the process whereby the split soul speaking two languages,—the symptomatic language of the repressed id and the rational, social language of the ego,—learns to make a translation of these tongues and thus becomes able to regain unity by the communication of its parts. Vd. *Dialectic,* New York, 1927: pp. 107–125. The maxim of the Greek wise men, "Know thyself", is the guiding rule of psychotherapy.

But such knowledge is not, by itself, the power to live well, to attain happiness. The psychoanalyst's therapy, therefore, seems to me predominantly negative. He has merely cleared the ground of obstacles to moral training, which is never merely an acquirement of knowledge, but always a right ordering of loves. He has done nothing positively to institute that training. While it may be true that a moralist would fail with neurotics because of the heavy burden of repression he could not cope with, the lightening of this burden by psychoanalysis can do no more than to make the individual more susceptible to moral training. Unfortunately, it seldom does even that. Vd. Note 62 *infra.*

A simple analogy may make clear the relation of psychoanalytic therapy to moral training. Consider the case of a paralyzed man who wishes to perform well gymnastically. His trainer might be prevented from developing these skills in him, or at least impeded, by the physical handicap he suffers. A surgeon is able to remove the obstacle of paralysis. When the paralysis is cured, the patient is much better able to learn what the gymnastic trainer can teach him. But the surgical cure of the paralysis is not in and by itself the same as a course of gymnastic training. The surgery as a negative step is here instrumental to the positive training. Psychoanalytic therapy is a kind of surgery, removing repression and curing neurosis,–the obstacles to moral cultivation. But the neurotic who is seeking to live well needs the positive help of a moralist, just as the paralytic needs the gymnast as well as the surgeon. Granted that repressions have kept the neurotic from being morally mature, their removal will not magically transform the infantile character into an adult. A child must be morally habituated. So must the psychoanalyzed neurotic if he is to grow up.

Human happiness depends upon the moral virtues, the rectification of the appetites through ordination to their due end, the moderation of the passions through prudence. The passions, after they cease to be submerged by repression and clandestine in their motions, must be positively disciplined. They must be habituated in obedience to reason. And reason itself must be disciplined in the habit of applying knowledge to the affairs of action and emotion, of making choices deliberately and in the light of counsel. The virtue of prudence must be formed,–prudence which is the operative habit of practical reason tending to appoint a mean between the extremes of too much and too little, and taking from the will its power to command.

Psychoanalysis may, as I have said, make a person, who would otherwise be intractable, susceptible to moral training. But the art of moral training exceeds its powers, and this is the art which positively aims to make men happy. It is the possession of those who have learned well the science of ethics, who not only know the principles and rules of human welfare but appreciate the inexactitude of these rules in practice, their relativity to particular cases. It is one thing to know the practical science of ethics academically. It is another to use it practically, in the guidance of one's own life or in counseling and training others. The difficult art of casuistry must be mastered. It cannot be learned in a classroom, but only through much experience. Unless the psychoanalyst is a sound moralist and practically wise, unless he understands the fundamental principles of ethics and is an accomplished casuist, he can cure men negatively but he cannot make them happy. It is obvious that if the psychoanalyst has these additional virtues and accomplishments, he does not have them as a psychoanalyst but as a man of wisdom and experience. Though the combination is rare, it is not impossible, unless the psychoanalyst makes it impossible by denying morality itself. Vd. Note 62 *infra*. Two things must, therefore, be said of psychoanalytical therapy: (1) that it is far from being indispensable; it is necessary, perhaps, only in those pathological cases in which special technique is required to prepare the ground; and (2) that even when it is necessary, it never by itself achieves the end of making men virtuous and happy. That is the work of morality. Without it, the accomplishment of psychoanalysis must be an empty, or at best, a partial gain. If, through psychoanalysis, the patient renounces morality or "transcends" it, the result is worse than a frustration. It is pernicious.

62. The preceding discussion (Note 61 *supra*) indicates that the final evaluation of psychoanalytic therapy depends upon the relation of psychoanalytic theory to morality. Sound moral theory recognizes the distinction between those principles which obtain universally in the direction of human life,–the analysis of its ultimate end and proximate means, the classification of the goods and the determination of their order, the definition of the virtues and their relation to pleasure and pain,–and the conventional determinations of these principles which constitute the customary regulations and the prevailing sentiments of a given people at a given time. One set of customs may not be intrinsically better than another, but all conventions are not indifferent in moral rectitude. In the light of principles a whole culture can be judged as better or worse, according as its conventions are more enlightened by reason, according as its ruling sentiments are sounder evaluations of fundamental goods. This judgment is not, as the contemporary sociologist would say, vitiated by the ethnocentric predicament of the moralist making it. He is not making it according to the *mores*,–the customs and sentiments,–of his tribe, but in the light of principles that are universal because men are everywhere men, and human society is everywhere essentially the same.

But the psychoanalyst claims to investigate morality as the natural result of the functional relationship between the individual and his environment. This in itself is not wrong, because morality has a natural basis in man's specific nature operating under natural environmental conditions. In fact, it is the psychological understanding of the fact of morality which shows us that its first principles are not merely conventional, not purely arbitrary, but rather intrinsically natural. The Freudian, however, has adopted the point of view of sociology and anthropology since the days of William Graham Sumner, the view that morality can be completely equated with the *mores*, that it is *nothing but* the prevailing sentiments and the ruling customs of a tribe or society at a given time and place. This is utter relativism. The reduction of morality to the *mores*, in the current understanding of the ethnocentric predicament, is an absolute denial of morality. The *Ethics* of Aristotle is nothing but the rationalization of Greek *mores* in the 4th century B.C.; as morality it is neither better nor worse than the practices of Hottentots or contemporary

Germans. It is superior only in having received a more cultivated literary expression or a subtler rationalization.

I wish to emphasize the fact that the psychoanalysts did not formulate this doctrine in the light of their own clinical data. They borrowed it from anthropology, as they made levies upon evolutionary biology for their genetic theory. Nor did the anthropologist or sociologist learn from their data that morality is entirely relative, entirely a matter of arbitrary *mores*. What their data showed them, —if they interpreted them properly,—was that *mores* differ from tribe to tribe and from place to place. The *mores* are the set of practices and values which prevail. So much the data can establish and no more. The next step is to understand the *mores* in the light of the principles of morality which are common to all men. The obvious fact that the *mores* are not everywhere absolutely different, but rather that they differ in details within a frame of similarities, should teach an open mind that the *mores* are conventional determinations of principles which are natural and common to all men and all cultures. The investigative scientist could not have made this interpretation, of course, if he did not understand the scope and character of the practical science of ethics, if he did not understand the relation between nature and convention, if he did know the difference between principles and casuistically determined rules. In short, unless he were a competent philosopher he had no competence to interpret his data beyond the simple fact they obviously established, the fact of the variety of conventions. But the anthropologist and the sociologist, like their brothers in the natural sciences, were not satisfied with being investigative scientists. The urge to "philosophize" could not be resisted, and so we have the false doctrine of the *mores*, which is nothing but a misrepresentation of the facts. Just as the physicist when he turns philosopher soon denies that there is any philosophical knowledge, and especially metaphysics, so the social scientist when he turns philosopher repudiates morality, denies that there is any practical philosophy that has a truth above and apart from the acknowledgment of custom.

This is the psychoanalyst's doctrine about morality. As a scientist he need not, in fact he should not, be a moralist. As a psychotherapist, he may perform the negative task of relieving repression without recourse to moral principles. But if he aims further to make the whole man healthy, in the full Greek sense of making him happy, then his denial of morality is serious. The reality principle is insufficient if it merely proclaims the reality of the customs and sentiments which prevail in the community in which the patient lives and to which he must conform in part. The full reality of those customs and sentiments is their natural basis, their rational source in the principles of human morality. Happiness does not consist in conformity to the *mores*. Such blind submission is the docility of a slave, the pusillanimity of a domesticated animal. The *mores* themselves must be judged. They are not the standards of judgment. Rather they are measured by conformity to reason and the practical principles it dictates. The reality principle, then, must be the rule of reason in human life. Morality transcends the *mores*. If the psychoanalyst denies this, the patient he cures is, at best, a "socialized beast", whose anti-social tendencies have become domesticated, or, at worst, he is a thoroughly vicious man who subverts reason to the degraded task of *rationalizing* his appetites and passions, and who uses his intelligence, not to seek the good and avoid evil, but only to avoid the painful consequences of transgression of society's laws. The philosopher, said Aristotle, does from wisdom and virtue what other men do from fear of the law. The maxim applies not only to the philosopher but to every good man. He who acts *only* through fear of the law is a bad man aided by cunning and abetted by all the contrivances of expediency.

I have tried to show how psychoanalytic therapy might be of some instrumental value in the larger task of making men good and happy. Even if the service is only negative, it may be praiseworthy as an aid, perhaps an indispensable one in some cases. But if, as appears to be the fact, psychoanalytic therapy is practised in the light of a false doctrine about morals, it is condemnable as frustrating its own potentialities. The psychoanalyzed patient is cured by being taught the errors of the psychoanalyst. He learns to psychoanalyze himself, which means that he learns to take a purely "scientific attitude" toward all moral problems. He becomes objective. He is at all points a student of life rather than a practitioner involved in its perplexities. The error here is the supposition that to be scientific entails a denial of norms, that to be objective means that knowledge by itself can decide practical questions. The fact of norms is the cardinal fact that there is good and evil in the world, which the human appetites must be trained to seek or avert. Knowledge is not enough, even when it is "scientific". Knowledge must be converted into moral principles by the acknowledgment of an objective difference between good and evil. This is a true objectivity, beside which the "scientific attitude" of the psychoanalyst and his patient is the worse kind of moral solipsism, which converts everything into a matter of personal or tribal taste.

But the root error is deeper. It is the prevalent positivism to which psychoanalysis subscribes. Just as, on the theoretical side, the psychoanalyst stumbles because he denies philosophy and then proceeds to philosophize beyond the scientific significance of his data; so on the practical side, he blunders when he denies morality and then imposes his a-morality upon the patient. In both cases he has exceeded the task for which he is disciplined. In both cases he has proclaimed that science is enough, only to reveal the error of this dogma by self-contradiction,–by going beyond science precisely because it is not enough. Of the two mistakes, the latter is clearly more important. In the first instance, he only fools himself. In the second, he leads other men astray.

EPILOGUE

I WROTE the foregoing notes as a commentary after I had re-read the text of the lectures. I have now re-read the notes and feel impelled to add a brief comment on them. The discussion in the notes engages, at many places, in intellectual history, not for its own sake but for the purpose of discriminating the true from the false. Historical positions have not been simply reported. They have been judged. But the fact that the positions have been recognized as belonging to this or that moment of the historical sequence must mean that intellectual *history* contributes something to the understanding of philosophical issues. This does not mean that they cannot be stated entirely apart from proper names and dates. But the history of the natural sciences is much less relevant, much less useful, to the understanding of what they present today as knowledge, than the history of philosophy is to the understanding of what a contemporary philosopher holds to be the case. Thinkers of a Platonic temperament do not find the history of philosophy embarrassing. It exhibits a continuous discussion of the few basic ideas which, in every age, are implicated in human discourse. Thus, Whitehead reports intellectual history as the adventures of ideas, their incidence and transformation according to the conditioning circumstances of different epochs. And an Hegelian describes these transformations as a dialectical development which marches along the straight line of progress to culmination in his own philosophy. But an Aristotelian finds the history of philosophy embarrassing precisely because he conceives philosophy as *knowledge*, and not as progressively enlightened controversy. Far from seeing in the sequence of historical positions a closer and closer approximation of the truth, he discerns error on all sides. He must face the question, therefore, why, if philosophy is knowledge obtained by reason from common experience, should most philosophers have been unable to speak without error, error often grievous though never unmitigated by some truth. This is the question I feel called upon to answer because of the historical portions of my notes.

In the first place, the obvious difference between the history of science and the history of philosophy must be noted. The line of progress in science is undeviating. In each successive period, the state of scientific knowledge is an improvement on what went before. There is both more and better knowledge. The history of science can be reported as a correction of errors and inadequacies, but once the correction is made, the advance is consolidated. There is no back-sliding, no atavism. A scientific error always occurs at an earlier time than the knowledge which corrects it. This is not true of the history of philosophy, which moves forward in spiral rather than rectilinear fashion. Aristotle corrected the errors of Plato and the pre-Socratics only to have these same errors recur throughout the middle ages, especially the neo-Platonic reversions. Aquinas corrected the neo-Platonism which dominated most of mediaeval thought only to have modern philosophy return to these same errors, as well as to materialism and other positions taken by the pre-Socratics. In this view of the history of philosophy, atavisms are the rule and advances are exceptions. But the fact, however startling, that error and its correction are not related in the history of philosophy as they are in the history of science, does not show that philosophy is not knowledge. On the contrary, it shows that philosophy is knowledge of a different sort from science. There is not, on the whole, more error in philosophy than science, but the way in which it occurs, and recurs, is different. This difference is to be explained by the difference between science and philosophy as distinct types of knowledge employing different methods. Science, concerned with the phenomenal order, is investigative and inductive. Its regular advance is due to the progressive exploration of the sensible world and to the new fields of data discovered by experimental ingenuity, under the impetus of technology and invention. Philosophy, concerned with ontological problems, is inductive and dialectical. If philosophy were merely inductive, it would soon achieve a dead stability. The same is true of science. Without the continual increment of data achieved by investigation, induction would soon exhaust the fertility of what data there were. The role which investigation plays in science, dialectic plays in philosophy. The great philosophers do not disagree about the data of common experience or even about the primary inductions which these yield. But the movement of philosophy is from these data and inductions upward to the principles of highest generality which are the sources of intelligibility, and then from these principles downward in more and more articulated analyses to illuminate the concrete. This is the upward and the downward way of dialectic as Plato describes it in the *Republic*. This is the technique peculiar to philosophy, as investigation is to science. Unlike some modern Platonists who rely upon portions of the seventh epistle, I hold that this technique does not make philosophy merely dialectical, that Plato as well as Aristotle valued this technique as an instrument for getting valid knowledge and not merely as an instrument of controversy or the clarification of discourse. Plato used "dialectic" to name both the philosophical process and the product it achieves,—the wisdom that Aristotle called *philosophia prima*. If I stress dialectic as method, it is because it is necessary to make clear that the method of philosophy is not demonstrative in the sense in which modern mathematics is; it is not linear inference, deducing theorems from postulated premises. Finally, it should be added that the dialectical method of philosophy is a completely natural process of knowing; whereas the investigative method of science is technical, involving many auxiliary arts.

Dialectic is the source both of advances in philosophical knowledge and of the multiple repetition of errors. It is a subtle technique, mastered only by a few. Although experimental ingenuity and inductive genius may be equally rare in science, division of labor in the scientific enterprise makes it possible for a multitude of drones to perform useful tasks which are within the competence of many. Science is always productively at work, even in the absence of great scientists. This is not true of philosophy. Here the many, lacking either great or distinctive dialectical skill, do little more than repeat old errors or old truths. And the errors are easier to repeat than the truths. Being the product of inferior dialectic, they are naturally more within the competence of the many. This partly explains why the errors of Platonism and materialism, originating in the ancient world, have been so often repeated in the mediaeval and the modern epochs; it also explains why the dialectic of St. Thomas improves upon, rather than merely repeats, Aristotelian principles and analysis. If Aristotle in his day was the master of those that know, St. Thomas, mastering Aristotle, was an even greater master in his day.

Philosophical truth does not stand to philosophical error as white to black, if one considers a whole philosophy and not merely its constituent propositions. A true and a false philosophical proposition are related as contradictory, but a true philosophy must be compared with a false one in terms of dialectical criteria. The measures of truth in a whole philosophy are its intelligibility, its coherence and its adequacy, as well as the truth of its propositions. One philosophy is better than another as containing more truth and more wisdom, better articulated. It is by such criteria that I have judged the superiority of Aristotle to Plato, and the superiority of St. Thomas to the neo-Platonic philosophies of the middle ages and modern times, not to mention materialism and the various confusions of doctrine which proliferate in all ages.

The history of philosophy in modern times is complicated, first, by psychologism, and second, by the rise of positivism. When the question, How do we know? is made to precede all other philosophical analysis, metaphysics and the philosophy of nature suffer from the priority of psychology, and it in turn suffers from occupying the improper position of "first philosophy"; but worse than that, philosophers soon become occupied with questions about philosophical method as prior to all other philosophical questions. This ultimately leads to positivism and the denial that philosophy is knowledge of the real, independent of science. However sharp the contrast between the history of science in modern times and the history of philosophy in the ancient and mediaeval periods, it is even sharper if the comparison be made with the history of philosophy in the era of science. Not only is there no progress in philosophy, but modern philosophers do not seem able to agree among themselves about their problems and methods. This is rarely the case among scientists; rarer, or even unthinkable, would be the case of a scientist who denied that science was knowledge, having separate problems and an independent method. Yet that is precisely the position of those paradoxical creatures, the philosophical positivists,—philosophers denying or, at least, abandoning philosophy. There is reason, therefore, for a philosopher to feel most embarrassed about the history of modern philosophy. He is confronted not only by the return to ancient and mediaeval errors, usually in a form that is less clear or significant, but also by the apparent loss of philosophy itself, or, at least, its degradation in the cultural nexus.

This last point brings me to another aspect of the notes which calls for comment. At many points explicitly, and generally in tone, they *seem* to condemn the whole of modern times. I say "seem" because the condemnation is really restricted to what is condemnable: not the whole of modern times, but the errors and misdirections which have unfortunately obscured and marred the genuine advances made in this period. As Maritain says, "to denounce a fundamental spiritual deviation in a period of culture is not to condemn that period. . . . An error in spiritual principle bears its inevitable fruit. We must expose the principle and avow the loss. During the same period there is an evolution in human affairs, an expansion of history; there are conjoined to certain evils, gains and achievements of mankind that have an almost sacred value" (*Freedom in the Modern World*, New York, 1936: pp. 84–85). The spiritual deviation of modern times is in philosophy and it is an evil that seems to have been necessarily conjoined with the gain and achievement which is science. We have already seen that positivism made a philosophical advance in so far as, beginning with Hume and Kant, it formulated a clear conception of the nature of science. So far positivism must be praised. It is to be condemned only for its negations and exclusions which originate in the psychologism of modern philosophy. Similarly, science must be praised without stint for its magnificent contribution to human culture, even though the advent of science in the household of human knowledge almost dispossessed the older children, philosophy and theology. Again, as Maritain says, "if the loss or lowering of the metaphysical spirit is an incalculable damage for the general order of intelligence and human affairs, nevertheless, the predominance of the metaphysical spirit, when it is not accompanied by exceptionally vigorous critical rectifications, serves as an accidental hindrance to the particular interests of experimental research. And this accidental hindrance is a heavy cost, for experimental research, and the least advance in the least truth of fact, is also a thing of the spirit, and the spirit does not tolerate any hindrance" (*Les Degrés du Savoir*, Paris, 1932: pp. 118–119).

In other words, if we take a more comprehensive view of intellectual history, in which philosophy is only a part, we shall see modern times in a better light, and in the altered perspective the career of philosophy in the epoch of science may also be better understood. We may even discern the promise of a new *Aufklärung*. To be brief, I shall report this more comprehensive view in a story. The characters are Plato (and his retainers), Aristotle (and his), Philosophy, Theology (and Religion), Science (and Technology). There are three episodes.

(1) In the ancient world, Philosophy, Theology and Science were together as relatively undifferentiated parts of Human Knowledge. Yet their different personalities can be dimly seen if we note three moments in the development of Human Knowledge in the ancient world. It is as if Human Knowledge appeared upon the stage successively wearing three masks: the pre-Socratic mask is the face of Science turned towards the changing world; the Platonic mask turns the eyes of knowledge upward theologically; the Aristotelian mask bears the features of Philosophy not yet perfectly composed, because the line of its vision shifts now in the direction

of Science and now in the direction of Theology. It is in its Aristotelian personality that Human Knowledge was most mature in antiquity. Although real differentiation of characters has not yet occurred, the Aristotelian moment is the one in which the eyes of Philosophy have at least distinguished three directions in which Knowledge can turn. That is the Aristotelian achievement. In a sense, it is the birth of Philosophy.

(2) In the mediaeval world,–a world made different by the Christian revelation,–Religion enters as a separate character. Human Knowledge is deeply moved by the part it must play, a role in which hospitality to this newcomer is mixed with strange fears. At first, and almost for a thousand years, Human Knowledge plays this part wearing the Platonic mask, but there are momentary, almost furtive, shifts of expression. Philosophy, having achieved some sense of its separate character in the ancient world, can no longer completely submerge itself in the personality of Theology. If it continues for many centuries to wear the Platonic mask, it is because that is most suited to expressions of hospitality toward Religion. The fears with which this geniality is mixed betray themselves in nominalistic caricatures of the face of Science, subtle reversions to a pre-Socratic mood. It is not until Aristotle is remembered and resurrected that this conflict of emotions is resolved. The happy climax is reached in the 13th century when Aquinas effects the full separation of Philosophy from Theology. Human Knowledge is still ambiguously personified as Philosophy and Science, but it is in the now clear character of Philosophy that Human Knowledge is self-conscious of its distinction from another sort of knowledge which is the heart of Religion. Far from being tragic, this sharp differentiation enables Philosophy and Theology to understand each other as never before, and out of that understanding is born their compatibility, their harmonious union. This is the Thomistic achievement. It is more than an echo of the Aristotelian moment of antiquity. It is a genuine advance toward the greater maturity of Human Knowledge, an advance in which Philosophy passes out of its infancy.

(3) In the modern world, Technology is the innovator. Again Human Knowledge is profoundly stirred; this time by all the promises which Technology makes. The gifts with which Religion came are not forgotten entirely, but Technology offers a new world to conquer. The dowry it brings is an obvious one, as measurable and assessable as the things of this world. Human Knowledge is torn between what seems to be an assured happiness and the bright novelties which make Technology alluring. The strain

is too much. There is a gradual alienation of affection. At first Knowledge avoids a real breach by being deceptive. When it stays at home with Theology it is clearly philosophical in character, but when it goes out into the world with Technology it puts on the mask of Science. What is at first only a mask becomes through much worldliness a more and more distinct character. It is now Philosophy which is torn between Science and Theology. And extraordinary things being to happen. Philosophy finds it easier to get along with both Theology and Science by wearing the Platonic mask which twice before it had discarded. It tries to be all things at once. But the difficulties increase as Science and Theology move further apart. Human Knowledge in its Platonic personality aids in establishing the autonomy of Science, as in the early Christian period it made way for Theology. Under these circumstances, Philosophy finds it increasingly difficult to retain its own character. It tries so hard to understand Science that it almost ends in utter self-abnegation and in fitful forgetfulness of Theology. The Platonic mask, which in the ancient world reflected theological light, assumes the self-effacing features of positivism looking only at Science.

The birth of Science is the achievement of the modern world. But unless one believes that Human Knowledge *is* Science and that Theology and Philosophy are immature expressions which it has outgrown, the historical drama is not yet concluded. The third act will not come to its happy ending until it reaches another Aristotelian moment in which Philosophy will attain full maturity, separate not only from Theology but from Science. Just as in the Thomistic synthesis, Philosophy and Theology became well-related through being well-separated, so in the synthesis yet to come Science and Theology will be united through being divided by Philosophy, itself in clear distinction from them both. If I am right in the prophecy of this next turn, the story is the tragi-comedy of human progress. There has been and will be a progressive differentiation of Human Knowledge. Theology, Philosophy and Science will be better related as three distinct characters than as three aspects of one. Religion and Technology will assume their proper places, together though differently encouraging this triumvirate of Knowledge. And Philosophy, which must play the central role because of its relations to Science and Theology, will have advanced to a better understanding of itself precisely because in our times it has almost lost itself in understanding Science, as once before it almost did in serving Theology.

The intellectual history of western Europe thus told is not only the story of a general cultural advance, but also the story of the progress of philosophy, in which Aristotle is the hero and Plato the somewhat benign villain. It was through correcting pre-Socratic and Platonic errors that Aristotle won the first fruits of *purely* philosophic wisdom. It was through correcting the many times multiplied neo-Platonic errors,—much more subtle than the original ones because colored by misunderstandings of Aristotle—that St. Thomas ripened these fruits. As heretics are the indispensable causes of a sounder orthodoxy in theology, so the increasing subtlety of philosophical error is necessary for the deepening of wisdom. St. Thomas was able to improve upon Aristotle, not only because he understood the master so well, but also because his understanding was magnified by the mastery of errors which were unknown to Aristotle. The neo-Platonists of the middle ages were more subtle adversaries for St. Thomas than Plato was for Aristotle. But St. Thomas did not finish the work of philosophy. Because of the rise of science in modern times, because of another tide of neo-Platonism,—this time complicated by a vigorous return to the materialism of the pre-Socratics and by the denials of positivism,—further philosophical tasks remain to be done. The fruits of wisdom can be brought to even fuller bloom in a third *Aufklärung*, provoked by the errors of modern times,—a consummation which may be achieved when men realize that Technology has failed to bring peace on earth. Their wisdom will turn upward again to the theological virtues instead of down to science and the industrial arts. These matters are too contemporary to permit an assured judgment, but I discern in Maritain's *Les Degrés du Savoir* the outlines, at least, of a synthesis of science, philosophy and theology which will do for us what St. Thomas did for philosophy and theology in the middle ages. In that synthesis, philosophical wisdom will be enriched. The understanding of science will make for an improved Thomism, as the understanding of theology enabled St. Thomas to improve upon Aristotle. Whether or not Maritain has accomplished this or merely forecasts it, he seems to me the only contemporary philosopher who has deeply sensed the movement of history and the point at which we stand. More than that, he has divined the principle of intellectual progress. It is a maxim which can be used as the title for the whole historical drama: *distinguer pour unir*.

If one turns from prophecy for the moment to survey the contemporary scene, one is forced to realize that the whole story is a tragi-comedy and that the tragic accent dominates the present. Positivism, which reached its high point in the 19th century, is still ascendent in many quarters. Marxian materialism has not yet become truly dialectical materialism. With its affinities for mathematical physics and relational logic, on the one hand, and for Theology, on the other, neo-Platonism in many subtle varieties is still attempting to fuse science and religion. Formal materialism, though it is renewing its ancient and mediaeval vigor, has still many obstacles to overcome and victories to win if it is to produce a modern *Aufklärung*. It must assimilate Marxism, by showing itself to be the true dialectical materialism which Marx failed to derive from Hegel. It must do justice to the insight of positivism with respect to science, but avoid its blindness with respect to theology. This it can do by proper discrimination of the kinds of knowledge, converting Hume's denials about philosophy into affirmations of the limits of science, and Kant's antinomies and paralogisms into indications of the philosophical mysteries which mark the boundary between reason and faith. And, finally, formal materialism, today as ever, must strengthen itself against Platonic weaknesses,—particularly in regard to the relation of matter and form in the doctrines of substance and abstraction,—weaknesses which appear as soon as dialectical vigor is the least relaxed.

In facing all of these tasks, in all that remains to be done, the position of psychology seems to me crucial because philosophy cannot be re-established in its separate autonomy until peculiarly modern epistemological errors are corrected. We have seen how complicated is the network of reciprocal influences here,—how Platonism and psychologism have converged, how both have led to positivism, and how that in turn has prevented the science of psychology from reaching intellectual maturity. The cure of Platonism, the cure of positivism, both depend upon the rectification of psychology, as a science and in philosophy. But that also means that psychologists must be cured of Platonism and positivism. Psychology, therefore, seems to me that part of the field of science on which philosophy must win its decisive victory. Contemporary psychology,—particularly the doctrines which proclaim themselves as scientific,—is the source of much disorder in the practical world: in education, in morals, in religion, and even in economics and politics. That this is so follows necessarily from the relation of psychology to all practical problems; it is the theoretic root of the moral disciplines. The view which one takes of human nature determines how one lives as a man, alone and with others. The modern view of man, produced by the divorce of psychology from philosophy and its wedding to science, brings man to a lower state than he fell to from grace. The nobility with which man walked as a rational animal in Greece, the spirituality of man as a person in the middle ages,—these have been lost or obscured. And in their place is the bare objectivity of the man whose nature has been equated to the limited devices of the laboratory and the clinic. The position of psychology in modern culture is crucial both in the practical and the speculative dimension. I have no doubt that it will be rectified and that man will again rise to proper self-esteem, because I have no doubt that philosophy will reach a new fruition, healing thereby the disharmonies and blemishes of modern times. But this is prophecy, and if the prophet turn his eyes from the future to the present, the note of hope in his voice must give way to the tone of a Jeremiad.

"If this belief from heaven be sent,
If such be Nature's holy plan,
Have I not reason to lament
What Man has made of Man?"

LIST OF PRINCIPAL NOTES